TELEPEN

6 00 135509 6

KU-546-314

DATE DUE FOR

SHORT LOAN COLLECTION

15. MAY 89 2

15. MAY 89 3

SHERMAN ROY KRUPP, *editor*

Queens College,
City University of New York

The
Structure
of
Economic
Science

essays

on

methodology

WITHDRAWN

PRENTICE-HALL, INC.

Englewood Cliffs, New Jersey

© 1966 BY PRENTICE-HALL, INC.

All rights reserved. No part of this book may be reproduced in any form, by mimeograph or any other means, without permission in writing from the publisher.

Current Printing (last digit):

10 9 8 7 6 5 4 3 2 1

PRENTICE-HALL INTERNATIONAL, INC., *London*
PRENTICE-HALL OF AUSTRALIA, PTY. LTD., *Sydney*
PRENTICE-HALL OF CANADA, LTD., *Toronto*
PRENTICE-HALL OF INDIA (PRIVATE) LTD., *New Delhi*
PRENTICE-HALL OF JAPAN, INC., *Tokyo*

Library of Congress Catalog Card No.:
66–16395

Printed in the United States of America
C–85466

237385

Econ a Soc. Hist

UNIVERSITY
LIBRARY
NOTTINGHAM

PREFACE

TO DISCUSS ECONOMICS IS MAINLY TO TALK ABOUT SUCH THINGS AS DEMAND and supply, inflation, growth, international trade, the monetary system, or public policy—the substantive problems of the field. This is as it should be. However, there is another kind of question which concerns the way in which the field organizes its inquiry. The first kind of investigation is properly the "science" of a discipline, its laws and relations; the second is its "philosophy of science," its methodology.

The methodology of a discipline is usually buried in its substance and in the intellectual activities of its scientists. Consequently, it is often extremely difficult for people who are not trained in a particular field to understand how a discipline arranges its thought. Philosophers who are well trained in the study of methodology are rarely trained in economics. People trained in economics find it difficult to stand aside and observe their own methodology. Philosophers do not know economics, and economists rarely know philosophy. This is the paradox of methodological investigation.

Conscious methodological inquiry within a discipline almost always arises during periods of great intellectual controversy, because substantive questions often have important methodological implications. For example, the *methodenstreit* at the end of the nineteenth century was a controversy between the historical school and the classical and neoclassical economists. In contrast, during the last fifty years in economics there has been declining interest in methodological questions. Indeed, the recent developments in the philosophy of science have had little direct application in economics. The older methodological concerns are today regions

iii

of comparative neglect. This is partially explained because modern economics has developed great areas of agreement in its substance and style of reasoning. It is indicative that the recent revolution in favor of mathematical economics and measurement has been as silent as it has been forceful. Almost all ·economists accept a large part of the main theorems of neoclassical economics for many applications, although the applicability and relevance for particular contexts is sometimes disputed. Nevertheless, the habits of thought should not be taken for granted. Some problems that arise in economics, such as intradiscipline disputes and disagreements as to the proper domain of a discipline, can benefit from methodological clarification.

The essays in this book are published here for the first time. Mainly, they are by economists who have strong methodological interests. Several of the authors are philosophers. The economists look within their discipline at their own habits of thought, at their axioms, and at their assumptions. They try to present their ideas in a way that will be comprehensible and beneficial to informed social scientists who have not had special methodological training. These essays have been written for the general economist who is mainly interested in the substantive problems of his field, for the undergraduate or graduate student who wishes to discover more about the precepts of economics, and for other scientists and philosophers who wish to learn more about how economists handle their substantive and methodological problems.

The collection is divided into four parts. Part 1 considers some general problems of methodology, theory construction and observation, analysis of the logic of controversy in economics, and discussion of economics relative to its doctrinal history and to the sociology of knowledge.

Part 2 includes a general discussion for the nonmathematician of the uses and limits of mathematical methods in the social sciences, the problems of observation and verification that arise in general econometric formulations and in econometrics.

Part 3 discusses the boundaries between economics and other disciplines, the relations between economics and institutions, and the difficulties in formulating theories that encompass both micro- and macrosystems.

Part 4 is composed of three essays which investigate the nature of values. The use, measurement, and verifiability of values in economic theory is examined in relation to individuals and to collectivities. ·

SHERMAN ROY KRUPP

Queens College
City University of New York

CONTENTS

v

vi

PART 1

THEORY

AND

DISPUTE

IN

ECONOMICS

INTRODUCTION

THEORETICAL KNOWLEDGE REQUIRES A HIGH DEGREE OF INTELLECTUAL organization. It consists of an orderly structure of logical and empirical relationships. What is essential to a theory is that this structure is purposeful, that the theory does the work for which it is designed. But the organization of a theory is rarely self-evident. The most highly developed branches of theoretical knowledge, in fact, are often the most simple in their form, and these simplifications, which give a theory its generality and analytical power, also conceal the organization. This is especially true of economic theory.

The five essays in Part 1 concern themselves with the problem of how theories hang together. What theories are, how they relate to observation, how they may be justified, how they may conflict, and how they interact with their social and historical environments are the basic themes.

First, Martin Bronfenbrenner broadly sketches some of the important links between the substantive problems of economics and its methodological underpinnings. He points to the diversity of economic reasoning. Can economics be meaningfully classified into "positive" and "normative" economics? What is the nature of economic controversy? What is the value of equilibrium theory? Is there validity to Marxian economics? What kind of assumptions do economists make, and how do these assumptions orient their vision? Bronfenbrenner raises many questions that are basic to the other essays of the volume and, thus, introduces the reader to the various topics of the book.

Henry Margenau develops the general character of scientific theory as

3

a varied relation between logical constructs (the C-field) and the elements of experience itself (the P-field). Since there is no rule for linking concepts to observation, a theory can rarely be decisively justified. Theories draw from both domains in widely assorted ways, but there are no rules for a perfect balance between the conceptual and the directly observable elements of a theory. Many different theories can be constructed to explain the content of the same field of observation.

If the rules for selecting concepts and for relating concepts to experience have wide variation, it follows that alternative theories cannot be preferred or rejected on the basis of absolute criteria for truth. Sherman Krupp develops controversy as an essential ingredient of theory construction in economics. He shows four kinds of possible conflict: conflict over fundamental concepts, over the justification of theorems, over the limits and boundaries of a theory, and over differences in valuations. Controversy arises from the varied ways in which concepts can be constructed and linked to the domain of experience. Theoretical conflict, he argues, is a necessary and valuable characteristic of theory formulation.

More specifically, Fritz Machlup questions the operationalist solutions to the problem of bridging between pure theory and observation. Operationalism asserts the close identity between the concepts of a theory and the means through which the concepts are translated into observation. Machlup shows that acceptance of too close an identity can seriously limit the development of theory. However, operational definitions are necessary to theory, not as a substitute for pure theory itself, but for answering particular questions or for verifying parts of the theoretical apparatus.

The concepts of a theory and the way experience is organized have an historical aspect as well as a logical one. The genetic and sociological components of theory are the subject of the essay by Lawrence Nabers. Economic formulations, he argues, occur in a social and historical setting and concern themselves with this setting. Hence, economic theory will contain some value elements. Because values help us screen experience, they are essential ingredients of the C-field. The attempt in economic analysis to expunge the normative elements brings about their re-entry through the backdoor of axioms and assumptions. Where the development of modern economics has been towards a "value-free" science, the result has been a removal of some of the more important problems of the field. Nabers' use of the historical approach offers a perspective on modern trends in economic theory.

MARTIN BRONFENBRENNER

Martin Bronfenbrenner, Ph.D., University of Chicago, is Professor of Economics at the Graduate School of Industrial Administration, Carnegie Institute of Technology. Previous affiliations include the Universities of Wisconsin and Minnesota and service with the U.S. Treasury Department, the Federal Reserve System, and the Occupation of Japan. He is a general economist whose published articles have been concerned primarily with (1) the theory of income distribution, (2) monetary and fiscal policy, and (3) aspects of the Japanese economy and its history.

ESSAY

1

UNLIKE MOST CONTRIBUTORS TO THIS VOLUME, I lack formal training in logic. What is presented here is merely a "middlebrow methodology" chapter adapted to an unwritten middlebrow economic theory textbook.

Let me, to offset this lack, disclaim a frequent bias which gives methodology much of its bad reputation. Methodological discourse tends to suffer from the animus inherent in the assumption that "What *I* know is correct and relevant, but what *you* know is wrong or irrelevant, unless I know it too." Let me admit in advance, therefore, that what I know is weighted down with excess baggage, and that you may know many things which I should have learned.

A

"Middlebrow"

Introduction

to

Economic

Methodology[1]

[1] In specific connection with this essay, my principal debts are to William W. Cooper, Richard M. Cyert, James G. March, Eugene Rotwein, and Herbert A. Simon, as well as to the editorial advice of Sherman Krupp. (My creditors do not always agree with each other more fully than with me.)

I. DEFINITION OF ECONOMICS

We begin with the lamentable fact that there seems to be no satisfactory definition of economics or economic science. A "satisfactory definition" would set up defensible boundaries between economics, on the one hand, and such related disciplines as business, history, politics, law, psychology, sociology, statistics, engineering, geography, etc., on the other. It should at the same time refrain from such tautologies as Jacob Viner's despairing "Economics is what economists do," or my daughter's "Economics is where Daddy draws those lines and writes those numbers."

My tentative choice of a definition of economics, modified from Lionel Robbins via Oskar Lange, reads: "Economics is the systematic study of social adjustment to, and management of, the scarcity of goods and resources." But this lacks the empirical content required to set up boundaries of the sort just mentioned.

Use of the term "scarcity" reminds us that it is a word of art among economists, which must itself be defined. As conventional economists use the term, a good or service is scarce if, as a free good with a zero price, the demand for it would outrun the supply. This does *not* imply that demand exceeds supply at the existing price, presumably positive. Neither does it rule out the standard "economy of abundance" criticism of our economy for adjusting to excesses of supply over demand at existing prices by reducing supply or stimulating "artificial" demand in preference to lowering prices.

Communists, technocrats, and other "maximalist" critics of the "economy of scarcity" school go further and deny that scarcity, even in the technical sense, is "natural" or inevitable. They anticipate that, in a rational economy with science and technology given a free rein, with demand not inflated by advertising and salesmanship, with no problems of defense and war, and with all individuals serving relatively short terms of civilian labor (analogous to present periods of compulsory education and military service), all goods and services can shortly be made free. Such economic maximalism is an analogue to Christian Science in the health professions. Like the sunspot theory of business fluctuations, it has not been proved wrong; the usual reaction remains, to say the least, skeptical.

II. THE MANAGEMENT OF SCARCITY

Solutions actually suggested for the social management of scarcity fall into three rough categories, with no "pure" solution in effect in any actual society. In primitive societies, customary solutions dominate in determining what and how much shall be produced, the production methods to be used, and also the "for whom" of the process—the methods and criteria for distributing the product. More advanced societies use either market solutions for the same problems—the United States being an example—or else authoritarian "planned" solutions—which dominate in the Soviet Union, China, and Eastern Europe.

Many writers have suggested criteria for choosing between and among these three solutions, not to mention the mixed ones both practiced and advocated. Let me suggest six such criteria, four of them "purely economic" and the others "quasi-economic" in nature.

The four economic criteria are fairly obvious. One is the standard of living of the mean or median citizen. Another is the growth rate of this standard, both the long- and short-run rate.[2] A third is the "equity" of the distribution of both the flow of income and the stock of wealth, joint determinants of the living standard. The fourth is the stability of the standard as against downward pressures in particular. Such pressures can be due to short-run oscillations known as "business cycles," or to longer-run ones associated with technological change, including what we now call "automation."

My quasi-economic criteria are compatibility of the economic system with civil liberties and with the physical and mental health of its citizens. A system which rests on slavery or forced labor, or where acceptability requires a monopoly of propaganda, violates the civil liberties criterion. A system which sacrifices industrial safety for increased production, or where competitive pressures breed ulcers and neuroses, violates the physical and mental health criterion in the same way.

III. POSITIVE AND NORMATIVE ECONOMICS

There is considerable dispute among economists and their critics regarding the difference between what is called "positive" and "normative" economics. Is there a real difference, and if so, what is it? Can either positive or normative economics be "scientific" or "objective"? If so, should it be? And if not, what of it?

Perhaps a diagram (Figure 1) can help clarify this issue. On this diagram, "economic analysis" and "economic facts" comprise what is usually called "positive economics," while "economic value judgments" and the resultant "economic policy recommendations" are normative in character.

---

[2] Special problems arise because policies which increase this growth rate in the short period may not do so in the long period, or vice versa. The successive Soviet Five-Year Plans are examples of planned sacrifice of the short-run to the long-run growth of the standard of living and perhaps also of the "national income," at least as measured in the West.

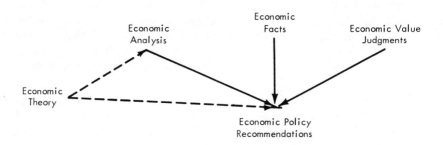

Figure 1

Nothing has yet been said of "economic theory," which has become a kind of weasel word with at least two commonly accepted meanings. One of these is "economic analysis" (positive) and the other "economic policy recommendations" (normative). To make matters more confusing, both meanings may be combined indiscriminately, and they often are. Questions relating to the applicability of "Western" economic theory in underdeveloped countries, or of "bourgeois" economic theory in socialist countries, have different answers depending upon which meaning of "economic theory" we use. The economic analysis of the effects of free international trade or of the rate of interest as a basis for allocating an investment budget are clearly more applicable outside their Western, capitalist homelands than is the recommendaton that free trade policies be adopted or that interest rates be used to ration capital. Discussions of "the theory of free trade" or "the theory of interest" are often unclear about which meaning (or mixture of meanings) is being applied.

Two perennial issues arise whenever economists make policy recommendations involving normative economic issues. Are economists entitled to make policy recommendations at all, *qua* economists rather than *qua* interested citizens? And if so, to what extent, if at all, should considerations of political feasibility limit the recommendations which they make? A possible compromise between extreme views on both sides might be this: When economists make recommendations, they should distinguish as carefully as possible between the positive and normative bases for them since their professional competence (if any) is concentrated on the positive side. They should also make as clear as possible whether a specific proposal is a second- or third-best compromise or concession to short-term political feasibility, and if so, what alternative recommendation they might have made in the absence of this restriction.

IV. ECONOMICS AS A SCIENCE

Is economics, either positive or normative, a science? Like medicine or meteorology, part of it is and part is not. More precise discussion is difficult because no definition of "science" has delineated boundaries with much clarity. A broad definition of a "science" as "an organized body of knowledge" will include more of economics (positive economics) than narrower definitions which place primary reliance on laboratory methods, or on quantitative testing which compares predicted with observed results.

While economics has clearly become an organized body of knowledge, it makes minimal use of the laboratory method in any rigorous way. It has of late attempted substantial quantitative prediction over both short and long periods. The results have not been uniformly successful; some of them have been downright discouraging. The closest analogies to economic method in the natural sciences are probably astronomy and meteorology. Like these other sciences, economics has made widespread use of mathematics and statistics as substitutes for laboratory work. Thus far, economics has not required *as much*, or *the same*, mathematical or statistical methods as are used in these natural sciences. Indeed, too close an analogy may be misleading. For example, the use in the theory of business fluctuations of the forms of harmonic analysis applied in the theories of tides, eclipses, and other astrophysical phenomena has not yet produced valuable results.

Until perhaps a generation ago, it might have been necessary to justify the use of mathematics in economics and the other social sciences, or perhaps to set up limits for such use. Since 1929, however, such issues have progressively disappeared in the United States and Western Europe.[3] The resolution of this problem has been due less to specialized methodologists, however, than to practicing economists who have derived qualitative or quantitative results with the aid of mathematics, when literary economists could obtain similar results, if at all, only with much more labor and much less rigor. The shoe now threatens, indeed, to pass to the other foot, with the nonmathematical practitioner laboring under a darkening suspicion (despite the history of economic thought) that nothing he does will be worthwhile unless formulated mathematically and subjected to statistical testing.

The mention of mathematics still gives rise, however, to another question: Are the theorems of economics, particularly mathematical economics, "true" in the same sense as those of algebra or geometry, or are they merely probable, like the propositions of the literary economists?

In dealing with this question, economists are indebted to Andreas Papandreou for making explicit in economics the logicians' distinction between "models" and "theories."[4] His distinction, briefly, is that a *model* (logical, economic, or what you will) follows from its premises or axioms

---

[3] In Japan it is considered presumptuous in orthodox Marxist circles to employ in economics mathematical techniques which Marx did not sanction by using them himself.

[4] *Economics as a Science* (Philadelphia: Lippincott, 1958).

and may be considered in this sense as absolutely true. At the same time, however, this model and its axioms may not be applicable to any real-world situation. The proposition that a given model (such as the perfectly competitive one, which includes the theorem that prices will approach minimum average costs of production) is reasonably applicable to a given set of situations, such as the American economy in the 1960's, may be called an *applicability theorem*. And since it relates to the actual world, an applicability theorem may be highly probable but is never absolutely certain.[5] An economic model with one or more applicability theorems appended may be called an economic *theory*, in the analytical rather than the policy-recommendation sense of our Figure 1.

Let us retrace our steps. An economic model may indeed be certain, but its applicability outside "Never-Never Land" is only probable. An economic theory, being a model to which something new (an applicability theorem) has been added, may be applicable to a number of real-world situations, but it cannot approach closer to Absolute Truth than its applicability theorem does. In this connection economics differs from physics, astronomy, or applied mathematics in one important respect: the *sizes* of the probability values of the applicability theorems for most propositions of economic theory are lower than physicists, astronomers, or applied mathematicians consider respectable. Yet this is a difference only of degree; economists not only hope to do better in the future, but are working actively toward this end.

Special effects, favorable or unfavorable, sometimes result from public reactions to some economic predictions (relating, for example, to stock prices and business fluctuations). These reactions may make the predictions self-confirming or self-disconfirming. The natural scientist need contend with this kind of "noise" only in a few special cases, like artificial seeding of clouds to produce rain or crash programs of immunization against threatened epidemics. Except for these reaction effects, which some economists hope to discount by special "reaction functions," I observe no feature of economic predictions sufficiently different from astronomical or meteorological ones to constitute "transmutation" into qualitative differences between them.

Strictly scientific or not, is economics at least "objective" in the sense that competent practitioners will approximate the same results from the same data? Only imperfectly so, we must admit; a possible analogy is medical diagnosis. Usually, however, the charge of "lack of objectivity" against economics has implied more than ordinary human error, subject to the laws of chance. It implies certain systematic biases related to the selection and training of economists. The issue of objectivity is kept alive

---

[5] The *scope* of the model's applicability may also be indicated by the appended applicability theorem, which may be general or special, broad or narrow.

by references to "bourgeois" versus "proletarian" economics, "developed-country" versus "developing-country" economics, "Aryan" versus "Jewish" economics, to "value-loaded propositions," "conventional wisdom," and so on.

What objectivity economics possesses is concentrated in its positive aspects—the facts, the technical analysis, etc. There is no particular reason to expect an economist's basic value judgments or policy recommendations to be independent of his social class, type of culture, and his country's degree of economic development, or to be surprised when they are not. In the capitalist West, for instance, with its individualistic traditions, there is a tendency to prefer free consumer choice to the forced acceleration of growth which might result from devices forcing the consumer to save and invest more than he desires; the opposing view is pilloried as "growthmanship." In the Soviet Union, on the other hand, the Western position is called "primacy of consumption over production" or sometimes "consumerism." It is a heresy; issues of "choice versus growth," as Peter Wiles has called them,[6] are (almost) automatically decided in favor of growth.

Even in positive economics, however, as Gunnar Myrdal takes special pains to point out,[7] objectivity may be impinged upon in a number of ways. The very facts to be studied and statistics to be computed can sometimes be selected in a biased manner. For example, in dealing with distribution of income, bourgeois economists concern themselves with the labor share in the national income and Marxist ones with the rate of surplus value or exploitation—both of which, incidentally, seem to be rising slowly in the contemporary American scene. Or, passing to models and theories, these may be constructed with "specialized" assumptions or concepts, as when structuralist and institutionalist writers treat prices as rigid or demand and supply adjustments to price changes as highly inelastic. Centralized economic plans, to cite another case, may be assumed either well or imperfectly articulated. Or, finally, the competitive market may be considered as a "system" or as "anarchy." Those who see it as a system will assume the existence of stable equilibrium "solutions" with well-behaved supply and demand functions for goods and services, and they will devote themselves to exploring the attributes of such solutions. Those who see the market as a jungle will assume that no solutions exist—or if they do, that they are inherently unstable and/or reached too slowly for relevance in historical time—and delight in exploring the implications of badly behaved supply and demand functions,

---

[6] *The Political Economy of Communism* (Cambridge: Harvard University Press, 1962), Chap. 11.

[7] *The Political Element in the Development of Economic Theory*, trans. by Streeten (London: Routledge, 1953).

or economic chaos "On a cloth untrue, With a twisted cue, And elliptical billiard balls." [8]

Another lapse from objectivity, even in positive economics, is the reliance on terms which, except to disinfected experts, are heavily "value-loaded" with a view to influencing policy recommendations. "Welfare," "efficiency," "utility," and "productivity" are frequent examples on the capitalist side. "Dynamic," "planned," and "structural" are favorite adjectives of socialists and planners. What is called "free enterprise" and "economic freedom" in the United States is "freedom to exploit" in the Soviet Union. What critics of the market economy call "competition," its defenders qualify as "imperfect," "cut-throat," or "monopolistic" competition, not to mention "oligopoly." "Right-to-work" and "union-busting" laws refer to the same legislation; so do "managed currency" and "fiat money," not to mention "rational planning" and "the road to serfdom." "Exploitation" is by no means the only term in positive economics which has "ceased to be a noun and become a noise."

And here, to close and illustrate this section, is the title of the (unwritten) volume of economic theory for which these paragraphs might be a "methodology" chapter: "A Dynamic Approach to Scientific, Behavioral, and Managerial Economic Analysis for Public Policy and Growth in a Time of Change for the Citizen at the Crossroads of Applied Values in a Free People's Planned Democracy."

V. IMMANENT EMPIRICISM AND PERPETUAL DISAGREEMENT

The easiest and least systematic way of acquiring a "feel" for economic methodology is perhaps to consider a few of the current controversies and unsettled areas in the field. Let us, accordingly, outline a few of them; I shall indicate my own half-formed conclusions where they exist.

The first of these controversies is, like the one about the legitimacy of mathematical methods, on its way to oblivion. Is technical economic analysis—the "economic theory" of the textbooks—necessary and useful? "Immanent empiricists" among philosophers and institutionalists among economists are inclined to answer in the negative. As I understand the doctrine of immanent empiricism, if one looks at enough facts or cases long enough and hard enough, general solutions (or acceptable compromises) will become clear, less by formal logic than by "insight," by "vision," by analogy, or sometimes by "compulsive comparisons." A Marxian variant of the same school accepts immanent empiricism as the basis for "scientific" value judgments on which reasonable men agree in a non-"decadent" society—but only after *both* knowledge of the facts *and* application of dialectical materialism.

---

[8] Gilbert and Sullivan, *The Mikado*, Act II.

Immanent empiricism, without much conscious analysis, is the philosophy of the practical man and the English Common Law. It dominates, with its "case method," our schools of law and of business, although its dominance has fallen off since World War II. It is generally out of favor in academic departments of economics; this difference in the official epistemologies of economists and "business school types" is one reason for the difficulty of maintaining peace and mutual respect within many Groves of Academe. "Fact finding" in the mediation of labor-management disputes and the "Dow theories" of stock market forecasting are other diverse examples of the immanent empiricist's anti-"theory" position.

Immanent empiricism is probably wrong as a general theory of knowledge. It may nevertheless be pragmatically right in particular cases. It may also be a good description of our thought processes—which I understand to be the Deweyan definition of "logic"—regardless of the validity of its results.

A second controversy is this: Does not the economists' notorious failure to agree suggest or prove the "prescientific" character of economics as such? I follow my professional bias (vested interest?) on the negative side of this proposition. Much of the disagreement is inevitable since it centers around economic values and policy recommendations and involves normative rather than positive economics. None would deny the claims of physics to scientific status, but physicists seem (to outsiders) no nearer agreement than economists as regards public policy questions involving their science. Consider for example the disagreements between physicists of the stature of J. Robert Oppenheimer and Edward Teller as to the desirability of developing hydrogen bombs and the feasibility of mechanical (nonhuman) policing of international agreements limiting the testing of atomic weapons generally.

This is not to deny the existence of disagreements in positive economics, of which there are plenty. (In 1963, President Edward S. Mason of the American Economic Association complained with justice in his presidential address that we have only opinions, not firm estimates, as to the effect of increased employment in the United States upon the American balance of payment position.) Yet we have faith that most if not all such positive disagreements will eventually be resolved, as parallel disagreements have been resolved in the natural sciences. The dispute between the Ptolemaic and Copernican systems of astronomy has apparently ended in the general acceptance of the latter (as a set of highly probable, if uncertain, propositions). The Darwinian-Lamarckian dispute in biology as regards the inheritance of acquired characteristics has (less completely) ended in favor of the Darwinian position. We anticipate that the disputed issue of the relationship between tobacco and lung cancer will also reach an accepted solution. So it is in economics. We grant that, at the present time, economists are divided as to whether increased American employment will increase or reduce the "dollar glut." We can and do hope, nevertheless, that further advances in economic science will some day permit not only qualitative but quantitative answers of high reliability. And should the answer be "it depends," we hope eventually to cite a manageably small number of factors on which the answer usually depends and estimate the relative weights of each one. (To an even greater extent than in the bio-medical controversy over smoking and cancer, however, agreement may be delayed, or withheld from the public, by incompetent amateurs and hired "mouthpieces" for pressure groups with special axes to grind.)

Amid all the suspicion directed against economists for failure to agree, we should not forget that they are attacked for agreeing too much as well as too little. American economists, in particular, have been attacked en masse as "learned lackeys of Wall Street," parlor-pink conspirators for socialism, refugees in mathematical obfuscation, dodgers of unpopular policy positions, and so on. We must admit that some certified economist or other, Ph.D. and all, is guilty of each of these crimes, as well as most other crimes in the book. This does not, however, make the discipline intrinsically "worse" than any other. (Readers of French will remember Molière's "philosopher" in Le Bourgeois Gentilhomme and his doctors in Le Malade Imaginaire.)

VI. "THE FRIEDMAN" CONTROVERSY

At a higher level of sophistication, economists have conducted since the early 1940's a controversy regarding the assumptions underlying economic analysis. The key questions of this "assumptions" controversy seem to be two: What is the role of assumptions in analysis, and what is the appropriate choice of these assumptions? The controversy (among professional economists, at least) owes more to the "positive economics" of Milton Friedman than to any other one individual, in the sense that Friedman is the man one is most apt to take a position "for" or "against." [9]

The standard textbook position expounded in elementary courses has been that no theory can be "useful" or command confidence of its underlying assumptions are "unrealistic." It is this aspect of conventional wisdom that Friedman and his fellow positivists seek to overthrow. To this writer, at least, the most dangerous aspect of the search for "realistic assumptions" is an implicit logical consequence: If one bases his reasoning on a sufficient number of sufficiently realistic assumptions, his conclusions can somehow evade our "applicability theorem," and combine cer-

---

[9] Essays in Positive Economics (Chicago: University of Chicago Press, 1953), Chap. 1.

tainty with applicability in a way Papandreou and I (and many others) insist is impossible.

There seem to be not two but five principal positions in the "assumptions" debate. One, the immanent empiricism which discards deductive analysis as such, has already been discussed. Let us concentrate, therefore, upon the four positions remaining.

Suppose that there are several different sets of assumptions which lead to approximately equally good qualitative or quantitative forecasts of some economic phenomenon. Which of these sets should the researcher choose as a basis for further investigation?

The *Positivist School,* including Friedman and centered at the University of Chicago, prefer, if I understand them correctly, the set which is mathematically simplest, that is, in the sense of involving the smallest loss of degrees of freedom. They prefer, for example, linear to nonlinear functions. They make free use of such simplifications as proportionality between the quantity of money and prices (in the short run), atomistic markets in which all individuals maximize profits and/or utility but where no individual has power to affect prices of anything he buys or sells, and measurable quadratic utility functions which yield linear marginal utilities. (Mathematical simplicity in this sense, of course, often involves statistical complexity. Witness Friedman's own "permanent income hypothesis," which makes consumption a relatively constant proportion of disposable income, the magical percentage being 88. This requires us to estimate the "permanent" components of both income and consumption, which differ from the immediately measured ones. The estimation processes, moreover, involve elaborate patterns of lagged relations distributed backward through time in patterns recommended a priori by mathematical considerations alone.)

A persistent danger in positivist thinking, although I do not accuse Friedman himself of yielding to it, is reasoning backward in an illegitimate manner. Because a given simplification like "pure competition" works, meaning that it predicts the future as well as more elaborate structures, it is tempting to conclude that these simplifying assumptions are therefore "true" and that the real world is in fact "that way," even when direct observation suggests otherwise.

At the opposite extreme from positivism lies the *Realistic* or *Quasi-Institutional School,* insisting (with Alfred Marshall) on short chains of reasoning from abstractions which deviate only marginally from facts as casually observed. We have mentioned the intuitive appeal of such a position to the practical man and its support in the textbook aphorisms of the conventional wisdom. It also has at least heuristic advantages in the explanation of historical events or existing situations, even if one follows Friedman (as the realists do not) in abjuring distinctions between explanatory and predictive power. A persistent danger in the realist position is, however, the piling of assumption on assumption, complication on complication, until their "model" (or equivalent logical structure) retains too few degrees of freedom to explain anything at all. It leaves us in the position of "whatever is, is." This is occasionally dignified as a "behavioral" theory of this or that, but it looks more like a collection of particular cases, which goes little further than formalizing the special circumstances of each case covered. Kenneth Boulding has put this problem into verse, as it relates to business behavior:

> Business men are rather dumb.
> Their model is the rule of thumb.
> Economists, it should be said,
> Prefer to have a rule of head . . .
>
> But though the head be blank inside,
> The thumb at least can hitch a ride,
> And so, from studying its illusions
> We draw behavioral conclusions.[10]

Friedman's "positivism" represented originally an assault less on institutionalism than upon general-equilibrium economics, associated with Léon Walras, Vilfredo Pareto, and their followers of the *Lausanne School* or *General Equilibrium School*. Walras aimed, I think, at assuring himself of the logical validity of economic theory (avoiding both circular reasoning and inconsistency), by reformulating it in terms of equation systems in which the number of independent equations and unknowns are equal.[11] In the hands of Walras' followers, Lausanne-type systems were expanded in generality to take a broader and broader range of phenomena into account. At the extreme, the general equilibrium school seeks the most universal set of assumptions possible, so as to be consistent with the greatest range of possible outcomes. It can explain almost anything *ex post,* but its models are difficult to apply for predictive purposes without further specification. It is interesting, however, to note that the "everything depends upon everything else" type of economics is being applied increasingly to planning problems in underdeveloped countries, usually with the added positive assumption (denied, however, by Friedman) that most production and many consumption relations are determined by technical considerations independent of relative prices. These are the "input-output" and "linear-programming" systems developed in America by Wassily Leontief and Hollis Chenery, in Western Europe by Ragnar Frisch and Jan Tinbergen, and in the Soviet Union by L. D. Kantorovitch and his followers.

The final participant in the assumptions debate is the *Axiomatic School,*

---

[10] *Models of Markets,* Alfred R. Oxenfeldt, ed. (New York: Columbia, 1963), pp. 369-371.

[11] In strict rigor, such balance is neither a necessary nor a sufficient condition for logical validity.

which prefers to start with the *weakest* mathematical conditions required for strictly rigorous models. The stress here is on mathematical and logical *economy* rather than on the simplicity sought by the positivists. The axiomatic approach shaves with Occam's Razor, seeking the maximum results from given hypotheses, and the "weakest" hypotheses for given results. The difference between the axiomatic and positivist positions may be clarified by an example from utility theory. We have mentioned the positivist preference for quadratic utility functions. Axiomatic work has moved in the direction of postulating nothing more than "revealed preferences" for one bundle of goods rather than another, and working with "lexicographic" preference relations under which the utility function is not only nonmeasurable, but also need not even exist. The persistent danger here, called "barren formalism" by its critics, lies in its concentration on re-proving what we already think we know, although more elegantly, more rigorously, or on weaker assumptions, rather than exploring matters of substantive novelty.

As the issues have been presented, there appears to be no one "right" answer. That is to say, one's choice of positions in the "battle of assumptions" reduces, in my view, to a matter of subjective preference. Figure 2, patterned after the standard indifference maps of economic theory, is designed to illustrate this point.

In this figure we consider only two alternatives, the *simplicity* of assumptions (horizontal axis) and their *realism* (vertical axis). We suppose that "simplicity," "realism," and "predictive efficiency" (or "explanatory

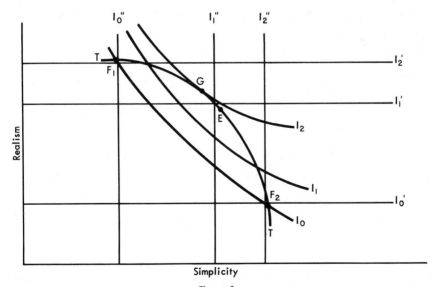

Simplicity

Figure 2

power") are all measurable. (This means operationally that there exist quantitative surrogates or proxy variables for these three qualities.) The curve TT on the diagram, analogous to a production possibility curve, bounds the efficient assumption sets available. That is to say, sets southwest of TT are inferior to sets on TT as regards both simplicity and realism, while sets northeast of TT are not attainable. Proceeding along TT in a northwesterly direction, we suppose each successive point to involve increased predictive efficiency or explanatory power [12] (corrected for degrees of freedom) until we reach E. Thereafter, predictive efficiency decreases monotonically. Let the two points F_1 and F_2 represent the minimum levels of predictive efficiency that we are willing provisionally to "accept."

The other curves of Figure 2 are three different families of indifference varieties, equally subjective and, to my agnostic way of thinking, equally "reasonable." The horizontal set I'_i is an institutionalist's; it results in the choice of a complex but realistic assumption set corresponding to point F_1. The vertical set I''_i is a positivist's; it results in the choice of the simple but unrealistic assumption set corresponding to point F_2. The set I_i is a compromiser's; it results in the choice of the half-way house corresponding to point G, which will not generally coincide with E unless the compromiser is a statistical pragmatist as well. We cannot tell a priori whether the F_i will lie on the same indifference curve (as I_0 here) or whether F_1 and F_2 will lie on different curves.

We might also guess with some reason that a moderate institutionalist's optimal point G would fall between E and F_1 (as in the diagram), while a moderate positivist's optimal point G would fall between E and F_2. In (almost) all cases, we suggest that some sacrifice of predictive efficiency is accepted in the interest of subjective preferences for realism in the first case and for simplicity in the second. (I do not agree with one critic who maintains that the institutionalist preference for assumptional realism is (a) inherent in normal human nature and (b) required for pragmatic explanation of past events along with predictive powers over future ones. But if he is right, G *must* lie between E and F_1 on the diagram.)

VII. THE "MYRDAL" CONTROVERSY

The last methodological problem for which we can take time is by no means the last live issue among economists (even within the Western

---

[12] Sherman Krupp proposes that "scope" be added to predictive efficiency and explanatory power as a desideratum of an assumption set. Except for uncertainty about the meaning of "scope," I accept this suggestion. For economy of space, however, we may perhaps include "scope" in "explanatory power," along with its usual meaning of applicability to past historical episodes.

world, and we omit any East-West dialogue). This problem centers about the Swedish Socialist Gunnar Myrdal, much as the debate on assumptions has been associated with Milton Friedman. The "Myrdal controversy" is about the relative usefulness of equilibrium and vicious-circle analyses [13] in policy proposals for underdeveloped areas like South and Southeast Asia and for underprivileged communities like American Negroes and Puerto Ricans.

Consider first the so-called Heckscher-Ohlin theorem in international economics. Economists generally agree that, under free trade conditions, countries specialize in commodities and production processes using their relatively more abundant resources more intensively, their relatively less abundant resources less intensively. Underdeveloped countries, for example, will specialize in labor-intensive agriculture and handicrafts plus (if they are fortunate) land-intensive natural resources, like petroleum and rubber. Developed countries, on the other hand, will specialize in capital-intensive manufacturing industries, particularly in heavy industry, to utilize their relatively abundant supplies of capital. The Heckscher-Ohlin theorem says that, in consequence of this specialization, wages tend to rise in underdeveloped countries relative to developed ones, and vice versa for interest rates. (Under certain special conditions, in fact, both wage and interest rates will eventually be equalized all over the world, even without migration or capital movements!)

If this equalizing and equilibrating tendency operates, clearly, the special problems of the underdeveloped countries will solve themselves through international trade with no need for positive planning. In the same way, the American Negro's economic problem can be solved by capital-poor Negroes concentrating on labor-intensive occupations like agriculture and services, while the labor-poor whites concentrate in capital-intensive ones like manufacturing.

Offsetting these equalizing and equilibrating tendencies, however, Myrdal finds pervasive vicious circles operating. Labor in the developed countries (or the American white community) has relatively good education, housing, health, and public services. Its efficiency and skill are built up over time. Its compensation and living standards rise. Labor in underdeveloped countries (or the American Negro community) lacks these advantages or enjoys them in a lesser degree. Its skills lie dormant, or may even fall when handmade products are displaced by factory-made imports. Demand for such labor falls off, at least relative to demand for better labor in developed countries. Its relative compensation and living standards also fall. Myrdal, therefore, argues that trade between developed and underdeveloped countries, or between Negro and white communities, sets off vicious circles which operate more certainly and rapidly

---

[13] See Gunnar Myrdal, *An International Economy* (New York: Harper, 1956).

than the Heckscher-Ohlin theorem itself. The result of trade is, therefore, increasing (relative) misery in the developing countries and underprivileged communities. It is the Marxian forecast in an internationalized revision. To avoid increasing misery, free trade must (says Myrdal) be modified drastically, with special privileges for developing countries (and underprivileged communities). The conventional economist's stress on equalizing and equilibrating tendencies is not only factually wrong, but it reflects bourgeois bias in favor of laissez-faire and against organized public action.

The facts of history seem at first glance to support Myrdal. The richer countries are growing richer, while many poorer ones are stagnating in terms of income per capita, departing from the market economy, or both. Two points are, however, in order before we discard the equilibrium notion out of hand. In the first place, and most generally, each case in dispute should be examined on its own merits. (There may be need to reinforce the law of gravitation for reasonable stability in a world of feathers in a high wind, but not in a world of leaden boulders in a dead calm.) The equilibrating mechanism may work more happily in Puerto Rico than in neighboring Haiti, more happily in the Philippines than in neighboring Indonesia. In the second place, Myrdal's reading of economic history fails to support his strictures against liberal trade policies insofar as these have been preached more fully in theory than practiced in fact. If poor-country wage rates have risen less rapidly than rich-country ones, has the villain been international freedom of trade or the protectionism of the rich countries? No American is a stranger to high-wage arguments for protection against so-called sweated, coolie, or substandard labor from the poor countries, and no elaborate analysis is needed to show that such protection is aimed directly at foiling the Heckscher-Ohlin theorem. In the same way, policies of agricultural protection in rich countries, especially when coupled with subsidization of agricultural exports, are aimed in the same direction.

Another element in the historical picture is the general tendency for population and the labor force to "explode" more rapidly in poor than in rich countries. This tendency is not opposed directly to the Heckscher-Ohlin theorem, as is rich-country protectionism. Nevertheless, it operates to delay or reverse the equilibrating forces on which the theorem relies.

VIII. METHODOLOGICAL TOLERANCE

Let me close this essay with a muffled plea for methodological tolerance rather than a set of definitive solutions to our set of methodological issues. This seems more than slightly anticlimactic—like announcing oneself moderately against sin. And yet it is not.

To explain why a plea for tolerance need not be anticlimactic is itself an embarrassing task. The explanation involves semipublic washing of some of the "economics profession's" dirty linen. Some of my examples may be unrepresentative and extreme. Even so, however, there exist numerous American research and teaching institutions of standing for which any plea for tolerance, however muffled, is meant as a shock. There are, for example, some in which Chicago School positivists will not be accepted, and others where nobody else is welcome. There are institutions where institutionalism is a "dirty" word; others in which the "conventional economist" is on a par with the man-eating shark; others in which one must confine one's interest to immediate problems of policy; still others in which one must claim at least "cookbook" proficiency in econometrics, mathematical economics, or preferably both.

Marxian economists present special problems on the American scene particularly during the Cold War. Many employers will not have them, any more than Russian or Chinese ones will have anyone else. A more common approach is to tolerate such Marxists as can prove familiarity and adeptness with other sorts of economic analysis as well. (This may appear reasonable, until we remember that nobody requires that a disciple of Marshall or Keynes have any familiarity with Marx.) A different double standard is practiced in Japan, which prides itself on greater academic freedom than America possesses. There a candidate should take a stand, be counted in one camp or the other, and if a Marxist, prove complete disinterest in "bourgeois economics." There is prejudice against the prospective eclectic compromiser and synthesizer "with both feet planted firmly in the air," who has joined neither church.

Considerations of professional purism are occasionally raised to justify intolerance. An econometrician is opposed not because he is an econometrician, but because he is "really" a mathematician or statistician rather than an economist. A labor economist of institutionalist leanings is voted down as "really" a sociologist or welfare worker; a development economist is rejected as "really" a geographer, historian, or anthropologist. The economic historian on joint appointment, who must prove professional purity in two departments simultaneously, often has the saddest fate of all. (He is currently also in short supply!)

The foregoing paragraphs have been limited to the "academic freedom" aspects of the toleration problem. An additional argument, from complementarity between disciplines, argues in the same direction. For example, the future economic theory of the business firm may gain from combining the standard model (which assumes the single goal of profit maximizing under certainty) with behavioral theories of both individual and organizational reactions to uncertainty, imperfect knowledge, and a multiplicity of goals. Similarly, the future economics of growth may combine the model building of formal economic dynamics with the facts of economic history and the socio-cultural insights of the social psychologist and cultural anthropologist.

Unfortunately, no pleader for methodological tolerance in this or any other discipline can avoid recognizing certain limitations. What about the Fascist, Red or Black, who preaches planning with the bull whip (plus the input-output table), and practices methodological intolerance on anyone else? What about the John Bircher who purges in the sacred names of laissez-faire and free enterprise? What about the "genius" (alias crank), self-taught or otherwise, reforming the world from one book, from his own unfinished masterpiece, or simply from "voices in the air"? What about the economic astrologer, the tea-leaf reader, the hired hack? What about the picker-over of the entrails of birds and computers? Is there a line to be drawn on either side of commitment to a mental institution? If so, where, and on which side?

If these are "academic" or "theoretical" issues, they are not insignificant ones. In the Pittsburgh area where I teach, an heretical sect has its headquarters, predicting our future by sine and cosine curves of varying lengths and amplitudes. In the exurbia of Boston, near the Inner Temple of American economics, other idiosyncratics reorder the economy from an index of (potential) inflation, which itself depends as much upon the "quality" of money—in practice, its gold backing—as on either its quantity or the observed movements of prices. Does methodological tolerance require me, in the limited time at my disposal, to invite worshippers of trigonometric tables to share my chalk and blackboard? Does it require my Harvard, M.I.T., or Amherst colleagues to do the same for mystical devotees of the golden coin and calf? Should we require our students, in the limited time at *their* disposal, to ponder at length what one or both of these cults have to say? I know what we do, but not why we do it. While feeling strongly (not without evidence) that most teaching and research institutions need more methodological tolerance rather than less, on the question of limits I throw up my hands and call for help. When better straws are built, this drowning man will grasp at them.

BIBLIOGRAPHY

SECTION I

Standard starting points for the student of contemporary economic methodology are John Neville Keynes (father of the more celebrated John Maynard), *Scope and Method of Political Economy* (London: Macmillan, 1891); Alfred Marshall, *Principles of Economics*, 8th ed. (London: Macmillan, 1920), Book i; and Lionel Robbins, *Essay on the Nature and Significance of Economic Science* (London: 1932). The reference to Oskar Lange relates to his "The Scope and Method of Economics," *Review of Economic Studies* (1945–1946). Of interest also are Fritz Machlup, *Essays on Economic*

Semantics (Englewood Cliffs, N.J.: Prentice-Hall, 1963), and Joan Robinson, *Economic Philosophy* (Chicago: Aldine, 1963).

On the current "scarcity" debate, see Robert Theobald, *Free Men and Free Markets* (New York: Pantheon, 1963), and Peter J. D. Wiles, *The Political Economy of Communism* (Cambridge, Mass.: Harvard, 1962), Part IV. J. Kenneth Galbraith, *The Affluent Society* (Boston: Houghton, 1958), while better known, deals with "private" but not "public" goods as "abundant." A shorter piece is the writer's "Scarcity Hypothesis in Modern Economics," *American Journal of Economics and Sociology* (July, 1962).

SECTION IV

With regard to the role of mathematics in economics, strong affirmative statements are found in Paul A. Samuelson, *Foundations of Economic Analysis* (Cambridge, Mass.: Harvard, 1947), Chap. 2, and "Economic Theory and Mathematics: An Appraisal," *American Economic Review* (May, 1952). More skeptical views may be found in George J. Stigler, *Five Lectures on Economic Problems* (London: London School of Economics, 1949), Lecture 4, and David Novick, "Mathematics: Logic, Quality, and Method," *Review of Economics and Statistics* (November, 1954).

Our discussion of the scientific character of economics, particularly the model-theory distinction, rests on Andreas Papandreou, *Economics as a Science* (Philadelphia: Lippincott, 1958). "Reaction functions" are developed in Franco Modigliani and Emile Grunberg, "The Predictability of Social Events," *Journal of Political Economy* (December, 1954).

SECTION V

I have not found reasoned statements of "immanent empiricism" in economics, but plenty of loose inductionist statements about "the facts speaking for themselves." The Mason reference is to "Interests, Ideologies, Stability, and Growth," *American Economic Review* (March, 1963), p. 2 f.

SECTION VI

Friedman states his methodological position most clearly in his "Methodology of Positive Economics," in *Essays in Positive Economics* (Chicago: University of Chicago Press, 1953); Eugene Rotwein, "On 'The Methodology of Positive Economics,'" *Quarterly Journal of Economics* (November, 1959), is an attack on this position. Friedman's "permanent income" hypothesis is developed in his *Theory of the Consumption Function* (Princeton, N.J.: Princeton University Press, 1957).

An institutionalist manifesto is Allan G. Gruchy, *Modern Economic Thought: The American Contribution* (Englewood Cliffs, N.J.: Prentice-Hall, 1947), supplemented by Ben B. Seligman, *Main Currents in Modern Economics* (New York: Free Press, 1962), Chap. 3. Of original sources, the most readable is perhaps Thorstein Veblen, *Theory of Business Enterprise* (New York: Scribner, 1904). Much of the argument dates from the *Methodenstreit* over German *Historismus* in the late nineteenth century; compare Seligman, *Main Currents,* Chap. 1.

The standard work on general equilibrium economics is Léon Walras, *Elements of Pure Economics,* trans. by Jaffe, (Homewood, Ill.: Irwin, 1954). Robert E. Kuenne, *General Equilibrium Analysis* (Princeton, N.J.: Princeton University Press, 1963) is at a higher level of mathematical sophistication. On Western planning applications, see Jan Tinbergen, *Economic Policy: Prin-*

ciples and Design (Amsterdam: North-Holland, 1956); also Hollis Chenery and Paul Clark, *Interindustry Economics* (New York: Wiley, 1959); on Soviet applications, P. J. D. Wiles, *The Political Economy of Communism,* Part ii. Friedman's attack is found in "Lange on Price Flexibility and Employment: A Methodological Criticism (in *Essays in Positive Economics,* pp. 277-300).

Two examples of the axiomatic approach are Tjalling Koopmans, *Three Essays on the State of Economic Science* (New York: McGraw, 1957), and Gerard Debreu, *Theory of Value* (New York: Wiley, 1959).

SECTION VII

Myrdal's concern with the "vicious circle" as distinguished from the "equilibrium" approach may be found most briefly in *Development and Under-Development* (Cairo: National Bank of Egypt, 1956); a fuller treatment is *An International Economy* (New York: Harper, 1956). For the Heckscher-Ohlin theorem, see Eli Heckscher, "The Effect of Foreign Trade on the Distribution of Income," in *Readings in the Theory of International Trade,* eds. Howard S. Ellis and Lloyd A. Metzler (Philadelphia: Blakiston, 1949), and Bertil Ohlin, *Interregional and International Trade* (Cambridge, Mass.: Harvard, 1933).

SECTION VIII

For possible enrichments of the economic theory of the firm by "behavioral science" insights, consult Herbert A. Simon "New Developments in the Theory of the Firm," *American Economic Review* (May, 1962); also Richard M. Cyert and James G. March, *Behavioral Theory of the Firm* (Englewood Cliffs, N.J.: Prentice-Hall, 1963). Everett E. Hagen, *On the Theory of Social Change* (Homewood, Ill.: Irwin, 1962) and W. W. Rostow, *The Stages of Economic Growth* (Cambridge, Eng.: Cambridge U.P., 1960), are two very different interdisciplinary approaches to economic development.

Two examples of viewpoints mentioned as "doubtful" for the extension of complete academic freedom are Edward R. Dewey and Edward F. Dakin, *Cycles, the Science of Prediction* (New York: Holt, Rinehart & Winston, 1947) and E. C. Harwood, *Cause and Control of the Business Cycle* (Great Barrington, Mass.: American Institute of Economic Research, 1957).

HENRY MARGENAU

Henry Margenau, Ph.D., Yale University, is Eugene Higgens Professor of Physics and Natural Philosophy at Yale University. Dr. Margenau has served in official capacities for numerous academic associations (President, Philosophy of Science Association, 1950–58; Chairman and Research Director, Foundation for Integrative Education, 1950 to the present). He has received many academic awards, honorary degrees, and honorary appointments. His writings include The Nature of Physical Reality *(1950),* Open Vistas *(1961), and* Ethics and Science *(1964). His research activities have been in the fields of atomic physics, nuclear physics, and the philosophy of science.*

ESSAY

2

TO THE POPULAR MIND THE WORD "THEORY" conveys something like fanciful conjecture, something in contrast with actual fact and pejorative to truth. A little of this flavor is present today in the historical, social, and behavioral sciences, indeed in the field of economics. The physical scientist rejects the implication that theory exists *a faute de mieux,* avows its necessity, and believes that a phenomenon is not understood unless a theory is at hand to "illuminate" it. The present article accepts this premise and endeavors to show what is meant by saying that a theory illuminates phenomena; for this, after all, is the characteristic role of theory, and to clarify that role is to clarify the nature of a theory.

There are theories in areas other than science, such as theology, literary criticism, aesthetics, and so-called value theory. These are based on principles differing from those employed in science and will here be ignored. When they are analyzed, they are seen to share features with scientific theory, appearing perhaps to be on the way toward

What

Is

a

Theory?

full scientific stature. Such comparisons are interesting and inviting, but this account is limited to scientific theory.

THE STRUCTURE OF SCIENCE

Science achieves a peculiar organization of cognitive experience. To lighten the load of this heavy, leading sentence, I shall comment in sequence upon the meaning of "experience," "cognitive," and "organization."

Experience in the present context shall be taken in its original literal sense to denote *all* phases of human awareness. The Latin *experiri* designated perceiving, thinking, feeling, willing—indeed every content of the mind, whether the latter be engaged in active apprehension, passive feeling, or contemplation. In current philosophy, and chiefly as a legacy of British empiricism, experience has come to mean outer, or sensory, experience. Here the word will be restored to its pristine sense.

Note also that experience differs from linguistic, and perhaps from every form of symbolic, expression. To say this is to suggest that there are ineffable experiences, fully significant private mental facts which cannot be expressed in language because of a lack of words, or which one does not bother to express. To this class belong certain unique experiences, creative acts not yet stereotyped in speech, and also trivial experiences to which no interest attaches. It is true that recurring states of awareness normally clamor for communication and hence for symbolic expression, and also that they usually achieve it in the end. But two points are perfectly clear in this context: Language and experience are not identical, nor are they isomorphic, for there are linguistic expressions (e.g., meaningless strings of words) which elicit no conscious response except auditory nonsense, just as there are unverbalized mental images and acts. The second point is this: When language matches experience, experience is the prior form. Hence, a philosophy which claims as its sole purpose the analysis of linguistic propositions puts the cart before the horse. It is a useful preliminary to true philosophizing but cannot be expected to yield more than linguistic analysis has been known to produce during two millennia, namely dictionaries plus grammatical rules. Here, therefore, science will deal with experience as distinct from language.

However, insofar as the accepted results of science *are* significant and *have* paved their roads into language—provided of course that term is taken to include symbolic logic and mathematics—the distinction just drawn is of little practical importance.

The word *cognitive* designates a vaguely definable part of experience, that associated with knowledge. To admit of vagueness here is to acknowledge the patent fact that experience defies simple classification, that it is a continuum which can be divided only in arbitrary and unstable ways. This is why logic and all other formal procedures render only imperfect and partial accounts of it. Vagueness characterizes above all those aspects of the flux of experience which are accented by sensory qualities; one cannot define the directly experienced color blue or the taste of mustard except by seeing and tasting. Vagueness is lessened in rational concepts; it is practically absent in some abstract mathematical ideas like group, integer, etc., where sensory elements are not involved. One reason for the vogue of analytic linguistic philosophy is this very vagueness of experience, which refined language does not share. Language tolerates the application of logic; experience often does not. The linguistic philosopher who ignores experience is like the mathematician who ignores the number continuum and limits himself to integers or rational fractions because they are easier to handle.

We encountered vagueness in the definition of cognitive experience, describing it as concerned with knowledge; by knowledge we mean, in turn, that which is distinct from aesthetic feeling, wishing, willing, purely appreciative enjoyment, sadness, approval or disapproval. All these are equally vague, and there is nothing that we can do about it. Across the ingredients of cognitive experience, traditional philosophy has drawn a broad line which divides—again vaguely—sensory elements (acts and results of seeing, hearing, etc.) from rational elements or concepts. In the present context we shall retain this broad division and speak of the former as protocol experiences, forming a P-field, and of the latter as constructs forming the C-field. The reason for this terminology and a more careful analysis of these ideas have been presented elsewhere.[1] Suffice it here to say only this.

The external data from which science starts and which theory seeks to organize are largely incoherent and devoid of rational relations. One cannot build a satisfying and integrated picture of the world out of the observed events and coincidences which sensory experience alone delivers. Nevertheless, these are the facts which ultimately matter for survival and comfort; ability to predict them confers power on man. Hence he develops science, which is a composition of data and concepts, a rational enlargement of the data by theory such that the whole functions to satisfy man's desire to understand, predict, be comfortable, and survive. Concepts and protocols together compose the bulk of *cognitive experience.*

The remainder of this section deals with the meaning of the word *organization,* used in the beginning to designate the result of the application of theory to cognitive experience.

---

[1] Henry Margenau, *Open Vistas* (New Haven, Conn.: Yale, 1961); *The Nature of Physical Reality* (New York: McGraw, 1950).

The word protocol (*proto-kollon*, first glue) refers to the initial page which carried the itemized but unconnected contents of a Greek book, was often prepared before the book was written, and presented the chaotic material which the book was to make coherent, reasonable, and acceptable. The "protocol" stood in much the same relation to the entire book as do the data to the whole body of science.

Concepts, on the other hand, are by their very nature, as elements of the reasoning process, endowed with logical connectivity. Propositions involving concepts entail other propositions; they have consequences. The number 3, as a concept, entails that $3 = 2 + 1$; the mere observation of three objects does not. Temperature, as a scientific concept, is related to the mean kinetic energy of molecules; the feeling of hotness in one's fingertip is not. The concept π means more than the ratio of an observed circle to its diameter, for otherwise it could not have been computed to 100,000 decimal places, as was done in 1962.[2] The price of a commodity which enters into economic theory is not the bargain price one happened to pay in a particular purchase. Concepts *correspond* to protocol data but are not identical with them. The P-experience (e.g., feeling of hotness) is often said to be subjective, while the corresponding C is called objective.

The character of protocols, which in a wider sense include raw sensations and one's memory of them as well as careful observations, the record of experiments, one's own and those performed by others, lies primarily in the fact that they are "given." They seem to assail us from without; they are coercive; while we may contrive having them or lie in wait for them, their content is beyond our control. We do not feel responsible for them until theory permits us to anticipate and regularize their occurrence. More will be said about them in the last section.

The concepts associated with P-facts, on the other hand, are, strictly speaking, invented by man; they are truly "constructed" for the sake of permitting reason to enter the scene. This is at once evident from the circumstance that the correspondence between P and C is subject to *choice* at the beginning when a theory is formed. What I select as the counterpart of hotness, whether it be the temperature registered by an alcohol thermometer or that by the efficiency of an irreversible engine, whether I use the Fahrenheit or the Kelvin scale; what I select as the meaning of time, whether it is made objective by a pendulum clock or the motion of the stars—such decisions are not controlled by the protocol events themselves. Ideas are freely created, to use Albert Einstein's phrase. Yet they are not arbitrary when science reaches a certain stage of coherent development. For the choices present in the construction of ideas must be subjected to the rigorous regimen of certain

---

[2] D. Shanks and J. W. Wrench, Math. Comp. 16 (1962).

methodological (i.e., metaphysical) principles and to the demanding requirements of confirmation, as will be mentioned below. Hence, at the end of the scientific enterprise, the constructs which correspond to incoherent protocol experiences congeal into the firmest kind of reality known.

The correspondence here in question is of greater complexity than this brief account can fully expose to view. Science develops rules for passing from a given P to its counterpart in C. These are the rules of correspondence. In the simplest instances they are unrecognized and automatic, as when we associate the idea of a star—perhaps no longer existing —with a bright spot in the sky. Even when we take the shapes and colors present in a visual sensation to be an external object, we perform an unreflective transition from a pure P to a C; we reify. In most sciences the rules of correspondence are largely procedures of measurement, and the constructs to which they lead are said to be operationally defined. Thus, operational definitions are the most important rules of correspondence in science, for they allow numbers to be attributed to P-experiences and make the reasoning about scientific constructs *quantitative*. By the same token they achieve objectivity: the reading of a thermometer is the same for all in spite of the irreproducible vagaries of the temperature sense.

The structure of science can be summed up in the sketch of Figure 1. Double lines designate rules of correspondence, circles stand for constructs, single lines between constructs depict logical or mathematical relations between them. Measurement proceeds along double lines; reasoning, theoretical analysis, calculation proceed along the single lines between constructs. *A theory is a complex of circles together with the double lines which connect them with the P-domain.*

This statement requires some qualification. There are, in fact, two kinds of science and, therefore, two kinds of scientific theory. Sciences may be classified as descriptive and explanatory. A purely descriptive science hardly exists; it would aim at a record of P-experiences. Old-style botany, zoology, and geography come close to this type. But many modern sciences are descriptive—comparative in the sense that their practitioners make careful observations and then correlate their findings. This pattern, which is reminiscent of the philosophies of Sir Francis Bacon and John Stuart Mill, has been refined in our day to form an intricate and highly refined branch of mathematics, the statistics of correlations. In terms of the diagram, correlations are linkages between the P-facts, such as are indicated by dashed lines within or near the P-domain. They, too, form rudimentary scientific theories and may be regarded as very slight excursions into the C-field. Pictorially, they result if, in an elaborate diagram like Figure 1, all circles are squashed against P. Many phases of the behavioral sciences, including parts of

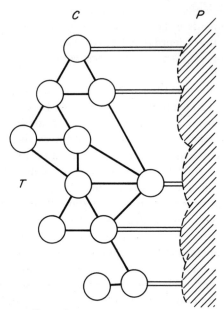

A theory is a complex of circles (constructs) held together by single lines (logical relations), e.g., the complex within the irregular envelope *T*, together with the double lines (rules of correspondence) which connect the circles with the P-domain.

Figure 1

economics, are of this variety. They may be called correlational to set them off from the theories involving more elaborate constructs, which are said to be explanatory. Again the contrast between sciences which have been termed (descriptive-comparative or) correlational and those called explanatory is not sharp.

One sometimes encounters a misconception which draws a similar distinction on the basis of the prevalence of mathematical symbolism. It is supposed that descriptive sciences use little mathematics, whereas the explanatory ones are profuse with equations. This is far from true; correlational science has become highly mathematical through the application of modern statistical techniques. But there is an important methodological distinction: Reasoning in correlational sciences is largely inductive, the conclusions are subject to probabilities. In the explanatory sciences, wherever the *C*-field is extensive, deductive reasoning is possible. This is the movement from left to right within that field in Figure 1. Constructs far to the left are abstract, general, and powerful. Propositions involving them function as premises from which other propositions, theorems, and laws of lesser range can be deduced. And as is well known, deductive inferences are not probable but certain, although true only if their premises are true. It may be said that the entire business of explanatory science is to make deductive reasoning possible, to open up for man's use the pleasing resources of deductive logic.

The distinction just drawn between correlational and explanatory sciences has thus given rise to a similar distinction between two kinds of theory, inductive and deductive. The course of scientific history seems to indicate that the former is usually a forerunner of the latter. The present essay deals with deductive theory only.

VERIFICATION OF THEORY

In the literal sense the question forming the title of this essay has now been answered. But this answer is incomplete and largely uninteresting unless it allows us to discriminate between correct and incorrect theories. Therefore, what is a *correct* theory?

The constructs which form its ingredients and the rules of correspondence which link it to protocols are arbitrary to a very considerable extent. Hence, it must be supposed that many theories can be set up to explain the contents of a given P-domain. The actual situation in most sciences clearly bears this out, at least in the early formative stages. Yet it is also apparent that among competing theories some are eliminated as time goes on, and there is, in general, even a semblance of convergence upon an ultimate limit, an asymptotic theory which might properly be labeled truth. Under what aegis, under what guiding principles does this progressive removal of obsolescent and useless theories take place? It is easy to say that the rejected ideas were false; but to specify precisely what was false about the geocentric theory of the world which did explain all known observations, or about the phlogiston theory of chemistry, or about Marxist economics is not easy at all.

In this limited space only a brief mention of the guiding rules is possible. They will be described under two headings: metaphysical requirements on constructs and empirical confirmation.

The latter are hardly subject to controversy—though not devoid of problematic features—and play a relatively simple role.

A theory is verified or, to use a more neutral word, confirmed—for a theory can never be regarded as absolutely true—if its consequences, via the rules of correspondence, meet the protocol facts. Explicitly, confirmation involves a circuit from P into C and back again to P. A set of observations (e.g., the position of a bright spot in the sky) is first fed in a theory (celestial mechanics). This means that certain P-experiences, through measurements with a telescope having marked scales of longitude and latitude, are converted into the construct: stellar body with specified position and velocity. The passage from P to C was made via a measurement routine, which is a rule of correspondence. Once in the C-field the astronomer can reason, moving as it were from one concept of the theory of celestial mechanics to another, arriving finally at a place in the C-field where another passage to P, via a rule of correspondence, is possible. That passage is called a "prediction." When the prediction meets the protocol, the theory is said to be confirmed. A theory which has sustained several, or many, such successful circuits of empirical confirmation is a promising candidate for scientific acceptance.

But it must also meet other tests, for there is the embarrassing fact that in many instances several scientific theories are successfully confirmed yet contradictory in their constructional contents. Whenever this happens, it is tempting to talk about "models," suggesting that reality has not been grasped as yet, but only a number of imperfect replicas of it. Such talk, however, is unavailing, for we never capture any static and unique "reality." We are always saddled with "models," and it is our duty and our predicament to choose among them, for reason will not allow us to live with ambiguities. And if empirical confirmation does not enable us to discriminate, we are forced to fall back on other regulative principles. These will be called metaphysical or methodological requirements on constructs.

A mere naming of them must suffice. They are often collected in a single phrase, such as economy of thought, Occam's Razor, or verifiability. When spread out into separate though closely related and continuously connected items, they present a spectrum with the following major components.

The constructs forming a theory must have as much *logical fertility* as possible. An idea entailing many consequences is better than a sterile one having few. This is why scientists prefer differential equations to numerical relations, mathematical operators to functions.

Constructs, or connected sets of them called theories, must be *extensible* to as large a P-domain as possible. On this score, quantum theory is better than classical mechanics.

Constructs must be *multiply connected*. A situation in which a simple phenomenon is explained by its own private set of constructs is suspect. One hopes and looks for connections between this set and others which account for a wholly different group of P-experiences. Ultimately, the dream of science is to explain all phenomena, those of economics as well as those of physics and chemistry, in terms of an all-embracive theory in which all constructs are logically related.

The constructs must be *simple*. What simplicity means is not very clear. Some seek it in the paucity of separate ideas composing a theory—but it is hard to count ideas. Some look for it in the forms of mathematical equations—unfortunately, however, the solutions of simple equations are sometimes very complex. Whatever the definition of simplicity, and it doubtless changes from generation to generation, every working scientist has a feeling for it which he respects and trusts. In some instances, of course, the import is perfectly clear. The simplicity of Copernican astronomy was numerically demonstrable, for it reduced the number of deferent circles required by Ptolemy from 84 to about 30.

Finally, there is a strong reliance on certain aesthetic features of a theory, on the *elegance* of its basic conceptions. Closely allied to simplicity, this regulative maxim separates what is ugly and cumbersome from sweeping ideas that carry élan and give pleasure upon comprehension. It casts its vote in favor of relativity and against a theory invoking a material ether, for the kinetic theory of heat and against the phlogiston. In modern theoretical physics the idea of elegance can be made mathematically precise in at least one context, for it means invariance with respect to a large class of well-chosen transformations.

The formal structure of a theory has thus been sketched. But perhaps sufficient attention has not been given to the solid primary stuff that makes theories necessary and possible. The meaning of protocols is still so loose that some consolidation seems in order, and this is particularly desirable because what is a protocol experience in one area of knowledge may not be one in another.[3]

DETAILED ANALYSIS OF *P*-EXPERIENCE

The foregoing discussion, which in the main followed philosophic tradition, drew the line between protocol experience and constructs approximately at the boundary separating sense impressions from concepts. Such a boundary does not in fact exist. Perceptory experience shades off continuously into the realm of concepts; to ask where one leaves off and the other begins is like asking for the point in the spectrum that separates red from blue. Nevertheless, the ideas "red" and "blue" remain meaningful. Even our attempt to characterize the *P* component of experience as the adventitious or coercive, whose origin lies outside ourselves, as the type of experience for which we disclaim responsibility, as the "unconstructed," can hardly do it justice, for there is nothing in our experience that corresponds to these descriptions with adequate purity. Every protocol experience worth the name already contains an admixture of constructional elements.

The simplest actual perception "of something" is already charged with interpretation. Its very claim to have an intentional object to which it refers loads it heavily with representational meaning. Furthermore, when language is used to communicate the occurrence of a perception, a passage to the world of symbolism and therefore construction has already taken place. Therefore, the word protocol will apply not to mere sensa-

---

[3] This was recognized as true in economics by the editor of this volume. See S. R. Krupp, *Western Economic Journal*, 1 (1963), 191.

tions devoid of meanings, which if possible at all are scientifically un-interesting, but to slightly more elaborate complexes such as *reified* sense impressions and to refined sense impressions which are occasioned (but not enforced) by such contrivances as measuring devices, for which we *are* responsible; roughly, then, the term is equivalent to *contingent* experience.

These groping efforts to define the meaning of protocol are, of course, as precarious as an attempt to define the sensed color "blue"; they will be lost upon a reader who is unable or unwilling to draw upon his memory of past occurrences which resonate with the attempted definition, just as a definition of "blue" is lost upon the color-blind. Strictly, therefore, it is necessary to use examples, and this will indeed be done. But first let us make a brief semantic analysis of the word contingent, which comes remarkably close to the heart of the protocol situation.

A given experience can be a contingent protocol fact in one sense and not in another. To the psychologist a brainstorm which sheds illumina-tion upon a problem in physics is a contingent, protocol fact, and to explain it he may invoke constructs like mental association, neural ac-tivity, or even chance, all in accordance with the foregoing sketch of the scientific method. But for the physicist, for whom P-experience is an ex-ternal observation or a measurement, the brainstorm is itself the act which reveals long-sought and welcome constructs of theoretical ex-planation. He does not count it as a P-fact, even though it is contingent in the psychologist's sense.

In short, the natural ambiguity of contingent protocol experiences breeds a variety of different sciences, permitting what goes as a construct in one to be viewed as protocol in another, and vice versa. Strictly speak-ing, every science has its own P-plane; these sometimes merge as progress is made, but even more frequently new protocol experiences call for new interpretations and generate new sets of constructs and thereby new sciences.

A survey of a few typical branches of science will expose to view what these disciplines regard as protocol. Physics comes closest to identifying it with traditional sense data, i.e., with John Locke's simple ideas, Immanuel Kant's *Wahrnehmungen,* or the contents of Rudolf Carnap's early protocol sentences. A direct observation of a physical phenomenon is a sense datum, but it is also a little more since, when recorded in objectively significant fashion, it already bears reference to physical objects which strictly are constructs. The measurement of a physical quantity is clearly more than a mere sensation. While the cul-minating act, e.g., the noting of a coincidence between a pointer and a scale, might be thus characterized, the arrangement of the measuring apparatus and the thought behind it, which are part of the measurement, pass beyond such description. The essential point here is that the outcome is contingent, cannot be predicted with certainty, and for that reason is regarded as crucial in some context of confirmation.

Refined observations (for instance, those involving microscopes, telescopes, amplifiers, and microbalances) fall into the same category as the indirect measurements just mentioned. An evident difference is encountered, however, in automatic recording devices which register measured values in the absence of any conscious perception. Here arises an epistemological question of great interest in quantum physics, where matters of this sort are crucial because of the highly abstract formalism relating to the measurement process. Suffice it here to say that an automatic record, unseen by man, is not a measurement, is not an observation, and does not count as a protocol experience in physics. Only when it enters someone's consciousness does it become one.

Contingent events are never certain; they are always surrounded by a penumbra of doubt. This uncertainty penetrates the nature and affects the use of protocol data in all sciences. It manifests itself first in the fact that one can never make an absolutely precise observation, but only one subject to some sort of error; secondly, it appears in the fluctuation of measured values that occurs when an observation or a measurement is repeated. The significant essence of a protocol experience is, therefore, almost never directly presented; it must be distilled from crude contingencies by elaborate procedures involving the *theory of errors*. Clearly, then, that theory, which regularizes the minutely deviant and erratic immediacies of observation on the basis of constructs of its own, is an important aspect of the philosophy of protocols in physics. Its extensive scope and technical complexity counsel against its inclusion in this discussion. But it should be recognized and greatly stressed that an adjustment of contingent data with the aid of the calculus of errors is necessary, not only in physics but also in every cognitive discipline, before any proper theory of that discipline can take hold of the data.

We have seen that a mere sensation rarely merits the "protocol" label in physics. If we think of a pure sensation, whatever this may denote,[4] as a plane bounding the volume called here the C-field (Figure 1), then a P-experience arises on and refers to that plane but extends some distance into the C-field. Figuratively, it may be convenient to think of it as a "bulge" on the P-plane. This bulge can be made to swell and to subside at the behest of theory because it contains constructs, which are made by the scientist. These constructs endow the observation or the measurement with more than operational meaning; they give it an affinity for a specific theory of science; they fit it into a niche within the orderly household of explanatory concepts. The more highly evolved

---

[4] I take it to be a wholly uninterpreted, preverbal, immediate, and pure sensory phenomenon like the sound of an explosion before its nature is apprehended.

and abstract the theory relating to a given observation as protocol, the larger the bulge.

Three physical examples of P-observations will illustrate this. The Newtonian theory of mechanics demands for its confirmation, and conversely explains, the motion of ordinary objects; it requires measurements of the position and the velocity of these objects. These are very close to simple sensations, and in this case the figurative bulge is small. Electromagnetic theory, when dealing with electrons, makes reference—via rules of correspondence—to scintillations on a zinc-sulfide screen and interprets them as impacts of electrons. There is still a good deal of visual immediacy in these observations, but the ideational baggage—the conception of an electron as a charged particle, the assumption that light is emitted when it collides with an atom on the screen—is considerable. Finally, think of the observation of a curved bubble chamber track photographed with a high-speed camera, a track signifying something about the motion of a hyperon. Without a great deal of theory this latter observation would never have been made. The constructional bulge is very large; the contingent event forms the culmination capping a complex network of ideas.

What has been described is a kind of *epistemological* feedback between the P-plane or field and the C-field. Only under the simplest circumstances and in the most primitive sciences does protocol experience remain unenlightened by constructs. Feedback normally causes the bulges of the P's to swell, but there are instances where it reduces them and drives protocol back to the sensory wall. This happens occasionally when theories and their demands as to confirmation become excessively complex, when the scientist begins to wonder whether nature can possibly be as cumbersome as the models he uses to explain it. Rejection of the ether theory in favor of the theory of relativity and the consequent redefinition of lengths, time intervals, and masses in closer alignment with concrete and simple measuring procedures, is a case in point.

As a last consequence of the union of ideas and sensation in protocol experience, we mention the changeability of the scientific significance of a given set of uninterpreted observations. The view of the sky and the horizon, the sun and the stars in their motions convinced the pre-Copernican that the earth stood at the center of the solar system; the same facts, coupled with certain others and with newer constructs, served as evidence for the heliocentric theory. The meaning, the bulge of simple observations, may change in a new climate of reasoning.

The preceding considerations relating to the nature of protocol experience, drawn from physics and astronomy, hold for all the physical sciences and with slight modifications for the *biological sciences* as well. In these, the kind of observation which, by way of correspondence rules, gives rise to significant constructs such as life, organic function, metabolism, growth, cell, chromosome, gene, organizer, etc. is primarily visual as it is in physics, and it is often coupled with the resources of chemistry. In the C-field, to be sure, procedures are different. Where the physical sciences place major reliance on causal, indeed on the simplest kind of causal explanation which is pictorial and mechanistic, biology is often compelled to invoke functional and teleological reasoning. The scientific method as such places no ban on teleology provided it is clear and disciplined, and not a mere cloak for insufficient analysis or lack of understanding.

A more radical departure from the physicist's choice of protocol experience occurs in *psychology* and *psychiatry*. Behavioristic psychology shows closest alignment with physics; it sees the protocol to be explained in external observations on animals and men. From these, and only these, it constructs notions like state of mind, consciousness, happiness or grief, intelligence, drive, disposition, character, and the like, and it couples these with observed behavior through operational definitions. Introspective psychology, along with certain branches of psychiatry, includes among its protocols the yields of introspection, dreams, and self-reflection, or at least a subject's report of them. These branches thus enlarge the P-plane beyond what is tolerated in physical science and thereby confer upon their activities a peculiarity which is wholly tolerable from any reasonable philosophical point of view, though they may require condemnation for loose and unprincipled handling of their constructs, e.g., for a disregard of the metaphysical requirements discussed in the second section of this chapter.

In *sociology* and *anthropology* protocol experiences are more complex; the bulge on the P-plane of which we spoke is larger. Indeed, here it is preferable, for the sake of exposition, to approach P from C by tracing backwards the rules of correspondence. In the C-field, we find simple constructs like family, siblings, tribe, nation; these are close analogs to the external common-sense objects of physical science and are related to simple observations almost by so primitive a rule as reification. But beyond this simple realm we encounter constructs like group behavior, values, and social norms, and these require for their stabilization very specific and elaborate operational definitions. The latter frequently take the form of interviews, personal inquiry, examination of the returns of questionnaires, and polls subjected to statistical analysis. What is primary and contingent here is always some aspect of the overt social behavior of people, a protocol experience which by itself is factual and irrational but becomes significant when placed in correspondence with such ideas or constructs as were listed (values, etc.).

The constructs, i.e., the elements of *economic theories*, are labeled wealth, assets, debts, market indices, business cycle, price, supply, demand, gross national product, and so forth. Their relation to protocol observations, again via operational definitions of these terms, is not unlike those mentioned in the preceding paragraph for sociology. Procurement of protocol data in this area is facilitated by existing institutions, financed by government and private sources; it involves large-scale cooperative efforts similar to those now made, belatedly, in the physical sciences. Somewhat in contrast to other social scientists, economists have begun to study and apply the full methodology of the scientific enterprise; have seen the need for careful, unambiguous, and reproducible rules of correspondence to effect the transition from P to C; and have come to recognize the unique value of exact mathematical theories and their confirmation. While the protocol data in their initial form are feelings and general observations about what people buy and sell, what profits they make and what losses they incur, how much one pays for specific commodities, these crude facts of personal economics are translated into objective constructs by very specific operational definitions which make these protocol facts objective, meaningful, quantifiable, and subject to logic and mathematics. And the theories which are blossoming forth take on increasing refinement and predictive power.

SHERMAN ROY KRUPP

Sherman Roy Krupp, Ph.D., University of California at Berkeley, is Professor of Sociology at Queens College of the City University of New York. He is the author of Pattern in Organization Analysis: A Critical Examination *(1961) and has written in the fields of methodology in economics and in the social sciences. He is currently active in organization theory, methodology, the history of social and economic thought, and the application of the concepts of economics to the other social sciences.*

ESSAY

3

SCIENCE IS POPULARLY IMAGINED TO BE A realm of serenity and certitude, a pleasant belief which scientists have not always bothered to dispel. However, it is clear that controversy is a permanent feature of the scientific landscape. Sometimes the conflict is clearly limited to a border dispute, but we can always find areas of settled belief and areas of controversy. The area of common belief is characterized by agreement about the terms of empirical reference and the criteria of confirmation. It includes a belief in the adequacy of deductive logic, the conviction that deduction can be fruitfully applied to substantive problems and that meaningful implications can be derived. It also includes some canons of relevance and use, recognizing that primitive concepts, definitions, and implications have been chosen on adequate grounds and for good reason. At the outer margins

Types

of

Controversy

in

Economics [1]

[1] For their criticisms and suggestions I am grateful to Melvin Bers, Douglas Fischer, John Moroney, Melvin Reichler, Eli Schwartz, Charles Smith, and Herbert Spitz.

of application, however, the accepted rules are often unclear and controversial. Scientific advance usually creates areas of disagreement.

Indeed, where inquiry acquires vigor it also breeds conflict, but the domain of controversy can be a very fruitful one. Disagreement can clarify issues and can make us aware of the need for new ideas or formulations that will be broader or more precise than the old ones. Hidden axioms and subtle preconceptions may be laid bare by the juxtaposition of opposing views. Dispute forces us to find the strongest grounds for our beliefs. It encourages the sharpening of concepts and the testing of propositions. Also, like the domain of agreement, dispute has analyzable forms. The nexus of conflict can be located as lying in one of four areas of theory.

First, the fundamental analogies, assumptions, and axioms of a theory may be challenged. A theory can be relatively well worked out and still present grounds for controversy. For example, economic theory, particularly micro-economics, is a well-formulated, highly axiomatized deductive theory which was developed on the equilibrium model of classical mechanics. Its primitive axioms define the individual units of the theory and assign properties to them. The maximization axioms account for the way things hang together in the theory. Maximization is to market equilibrium what gravity is to physical equilibrium. The axioms of maximization are among the fundamental assumptions of micro-economics, and the market forces of exchange and production express relationships derived from them. Nevertheless, both the equilibrium model and the principle of maximization have often been challenged.

Second, there may be disagreement about implications derived from fundamental axioms. This can occur because the choice of theorems and the definition of their empirical meanings result from the discretion and creativity of the theorist. Theorems are discovered. Their empirical meanings are constructed. Then the empirical content of the developed theory, beyond that which is contained in the axioms, is extended by attaching conditions of application to the general statements of the system and by supplying verification procedures. Although the value of the initial theorems and definitions is revealed in the elaboration of the expanded theory, critics may accept the initial axioms and still disagree with subsequent formulations. The more elementary theorems of economics include supply and demand, price elasticity, and substitution. The elaborated chains of reasoning yield concepts such as monopoly, welfare, and efficiency. One may contest the meaning of these derived concepts as well as the adequacy of their empirical support.

Third, it is possible to discuss the range and applicability of the theory. Definitions confine the theory to some ranges of application and exclude it from others, and basic assumptions tend to limit the theory's scope. Nevertheless, questions of applicability arise. Can externalities be comprehended within micro-economic theory? Can this theory be applied to the problem of race relations or to noncapitalist economies? To macro-consumption functions? What are the possible extensions of a theory to neighboring disciplines, or can nearby disciplines be extended into the theory?

Fourth, conflict may arise about problems of values and policy. How do we derive our grounds for choice between alternative means to achieve a single goal? What is the possibility of achieving collective values? Is there an ideological element in scientific theories?

Controversy over basic assumptions, over the derivations from those axioms, over the scope of theory, and over the role of values constitutes four major areas of theoretical disagreement. These areas often overlap, for economic theory is so highly developed, and its axioms are so coherently organized, that the specific function of an axiom is not always immediately apparent.

What are the functions of axioms? First, the primary axioms establish and characterize the basic units of economics. This classifying framework need not specify the relations that hold between the units. Second, the fundamental relations that hold between the units are stated as axioms. The maximization axioms, in conjunction with the elementary relations of exchange and production, form the rules of deductive combination, that is, the basic laws of the system. Third, because the laws of the system will rarely have universal application, some specification of the limits within which a given relation or law will apply is usually required. The statements which specify these limits are also axioms, known as com-position laws. Axioms which assert the strong independence of the in-dividual units and thereby limit the application of the basic relations are also composition laws. Application of the theory is thus limited to sectors where neither interdependence of tastes nor direct physical inter-dependence in production invalidates the theorems based on combina-tions of independent individual units. Clearly, the axioms which state the definitions, relations, and composition laws of a theory are continually open to refinement and challenge.

Perhaps the most important observation that can be made about the kind of theoretical controversy we have been discussing is that these arguments cannot be resolved on strictly empirical grounds. This is not to say that the empirical consequences of alternative forms of a theory are irrelevant, but merely to note that we cannnot directly appeal to them in making theoretical choices. The body of this paper will examine each of our four types of controversy as it relates to the principle of empirical confirmation.

FUNDAMENTAL ASSUMPTIONS AND AXIOMS

There are many possible strategies for the pursuit of inquiry and the framework chosen focuses the direction of a theory's development.

Explanatory frameworks may be mechanical, teleological, statistical, or historical.[2] Ideas can be presented in mathematical form, in the specialized language of a science, or in the language of everyday discourse. At the end of the nineteenth century, for example, the fundamental framework for economics was at issue in a debate between those who advocated explanations analogous to those of mechanics (the marginal utility school) and those who favored genetic explanation (the historical school). The argument turned on which of the two kinds of explanatory procedure would be more fruitful. It was a matter of deciding what questions the new science of economics was to ask and how they were to be formulated. This meant selecting a methodological model for inquiry. In the end, the controversy between economics as the "allocation of scarce means among competing ends" or as the study of historical and institutional configurations of development was resolved in the English-speaking countries in favor of the allocation question. The strategy for conceptualizing the allocation problem took the logic of mechanical equilibrium as its basic model. In the mid-twentieth century, statistical and probabilistic explanations, particularly in the resolution of problems connected with uncertainty, have gained a certain vogue. But the natural sciences have used all the methods as organizing themes for inquiry. Each strategy is differentially effective for resolving special types of problems. Statistical frameworks provide especially effective tools for resolving problems of decision under uncertainty or for problems which allow a great deal of ordering of the data. They also permit the treatment of aggregates where the behavior of individual components cannot be specified. Teleological models based on biological analogies can be extremely useful in single-goal oriented systems, such as managerial models of the firm. They can also be adapted to more complex systems where the laws of relationship are not reducible to simple forces like maximization: for example, Boulding's balance sheet model of the firm.[3] Historical and genetic methods are particularly useful in relation to problems of development. Areas of intersection between these alternative frameworks of inquiry are numerous, and such areas are often sectors of controversy.

If the strategy of theoretical inquiry is that of mechanical equilibrium, a set of basic axioms is introduced to establish the elementary units of the system, to describe their properties, and to distinguish their relations. Economics, defined as the allocation of scarce means among competing ends, takes its basic units to be the individuals or firms engaged in this activity. The primary axioms of economics endow these basic units with their characteristic properties and relations. They assert rational behavior and describe its elementary implications. The strategy of inquiry

<hr />

[2] Ernest Nagel, *The Structure of Science* (New York: Harcourt, 1961).
[3] Kenneth Boulding, *A Reconstruction of Economics* (New York: Wiley, 1950).

and the axioms, taken together, delineate the logical form, the domain, and the fundamental laws of economics.

Recently, there has been a basically healthy effort to integrate empirical research with the axiomatic framework of economics. This attempt to combine the theoretical terms of classical equilibrium theory with direct observational contexts is especially favorable to the elaboration of contexts for application. But the attempt to identify theoretical terms with directly observable phenomena has been extended by the more extreme empiricists to include the primary axioms as well. According to the more extreme applications of empirical methods advocated by some logical positivists, all the terms of a theory are required to be made operational. Theoretical issues are treated as though they can be resolved by empirical research, by the formulation of propositions in verifiable form. Little distinction is made between the empirical content of the axioms and the empirical relation of the more elaborated terms of a theory; both are regarded as being made meaningful by their direct reduction to observational terms. Consequently, the validity of the axioms is judged by their amenability to operational empirical translation rather than by their logical form. The logical role of axioms and their significance for the scope of a theory and the elaboration of theorems tends to be ignored where the stress is on questions of the empirical testability of the assumptions. But the consequence of axioms that can be highly identified empirically is that the theorems that can be derived are correspondingly limited. It is not always recognized that such restrictions can reduce the explanatory value of a theory.[4]

In micro-economics the attempt to operationalize the maximizing postulate of production theory takes the form of a familiar and apparently verifiable question: "Do firms maximize?" An empirical investigation of this question does not test the axiom at all. Rather, it serves to describe the scope and range of application of the elaborated theory, testing the relevance rather than the truth of maximizing propositions. Thus, dispute as to whether the business firm is a "theoretical entity" or an "empirical

---

[4] This controversy is continual in economics. Among the writers representative of the empiricist position are: G. P. E. Clarkson, *The Theory of Consumer Demand* (Englewood Cliffs, N.J.: Prentice-Hall, 1963); T. W. Hutchison, *Significance and Basic Postulates of Economic Theory* (London: Macmillan, 1938); Eugene Rotwein, "On 'The Methodology of Positive Economics,'" *Quarterly Journal of Economics*, 73 (November, 1959); Paul Samuelson, "Discussion," *American Economic Review Papers and Proceedings* (May, 1963), pp. 231-236; Sidney Schoeffler, *The Failures of Economics: A Diagnostic Study* (Cambridge, Mass.: Harvard, 1955).

On the other side stand: Milton Friedman, *Essays in Positive Economics* (Chicago: University of Chicago Press, 1953); Frank Knight, *On the History and Method of Economics* (Chicago: University of Chicago Press, 1956); Fritz Machlup, *Essays in Economic Semantics* (Englewood Cliffs, N.J.: Prentice-Hall, 1963); Lionel Robbins, *An Essay on the Nature and Significance of Economic Science* (London: Macmillan, 1932).

construct" or between "revealed preference" and the less testable cardinal or ordinal preference functions presents the same kind of situation. The choice is to test many of the important deductive consequences of pure economic theory, on the one hand, or to limit the scope of economics to contingent, empirical generalization, on the other hand. Pure economic theory introduces much of its empirical content by specifying contextual conditions for its elaborated theorems rather than by introducing empirical reference at the level of its axioms. It can thereby achieve greater levels of generality than a more directly empirically constructed counterpart. On the other hand, an empirical decision function such as revealed preference increases the reliability of propositions in specific contexts. We should distinguish among questions about the logical form of axioms and theorems, about their empirical content, and about their relevance to particular kinds of problems. High empirical content given to axioms reflects a preference for theory narrowly based on empirical generalization. Such theory will often have high descriptive capability, but it will be of a limited range. It also presupposes that the problems to be investigated be of a specific kind. One can choose to give axioms either high or low empirical definition; this is a free decision. Once it is made, however, restrictions are placed on the implications that can be drawn.[5] How, for example, do we formulate theories of general market behavior if we deny the maximization postulate? How can we derive propositions of general welfare if we confine our reasoning to the empirically known regions of choice entailed by the "revealed-preference" formulation of choice?

The choice of axioms, therefore, is a problem that eludes any simple solution. The import of axioms lies in the complexities of theory construction—in their scope-defining properties, in the function of theoretical terms in science, in the relations between theoretic terms and theories—as well as in the axioms' ability to clarify immediate practical problems. Uncertainty about the choice of axioms, contrary to the logical positivists, cannot be resolved by empirical test. Indeed, this question is often more meaningfully understood in terms of a philosophical bias preceding inquiry—a preference for empiricism, humanism, logical form, or practical applicability. Philosophical analysis and methodological inquiry are far more potent in clarifying these issues than a blind insistence on the primacy of operational definitions and procedures of verification.

DERIVATIONS

The second major area of theoretical controversy involves that of the confirmation of derived propositions. Any theory contains propositions

[5] Tjalling C. Koopmans, *Three Essays on the State of Economic Science* (New York: McGraw, 1957).

that are testable within some field of observation. However, a theory is only testable within a discriminated field, and usually only some parts of the theory can be represented by observables. The selection of a field of observation is achieved by describing the conditions for empirical testing or by defining the conditions within which the theorems will hold. This linkage of theoretic terms to the observable world so that verification procedures may be applied is accomplished by operational definitions.

The claim to empirical verification can usually be contested on the grounds that the operational definition does not match the original theoretical meaning; that is, the field of observation which the operational definition describes does not satisfy the conditions of the theorem. For example, should decreasing returns to scale be observed in the technology of the plant,[6] it could also be argued that the firm is made up of many plants which collectively could yield increasing returns or that the total economic environment could yield economies for the firm not inferable from the technology of the plant.[7] Distinguishing sharply between the plant and the firm alters the operational translation of "returns to scale." Because the adequacy of operational definitions can always be brought into question, theories are resistant to simple disconfirmation by the usual application of testing procedures.

All theorems and propositions require a statement of the conditions under which they apply. The *ceteris paribus* condition is an example of this in economic theory. Statements of "tendency," likewise, always contain important conditionals as qualifiers. In the social sciences, where historical, geographic, cultural and policy contexts must be included, the use of conditionals is especially necessary. As a consequence, social theory is hard to verify. The capacity of a theory to resist empirical disconfirmation is sharply increased by this introduction of qualifying conditions and when predictions do not support a theory, one may point to exceptional circumstances that operated in this special case. By introducing a general conditional into the fundamental axioms, especially a conditional whose scope is itself elastic, a theory may survive major empirical assault. Conditionals provide an escape clause against disconfirmation.

A good example of this use of conditionals occurs in the controversy over the Malthusian theory of population. In the first edition of his *Principles of Population* in 1798, Malthus stressed the geometric growth of population as a fundamental proposition and offered merely the positive population checks of misery and vice. The law of population seemed to be observable in the actual world. In the second edition of 1806 he qualified his theory by introducing the possibility of moral restraint, his

---

[6] George Stigler, "The Economies of Scale," *Journal of Law and Economics*, 1 (October, 1958), pp. 54-72.

[7] T. R. Saving, "Estimation of Optimum Size of Plant by the Survivor Technique," *Quarterly Journal of Economics*, 75 (November, 1961), pp. 569-607.

preventative check. Thereafter, when it was observed in concrete historical circumstances that population did not actually press against
resources according to the law, the preventative check could be called
upon to explain the lack of correspondence between the theory and
actuality. This introduction of the preventative check into the formulation
of his fundamental theorem effectively reduced the possibility for disconfirmation. Consequently, when Malthus' population theory was
integrated into a general theoretical system by Ricardo, it dominated
social thought in the nineteenth century.[8]

Another aspect of this problem of confirmation is important for the
social sciences. It is extremely hard to devise crucial tests in the social
sciences; consequently, tests in these disciplines are rarely decisive in
their results. Empirical support usually can be mustered either for or
against any particular proposition. It is generally necessary to evaluate
the weight of evidence or the relative significance of various kinds of
tests. The problem then emerges of deciding how a body of evidence or
a group of experiments supports a particular set of propositions. Thus, the
degree of confirmation offered by empirical evidence is itself a matter
for evaluation. A theory is an interlocking set of logically related propositions. How shall we evaluate disconfirming evidence against one proposition if the others have secured evidence in their support? The importance
assigned to a body of evidence must vary with the effectiveness of the
test that supplies it, but this is often a matter of very delicate judgment.

The problem of confirmation may be further illustrated by examining
attempts to develop an operational measure of economic concentration.
According to simplified economic theory, firms produce single commodities, and an industry is a collection of firms using similar techniques and
producing a homogeneous product. The distribution of firms according
to number and size, to the ability to differentiate their product successfully, combined with the set of conditions that determines entry into the
industry, would together yield a fair approximation of intra-industry concentration. While problems arise in the identification and measurement
of these variables, an even more elusive difficulty emerges with regard
to the definition of the field of observation. The measure of the degree
of concentration increases as the industry is more narrowly defined. The
canning industry, for example, should show a much higher degree of
concentration than food packaging. By expanding the field of observation the number of firms will increase, and the predominance of the leading few will usually decline. Because few commodities show sharp breaks
in the chain of substitutes, the definition of an industry is expandable.
Moreover, it is always possible to introduce competition on an interindustry basis (that is, furniture may be a substitute for automobiles).

---

[8] Kenneth Smith, *The Malthusian Controversy* (London: Routledge, 1951).

Consequently, an adequate measurement of concentration becomes an extremely difficult question to resolve. Good reason can always be provided for rejecting the adequacy of whatever empirical argument is devised, despite the fact that the solution of the concentration problem depends crucially upon the ability to identify, measure, and test these basic derivations of the theory.

Disputes of this second type concern the adequacy of operational definitions, the nature of conditionals, the degree of confirmation a test can afford for a particular proposition, the confirmability of clusters of related propositions or of theories as a whole, and the problems of choice between apparently divergent collections of observations. Attempts to resolve problems of this type are among the main concerns of modern empirical research and statistical theory.

THE SCOPE OF A THEORY

Controversies also arise concerning the boundaries and limits of a theory. Questions of scope are not verified in the ordinary usage of "verification." To verify an assertion of scope is to answer the question: "Where, when, how, and to what extent does this theory apply?" Formally, the scope of a theory derives from the axioms, the derivations, and the limiting conditions imposed on the theorems and operational definitions. Because problems of scope are usually not recognized as such, they represent one of the least understood aspects of theory construction.

Axioms include definitions which classify some things as belonging to a particular program of inquiry. They also include laws (composition laws) which determine the range within which a particular basic relation will hold. The axioms for ordering a rational preference function are illustrative. These axioms—comparability and known preferences, the transitivity of preferences, continuity in the ordering of preference and that of utility maximization—together restrict the elaborated theorems to domains where these conditions hold. Thus they do not apply to conditions of high uncertainty or rapidly changing tastes, nor can they cover situations where choices tend to be noncomparable, as in the redistribution effects of a simplification of the tax laws. These axioms would also include a composition law if they contained, for example, a specification of the independence of individual choice. The theorems would then not apply to sectors of interdependent preference functions or to group decisions.

The derivations acquire some restrictions on scope from the axioms, but within a given set of restrictions the permissible deductions are virtually endless. The particular choice of implications from a group of axioms will be determined by the theorists' sense of relevance, urgency, verifiability, or curiosity. Scope, therefore, will be based on empirical, practical, and logical considerations. Specification of hypothetical and theoretical conditions, operational definitions, as well as considerations of place, time, and policy further restrict scope by establishing the conditions in which the segment of theory can be applied. In part, they form a particular interpretation of a theory. Generally, theories which have relatively few and unrestricting conditions will apply more broadly than theories which introduce larger numbers of constraints. The scope of a theory refers to the manner or form in which restricting conditions are introduced as well as to their number.

The concept of time, which is basic to so much economic theory, may be introduced into a theory as a condition of scope. Concepts of the "short run" or the "long run" can be defined logically by sets of conditions of a theoretical sort (e.g., *ceteris paribus*) so that the operation of forces is confined to the logical span within which the restrictions hold. "Run" in this sense limits the context of analysis to a set of prior conditions which, in turn, may or may not be operationally translated into observables. Here the run is defined by a set of theoretically imposed conditions. Run may also be defined more directly as clock-time, or on an historical time axis which restricts the context to a time-place dimension. In the logical discussion of run the temporal identification of one element in the set of restricing conditions is sufficient to give analysis a concrete historical dimension, however incomplete it may seem (for example, the period of free market capitalism). The more numerous the clock-time restrictions, the more the analysis is restricted to the conditions imposed, and the more contingent the generalizations become. A crucial and largely unresolved problem of composition is how to aggregate short runs to deduce the long run.

According to its restrictions, a theory can explain and predict well in one area, with debatable success in another, and completely inadequately in a third. Nevertheless, extraordinary success in one area often encourages attempts to extend the theory's range over increasingly wider circles of inquiry. Lack of clarity over the range of applicability is a fertile source of conflict between theories.

The problem of externalities in micro-economic theory is an important example of a scope problem arising at the boundary of a theory.[9] The theorems derived from conventional assumptions of independence among individual units cannot be applied to problems of collective choice or to the interdependence which may arise in aggregation. Normally, qualifications of the independence assumptions occur in the form of new conditions or new variables which adapt some of the theorems to special

[9] This problem was more fully developed in the author's paper: "Analytic Economics and the Logic of External Effects," *American Economic Review Papers and Proceedings* (May, 1963), pp. 220-226.

contexts. For example, a rising supply curve may be explained by rising transfer payments, a relationship not directly derivable from the simple aggregation of individual cost curves. In this case, transfer payments can be introduced as a new variable to the aggregation. But where direct physical interdependence exists (for example, the social consequences of industrial smoke), the theorems of micro-analysis do not apply and cannot be extended without radical reconstruction. The relations of the pricing system can give an adequate account of the aggregate of micro-units, but the same theory will not explain the phenomenon of similar aggregation in the situation of direct physical interdependence. The explanations of micro-economics become less adequate as they approach a boundary that delineates the scope of what may be a perfectly adequate theory within its range. Thus, micro-economic theory develops a relatively adequate theory of comparative efficiency for the smaller sectors in the market mechanism, but it fails to develop systematic criteria for evaluating other economic systems or for the market mechanism as a whole. A more obvious example of theoretical conflict occurs at the border line of economics and sociology, when principles of efficient allocation are applied to underdeveloped areas. Disregarding the structure of social institutions creates the risk of significant negative feedback in the form of social disorganization.

VALUES

Controversies over values are complicated by the fact that values may be explicit or implicit within a theory. Full employment is often an expressed value, as are other goals such as price stability, growth, income equality, and so forth. However, in choosing definitions or in judging rival bodies of evidence for an hypothesis, implicit values are often introduced. They appear when one kind of relationship is singled out for control while others are treated as more or less independent factors. Thus, John Maynard Keynes' emphasis on the control of investment rather than on the redistribution of income to increase aggregate demand implies a value judgment. However, if, for a cross-section consumption function, the marginal propensity to consume can be shown to be constant, Keynes' value judgment is changed into an empirical problem. As an empirical question, however, this issue has never been settled.

In equilibrating systems values appear in a number of ways.[10] They help frame the questions that are being asked and thus provide principles for the selection of some of the important variables for the system. A theory may have an inadequate formulation if the values are not properly structured. Theoretical systems that are oriented toward the fulfillment

---

[10] This point was more fully explored in the author's book, *Pattern in Organization Analysis* (New York: Holt, Rinehart & Winston, 1961), pp. 32-50.

of a single explicit goal often fail to specify fully the variables that determine this fulfillment. Or values may be specified, but the range of variation of a given variable is too widely or too narrowly postulated, which
restricts the explanatory possibilities of the system. Also, the way the
variables are singled out will lead policy makers to assume that some
variable is more or less responsive to control than is indeed the case.
When this occurs, the policy maker will overstate or understate the possibilities of goal realization. These are errors of judgment, not flaws of
equilibrium analysis itself. Nonetheless, they are extremely common in
the social sciences.

In systems where goals are implicit an even greater bias can be introduced. The introduction of implicit value judgments into multiple goal
systems is a central problem because goals are rarely consistent. If
there is no reconciliation at points of intersection, such systems will be
incomplete. Keynes' criticism revealed this to be the case in classical
equilibrium theory, which emphasized the allocation of resources and
assumed full employment. It was believed that the system would be automatically self-adjusting near full employment because if a variable
reached a magnitude inconsistent with full employment, forces would be
unleashed which would change this magnitude in the direction of a
full-employment value. No one supposed that savings could rise significantly enough to create long-term disturbance, but if they did, a
compensating change in interest rates would stimulate a level of investment high enough to offset the fall in consumption. The self-regulating
character of the system was guaranteed by the variables chosen and by
setting restrictions on their number and possible range. It was also believed that deviations from full employment could readily be reduced by
monetary manipulation, a form of policy that intrudes least on the conventional mechanisms of economic allocation. The Keynesian framework,
in contrast, took full employment as its organizing value, minimized the
problems of inflation, and gave monetary stability a minor place on the
scale of values. People who do accept the efficacy of competitive equilibrium pricing as an effective system of explanation and those who do not
differ greatly in their treatment of empirical matters, explanatory frameworks, and policy questions. Differences in values affect many questions
that seem to be empirically determinable. This situation arises because a
judgmental factor is usually introduced at the level of testing hypotheses.
A decision about the adequacy of an individual hypothesis requires the
assignment of weights to various kinds of support and degrees of confirmation, not all of which are directly comparable. The degree of confirmation is, therefore, itself a variable with relatively wide flexibility.[11]

---

[11] C. West Churchman, *Theory of Experimental Inference* (New York: Macmillan,
1948).

The degree of confirmation of an entire theory is highly intertwined with value judgments which reflect, among other things, the selection of its constituent hypotheses. It is not coincidental, therefore, that the advocates of the theories of competitive price will simultaneously defend diminishing returns to scale, a low measure of economic concentration, the demand-pull explanation of inflation, a high consumption function, the effectiveness of monetary policies on full employment, the insignificance of externalities, and the general pervasiveness of substitution rather than complementarity as a basic relation of the economic system.

CONCLUSION

Theoretical controversy is closely intertwined with the procedures of science. It is not a pathology of scientific exploration to be deplored in favor of a consensus among intelligent men. Indeed, when consensus appears, there may be a sharp reduction in scientific discovery. Nor are differences in position usually clearly understood. A discussion may have to continue for a long time so that the issues become clarified before controversy can be located as impinging on a particular area of a theory. The philosopher, Gilbert Ryle, vividly stated the grounds for controversy when he wrote:

> a theorist is not confronted by just one question, or even by a list of questions numbered off in serial order. He is faced by a tangle of wriggling, intertwined and slippery questions. Very often he has no clear idea what his questions are until he is well on the way toward answering them. He does not know, most of the time, even what is the general pattern of the theory that he is trying to construct, much less what are the precise forms and interconnections of its ingredient questions.[12]

BIBLIOGRAPHY

AEA Readings in Industrial Organization and Public Policy, Vol. VIII. Richard Heflebower and George W. Stocking, eds. Homewood, Ill.: Irwin, 1958.

Broad, C. D., The Mind and Its Place in Nature. New York: Harcourt, 1925.

Churchman, C. West, Theory of Experimental Inference. New York: Macmillan, 1948.

———, Prediction and Optimal Decision. Englewood Cliffs, N.J.: Prentice-Hall, 1962.

Hanson, Norwood, Patterns of Discovery. New York: Cambridge U. P., 1958.

Hutchison, T. W., Positive Economics and Public Policy. Cambridge, Mass.: Harvard, 1964.

Kaplan, Abraham, The Conduct of Inquiry. San Francisco: Chandler Pub. Co., 1964.

---

12 Gilbert Ryle, Dilemmas (New York: Cambridge U. P., 1954), p. 7.

Krupp, Sherman, *Pattern in Organization Analysis*. New York: Holt, Rinehart & Winston, 1961.

Machlup, Fritz, *Essays in Economic Semantics*. Englewood Cliffs, N.J.: Prentice-Hall, 1963.

Majumdar, Tapas, *The Measurement of Utility*. New York: Macmillan, 1958.

Margenau, Henry, *The Nature of Physical Reality*. New York: McGraw, 1950.

Myrdal, Gunnar, *Values in Social Theory*. London: Routledge, 1958.

Nagel, Ernest, *The Structure of Science*. New York: Harcourt, 1961.

Papandreou, Andreas, *Economics as a Science*. Philadelphia: Lippincott, 1958.

Rothenberg, Jerome, *The Measurement of Social Welfare*. Englewood Cliffs, N.J.: Prentice-Hall, 1961.

Ryle, Gilbert, *Dilemmas*. New York: Cambridge U. P., 1954.

FRITZ MACHLUP

Fritz Machlup, Dr. rer. pol., University of Vienna, is Professor of Economics and International Finance at Princeton University. Besides general methodology of the social sciences, his research activities include pure economic theory, monetary theory, international economics, and industrial organization. He is the author of fifteen books and over a hundred articles in professional journals. Among his most recent books are The Production and Distribution of Knowledge in the United States *(1962) and* Essays in Economic Semantics *(1963).*

ESSAY

4

SOMETHING LIKE A "CULTURAL LAG" CAN BE found if one compares different fields of learning. Certain methodological ideas have arrived in some fields many years later than in others—sometimes after they had been discarded by the others. Certain "teachings" about scientific method and about the "proper" formation of concepts and theories have reached a particular discipline long after other disciplines had recognized them as errors.

Cases in point are the rejection of "causality" and all causal theories; the championing of "description" in opposition to "explanation"; the taboo against "nonobservables" and against mere "constructions of the mind"; the contemptuous characterization as "pseudo problems" of all questions to which only nonverifiable answers can be given; the insistence that only "operationally defined" concepts be used in scientific theories; the demand that every assumption employed in a theory be tested independently; the assertion that theories are "empty" (of empirical content) if they

Operationalism

and

Pure

Theory

in

Economics

include postulational propositions; the contention that theories must not be wider in scope than the empirical evidence available for their support. It might be possible to date the birth of each of these positions and to supply a time schedule of their arrivals in various disciplines.

The time schedule of "departures" of these ideas from the various disciplines would be difficult to ascertain, for there are cultural lags also among different representatives of the same discipline. Although most physicists, for example, have outgrown virtually all the positions enumerated, others—including some well-recognized authorities in special areas —may not have been keeping up with developments in the philosophy of science and may repeat the methodological precepts they were taught when they were students decades earlier. This holds for biologists, psychologists, sociologists, economists.[1]

It would be an interesting undertaking to show how little the methodological propositions stated by a writer are related to his own research and analysis. Many do the things they pronounce impossible or illegitimate, and many fail to do what they declare to be essential requirements of scientific method. These differences between the actual formation of substantive scientific theories and the statements of "theories of theory formation" should not surprise us. Most of us know how to walk, but do not know what our brains, nerves, muscles, etc., have to do in order to make us walk. Some great athletes have quite outlandish theories about the superiority of their techniques, but these ideas, however silly, do not affect their performance. Hence, a great physicist or a great economist may, without any consequences for his scientific work, embrace and proclaim the most naïve and outdated methodological principles. Students of methodology should beware of the temptation to rely on authority in accepting the methodological pronouncements of a great figure in his field.

The present essay attempts neither a survey of methodological thought in economics nor a review of the debate on a particular methodological issue. Its aim is much more modest: to offer a clear, but critical, presentation of the principles of "operationalism" (or "operationism") in economic concept and theory formation.[2]

---

[1] Perhaps some examples may be in order. The rejection of causality and the championing of mere description (rather than explanation) became fashionable in the last quarter of the nineteenth century. Many years later, Schumpeter was one of the first economists who embraced the excommunication of causality (1906), but later he was one of the most vigorous to plead for its reinstatement. The anathema against explanation and the exhortation for "description only" are still maintained by Samuelson (1964). I know of no philosopher of science who still clings to such views.

[2] For a more elaborate analysis of operationalism in physics and economics, see my article on "Operational Concepts and Mental Constructs in Model and Theory Formation," *Giornale degli Economisti*, 19 (September-October, 1960), 553-582. Reprinted in Università Commerciale Luigi Bocconi, Milano, ed., *Studi di Economia, Finanza e Statistica in Onore di Gustavo del Vecchio* (Padova: Cedam, 1963), pp. 467-496.

THE TENETS OF OPERATIONALISM

Operationalism insists that "the proper definition of a concept is . . . in terms of actual operations"; claims that pure constructs, designed "to deal with . . . situations which we cannot directly experience through our senses," should (although sometimes indispensable) be replaced as soon as possible by operationally defined concepts; denies that a "question has meaning" if one cannot "find operations by which an answer may be given to it"; and demands that "the operational mode of thinking [be] adopted in all fields of inquiry." [3]

This program concerns both the formation of *concepts* and the formation of *theories*. It is possible to accept a modified "operational" position for theory formation without accepting the program for concept formation. However, since this modified position removes the idea of operationalism far from what it originally meant—and employs the word "operational" merely as an equivalent for "verifiable"—we shall understand the principles of operationalism as they were originally proclaimed.

Whose operations were referred to? Clearly, the scientist's, observer's, experimentalist's, surveyor's, technician's, interrogator's, statistician's operations were meant. *What kind* of operations? "Physical operations" were required for physical concepts; this, evidently, meant chiefly experimental operations. In other empirical disciplines the operations would include setting up instruments, taking certain measurements, making controlled observations of all sorts, going through certain routines in recording, compiling, computing, and so forth.

Two contentions in the early operationalist position cannot meaningfully be maintained: (1) that the operations defining a concept are "identical with the concept"; and (2) that "mental operations" are still within the compass of the requirements of operationalism.

The asserted identity between the concept and the set of operations that defines it can conceivably be maintained for certain metric concepts (distance, time, velocity, weight) but not for other things. Concepts of (sensory or imagined) objects or events can be defined through sets of operations, but these operations are not identical with the concepts. The operations by which scientists identify a chemical substance, a gas, an animal, a disease, an earthquake, a revolution, an inflation, a strike, etc., are surely not "identical" with the things defined.

The admissibility of "mental operations" was probably only a momentary lapse, induced by the need to reconcile the exaggerated statement

---

[3] All quoted phrases are from Percy W. Bridgman, *The Logic of Modern Physics* (New York: Macmillan, 1927), pp. 6, 53, 28, 30.

about the prescribed operations being "a criterion of meaning" with the recognition that the formal disciplines—mathematics and logic—cannot be condemned as "meaningless." If "operations" are a prerequisite of meaning and if mathematical propositions evidently have "meaning," mental operations must be approved. However, if this approval is extended to empirical sciences, the entire platform of operationalism is compromised. For the formation of concepts in empirical sciences, definitions can admit only operations with data of experience, with records of observations, with "protocol statements."

The question is only whether the operations that define concepts must be *actually* performed (or performable) or whether merely *conceivable*, but not practically possible, operations are also acceptable. Conceivable operations with not yet invented instruments or not yet discovered techniques are perhaps acceptable if there is an honest expectation that these operations may soon be practically possible. On the other hand, conceivable operations of a more "imaginative" character, based on developments which nobody can reasonably expect to become reality, ought to be disqualified as criteria for allegedly "operational" definitions (for example, operations with a mind-reading device that records the hypothetical thoughts and choices of millions of people in thousands of hypothetical situations). If such fictitious operations were admitted, the difference between operational concepts and pure constructs would disappear and the demand for "operational definitions" would become senseless. This demand, in essence, is for concepts of things *observed,* for empirical data from the sensory domain, in contradistinction to concepts of things *imagined* or *postulated* in the domain of mental construction.

For the operationally defined concepts of economics the relevant operations are largely based on reports and on records compiled from reports, such as balance sheets, profit-and-loss statements, bank statements, market quotations, price lists, customhouse statements, income-tax returns, census returns, and so forth. Most of the data, both the raw data from the original reports and the manipulated data from the compilations, are numerical; but also nonnumerical "events," reported in newspapers, trade journals, and other publications, may be among the data entering into and emerging from the operations described or prescribed in the definitions.

It is one of the commandments of operationalism that the propositions which form a "theory" should be composed solely of operational concepts. Unfortunately, "theories" made of such material are only what some philosophers have called "low-level generalizations" or "statements of empirical uniformities and regularities." The "general theories," the "high-level generalizations" of a "theoretical system," from which any number of propositions about all sorts of relationships can be deduced, are made of different stuff. The differences between these two types of theory will be examined presently, but first we have to make sure that we understand the nature of the building material of theoretical systems, namely, "pure constructs" and how they differ from operational concepts (as "operationally defined terms" may be called).

PURE CONSTRUCTS AND OPERATIONAL CONCEPTS

What is given to us and what is constructed by us are obviously different things. Concepts based on operations with data from the *protocol* domain,[4] on records concerning sensory observations and experiences, on knowledge about concrete objects, magnitudes, and events, may be regarded as *empirical* and as containing all the impurities and the inexactness inevitable in the reporting, recording, and computing by erring, perhaps lying, and certainly not infallible humans. Concepts based on imagination, invention, and postulation, on pure reason in the domain of mental *construction,* on idealization, hypothecation, and heuristic fictions, on nominalistic conventions adopted because of their analytical convenience and logico-deductive fertility, may be regarded as *theoretical* and endowed with the purity and fictional exactness afforded by uninhibited, abstract speculation.

I am deliberately overstating the contrast between the two types of concepts when I stress the extreme polarities empirical–theoretical, concrete–abstract, given–constructed, reality–fiction, observation–idealization, impure–pure, and so forth. One could immediately show that the empirical concepts contain plenty of theorizing, abstraction, purification, and so forth and that the theoretical concepts are not all that free, uninhibited, and speculative (or they could not serve in theories applicable to explain observations of the real world). The *operations* with the data of observation are usually designed to produce empirical concepts that somehow fit the constructs of a theoretical framework, and the *construction* of purely fictitious ideal types is usually designed to aid in the formation of theories of explanatory and predictive usefulness. The requirements of *theoretical* usefulness of operational concepts and *empirical* usefulness of pure constructs are powerful constraints in the formation of the two types of concepts.

These constraints both in the choice of operations with the "givens" and in the choice of design for the "construction" should not be understood to reduce a difference in kind to a difference in degree. Despite all

---

[4] The term "protocol" was introduced by the early neopositivists of the Vienna Circle, evidently because in German this word stands for the "record" (of a testimony) or the "minutes" (of a conference). The idea is that the data given to the scientist are in the form of a record ("protocol"). Bridgman's "operations" refer to the original observations that are recorded, to the manner of recording, and to what is done with the data recorded. Hence, operationalism is by its very nature associated with the "protocol domain."

psychological and practical similarities, the logical difference remains. Its chief implication is that the various constructs ("constructed concepts") in a comprehensive theoretical system are *logically interrelated*, whereas various empirical concepts ("operational concepts") are at best linked by *inductive generalization* or statistical correlation. Conclusions deduced from a set of hypothetical propositions containing only pure constructs follow by *logical necessity*—though they may not be applicable to the concrete situations in need of explanatory or predictive judgments. Conclusions based on inductive generalizations about observed objects, magnitudes, or events possess some more or less definite *probability value* —though they may not be helpful in conveying any genuine understanding of the causal connections involved.

Illustrations may be needed to clarify matters, and I shall choose some from economics. The term "price" in the proposition "an increase in supply will lower the price" has a different meaning from the term "price" in the proposition "the price of steel in 1933 was 15 per cent lower than in 1932." In the first proposition, "price" is a pure construct; in the second, an operational concept. What are the operations employed in ascertaining the steel price in a particular period? A large variety of operations could be used: One could procure the price lists of all steel producers and compute some sort of average, weighted or unweighted; one could ascertain their sales proceeds—gross or net of discounts, commissions, transport costs—and divide them by the total tonnage shipped; one could secure reports from steel buyers and arrange, weight, or otherwise manipulate their figures in various ways; one could rely on reports from the largest middlemen; one could propose as many as fifty different sets of operations, all sensible and reasonable, but yielding different findings. Depending on the changes in the composition of steel shipments, the average per ton may have fallen while list prices were raised (but more of cheaper types, shapes, or qualities were shipped). The average of "delivered prices" may have increased while the average of f.o.b. prices declined (transportation costs being higher, perhaps because of steel being shipped over greater distances). The average of prices may be different depending upon whether new orders received, or production, or actual shipments are taken into account.

None of these operational concepts of "steel price" corresponds completely to the simple construct "price," because the latter abstracts from the score of complications presented by "reality," particularly from differences in qualities, shapes, alloys, etc.; from differences among producers; from differences between prices quoted and prices agreed; from differences between prices paid by the buyer and prices received by the seller (net of commissions, sales taxes, transportation costs); and so forth. Many statements about the pure construct "price" would not hold for some of the operational concepts. It is perfectly possible, for example, that an "increase in supply" of steel—provided an operational counterpart could be found for this construct [5]—will under certain conditions be associated with an increase, not a reduction, in the price of steel. This could happen either because of a particular choice of operations—computing, for example, average proceeds per ton, although the increase in supply had caused also a change in the composition of physical sales in favor of more expensive qualities—or because other things changed at the same time. *Ceteris paribus* is always a construction rather than an operational concept.

Many more illustrations could be chosen from micro-economic analysis. Among the most revealing are the concepts of "cost" and "profit," but the reader may be left to his own devices in comparing the wide variety of operational concepts and the smaller selection of pure constructs designated by these terms. The fact that the underlying data available for the statistical operations by disinterested observers come from reports derived from accounting operations that leave much leeway for subjective judgment by interested parties is only one of the difficulties in choosing appropriate operational concepts of cost and profit; much more significant is the fact that virtually all practically possible operations refer to historical (*ex post*) data, whereas most of the pure constructs that are relevant for the theoretical system refer to expected (*ex ante*) values.

Macro-economic terms present the same problems. Against the fictitious purity, simplicity, and exactness of the pure constructs of national income, consumption, *ex ante* saving, investment, imports, trade balance, and all the rest, the impurities, complications, and inaccuracies of their operational counterparts are appalling. Anyone who has done empirical work with national-income statistics or foreign-trade statistics is aware of thousands and thousands of arbitrary decisions that the statisticians had to make in executing the operations dictated or suggested by one of the large variety of definitions accepted for the terms in question. One cannot expect with any confidence that any of the theories connecting the pure constructs of the relevant aggregative magnitudes will be borne out by an examination of their operational counterparts. If imports, for example, are measured by the declared values of merchandise crossing the border of the nation and passing the customhouse during a stated period, this cannot be but a very imperfect surrogate of the imports supposedly purchased in consequence of certain changes in relative prices or total income, according to some general theoretical propositions.

Of course, passages or cross-connections between the domain of construction (the pure theories with their pure constructs) and the

---

[5] See Footnote 7, page 63, for an explanation of this doubt. The point is that an observable increase in the "quantity supplied" (perhaps in response to an increase in demand) may be associated with an unchanged or even reduced "supply."

domain of recorded data are needed; these connections are possible wherever an operational concept comes particularly close to a pure construct.[6] At these points "rules of correspondence" will direct the theorist to the data, and the empirical researcher to the pure theory. But from what has just been said about operational concepts and pure constructs, it should be clear why only the latter qualify as building material for general propositions within theoretical systems.

EMPIRICAL THEORIES AND PURE THEORY

Although most writers use the terms "empirical" and "theoretical" as opposites, and thus contrast "empirical correlations" with "theoretical relationships," there are some who speak of "empirical theories." The term "theory" in this phrase means nothing but "inductive generalization," that is, a statement of an expectation or probability that the same co-existence, sequence, or numerical relation that has been observed among certain objects, events, or magnitudes in the past will also be found in future constellations of the same classes of observations. If such inductive generalizations are termed "theories" by some writers, one has to understand it as an extension of the dictionary meanings of theory. There are others, who use the designation "empirical laws" for this sort of proposition. If my reading of contemporary philosophers of science is correct, they prefer to speak of these generalizations as "correlational statements," "observed links among protocol data," or "statements of empirical uniformities." The term "theory" is more frequently reserved for those general constructions which, by permitting logical inferences from premises to conclusions (and from causes to consequences), help us understand (interpret, explain) some observed "facts" from the protocol domain.

Empirical (correlational) statements are necessarily composed of operational concepts. This does not mean that no theoretical elements are contained in these concepts. There is no such thing as "mere description." The pre-scientific reports are already permeated with some theorizing on the part of the reporters as well as of those whose instructions or directives they follow. In addition, the subsequent operations with these protocol data are influenced by theorizing of a higher order, especially if the arrangement of the data is designed for "scientific" purposes. But still, despite the treatment which the raw data must undergo, despite selections, abstractions, adjustments, corrections, and other manipulations, they still belong to the protocol domain. For, since the treatment of the recorded data must be equal and uniform in accordance with technical rules stipulated for particular classes of data, the "facts" are still "stubborn," at least in their relative dimensions. The admixture

---

[6] On "The Need for Operational Concepts," see page 65.

of theory, however, may be substantial; indeed, the operations for the production and processing (or perhaps "fabrication") of the empirical data are designed and redesigned to make the resulting operational concepts as closely corresponding to some theoretical construct as possible.

Theoretical systems are composed entirely of pure constructs. This assertion, plausible though it is, contradicts the pronouncements of a large number of scientists and philosophers. They accept a constructed, nonempirical concept only where some notion is indispensable but no suitable operational concept can be found. They want as many terms as possible, within a theoretical system, to be operationally defined. Only where operational concepts are unavailable would they provisionally admit pure constructs; and they see progress in science when theoretical concepts are replaced by empirical concepts.

The opposite position, argued in the present essay, also has numerous supporters. They see progress in science when empirical concepts are replaced by theoretical concepts, for only by redefinitions, transforming all terms into pure constructs, can a logico-deductive system be developed. Fortunately, such redefinitions require only some superior constructive minds; it is always possible to replace 'an empirical concept by a theoretical construct. (On the other hand, attempts to discover practicable operations to obtain an operational counterpart for a pure construct may be frustrated by the nature of things. The search for operational proxies for some theoretical constructs may be quite hopeless.) The replacement of empirical by theoretical concepts, or of operational by pure concepts, is, to state it once more, needed for the following reasons: The roughness, or degree of exactness, of empirical concepts depends upon the technical possibilities provided by the state of the arts. The impurities and inaccuracies inherent in most or all practicable operations with sensory observations and recorded data destroy the logical links between different concepts. But without logical interrelations the propositions containing these concepts do not afford logically necessary conclusions. In the possibility of deducing such conclusions lie the sole purpose and value of any theoretical system.

ILLUSTRATION: A THEORETICAL ARGUMENT AND THE CONCEPTS USED

The entire discussion of empirical generalizations and theoretical systems—especially with all the jargon used about "operations with data from the protocol domain" and the "purity and exactness of concepts in the domain of construction"—may be lost on readers who are not given an opportunity to see "what's what" in an illustration. Hence, we shall offer an example of a theoretical economic argument, followed by an examination of the nature of the concepts employed.

In 1964 the new Labor government of the United Kingdom imposed a 15 per cent tax on imports. Economists were probably asked to analyze the probable and possible effects of this measure. The following argument might have been formulated by an analyst using his knowledge of economic theory.

0. Effective on a certain day, a tax of 15 per cent ad valorem is levied on all imports.

1. Assuming that both the foreign supply of imports and the domestic demand for imports have elasticities greater than zero and smaller than infinity, the prices of imports including the tax will rise by less than 15 per cent; that is, foreign suppliers will obtain reduced net prices. The physical volume of imports will decrease.

2. The amount of foreign exchange demanded for payments for imports will decrease, both because of the reduced quantities of goods imported and the reduced foreign prices of some of these goods.

3. Depending upon whether the elasticity of the domestic demand for imports is greater or smaller than unity, the total amount of domestic money spent for the reduced quantity of imports will be decreased or increased, but a portion of this expenditure (less than 15 per cent since the tax is on import values, not retail prices) will go to the Treasury.

4. With consumer expenditures for imported goods decreased or increased, expenditures for domestic products may increase or decrease; however, only if the elasticity of the demand for imported goods were less than unity (which one may doubt) would consumer expenditures for domestic products decrease. In addition, if the Treasury were to spend some or all of its revenue from the import tax, this would further increase total effective demand for domestic products.

5. Increased demand for domestic products will sooner or later result in (a) higher prices, (b) increased profits for domestic producers, (c) increased demand for, and prices of, productive factors, especially labor, (d) increased costs and supply prices, not only of import substitutes and domestic goods, but also of export goods.

6. The increased prices of domestic products will lead to an increase in the (domestic) demand for imports and to a reduction in the quantity of exports demanded (abroad).

7. With regard to some particular imports, special situations—in terms of elasticities of competitive foreign and domestic supply and demand or in terms of monopolistic market positions—may require special analysis.

8. With regard to some particular countries, the possibility of retaliatory measures and their effects may require special analysis.

9. With regard to the labor market, the possibility of escalated trade-

union pressures because of increased costs of living may require special analysis.

10. With regard to the domestic credit market and official monetary policy, the possibility of an increased demand for funds and of an expansion of bank credit may require special analysis.

11. With regard to international capital movements, the possibility of increased or reduced outflows of foreign long-term and short-term funds, in the light of expectations induced by the tax measure, may require special analysis.

Although this argument is far from complete, it more than suffices for our purpose—for an examination of the nature of concepts employed.

(1) "Foreign supply of imports" and "domestic demand for imports" mean hypothetical quantities as functions of hypothetical prices. No operational concept can be devised to ascertain these functions. Even as pure constructs the imagined functions can be unambiguously visualized only for one import good, or for a bundle of import goods of uniform composition. For many import goods, each with a separate set of supply and demand functions, the problem of "aggregation," even in imagination, would present difficulties. The theorist, however, accepts the single-commodity function as a satisfactory analogy for the many-commodities case. But even if there were "in reality" only one import commodity, the supply and demand functions would still not be operational. A so-called "statistical demand function" is a *tour-de-force* and its results cannot be accepted as a usable operational proxy for a construct, let alone as a part of a theoretical argument.[7] The other concepts, in this first point of the argument, are "domestic prices of imports," "net prices obtained by foreign suppliers," and "physical volume of imports."

---

[7] "Every beginning student of economics is (or should be) repeatedly warned of the hypothetical nature of the functional relations between the variables. There are no 'observable' supply or demand functions—unless one means merely the chalk symbols which the teacher produces on the blackboard for students to observe. All the values of the functions are imagined; the supply function assigns hypothetical quantities offered in the market to hypothetical prices paid, and the demand function assigns hypothetical quantities demanded to these prices, but since the prices and quantities are hypothetical only, they cannot be observed by anybody. (It may be said for the benefit of readers who are comforted by the thought of 'conceivable operationality' that with much fantasy one may design a grand 'experiment,' with heroic controls of all relevant factors, to ascertain all values of the functions. But one must add, in all honesty, that the 'operations' required to establish the functions as empirical observations are not practically possible.) The so-called statistical supply and demand curves have not really been 'observed'; they are the result of highly imaginative computations with data recorded at different times under different conditions and manipulated on the basis of unverifiable assumptions which range from 'plausible' to 'contrary to fact.'" *Giornale degli Economisti*, Vol. XIX, p. 574.

They all have operational *counterparts*, but they are pure constructs as used in the argument.

(2) The "amount of foreign exchange demanded for payments for imports" is another pure construct. An operational counterpart is available in countries with strict foreign-exchange controls, where each application for foreign exchange must specify the purpose for which the foreign payment is made. Even there the operational counterpart will be quite inexact for several reasons, one of which is that payments made in one period may be for goods ordered much earlier.[8] In any case, an operational concept corresponding to this pure construct is "practically possible," but in countries with convertible currencies nobody will bother actually to perform or direct the relevant operations.

(3) For the construct "expeditures for imported goods" operational counterparts could be obtained if necessary. The cost would be inordinately high if complete enumeration were wanted, but estimates could be made without a large bureaucratic apparatus. For purposes of the present theoretical argument, the theoretical construct is all that is needed.

(4) The same comment applies to the construct "expenditures for domestic products." For "Treasury expenditures" the operational counterpart is actually available, though it would be difficult to ascertain whether increased expenditures were in fact induced by the increased revenues, or would have been made in any case. Actual expenditures, public and private, may serve also as a proxy for "effective demand," though this term stands again for a pure construct in the argument.

(5) For some of the concepts used here as theoretical constructs one could obtain more or less approximate operational counterparts. Exceptions are (a) "increased profits" because *ex post* reported figures would not correspond to the *ex ante* ideas of those who decide on higher production volumes; (b) "increased demand for productive factors" because one can at best ascertain purchases, employment, prices, and wage rates but not "demand"; and (c) "supply prices" because one can ascertain only prices actually paid or received but not the hypothetical prices for hypothetically supplied quantities.

(6) The "demand for imports" has already been disqualified as a candidate for operational ambitions. The "quantity of exports demanded" stands a better chance.

(7)–(11). Only two more concepts which would present serious dif-

---

[8] Another reason is that under exchange restrictions many invoices will be a little "padded" so that the payor can get a little more foreign currency than he needs to pay for the particular import.

ficulties if they had to be operationally defined will be mentioned: "monopolistic market positions" and "trade-union pressures" (since demands for higher wages are made almost constantly, how can "pressures" be quantified?).

What this exercise has shown is that for *some* of the concepts used in the theoretical argument operational counterparts are available; for *others* they could be obtained if it were really necessary; for a *third group* they could not be obtained even with the greatest expense and ingenuity; but that in the theoretical argument itself *all* concepts were pure constructs, not operationally but nominalistically defined.

THE NEED FOR OPERATIONAL CONCEPTS

If operational concepts are not wanted, not even admitted for membership in a purely theoretical argument, does this mean that there is no use for them at all? No, they are wanted, indeed urgently needed, for two purposes: (1) when one has to decide what kind of theoretical apparatus will be suitable for answering particular questions, and (2) when one wishes to verify or test the theoretical apparatus.[9] (Regarding these two purposes, the significance of the "rules of correspondence" should be recalled.)

The theoretical economic argument, used above as an illustration, was intended to answer the question "What consequences could be expected from the imposition of a tax on imports?" This presupposes that we possess an empirical concept of "tax on imports" and can define it by unambiguous operations. We do have such a concept at our disposal, and we can define it explicitly. The operations may consist in looking for a law enacted by the legislature, for decrees making the law effective, and for records of tax offices about the law being executed. An even simpler set of operations would be to look for reports by importers paying the tax. There is no difficulty at all concerning an operational definition of "tax on imports."

For purposes of verification it does not suffice to have an operationally defined concept as the clear counterpart of the starting step that sets the theoretical apparatus in motion. We also need operational counterparts for some of the conclusions furnished by that apparatus, that is, for the consequences deduced from the propositions in the logical argument. Fortunately, some of the "consequences" inferred in our illustration have operational brothers or cousins. This is true at least for the prices and quantities involved. Several other "consequences" have no operational relatives and are, therefore, not testable. But no one expects a theoretical

---

[9] See the author's article, "The Problem of Verification in Economics," *Southern Economical Journal*, 22 (1955), 1-21.

system to be tested at every use. Occasional tests under favorable conditions suffice to establish confidence in the system, which will then be used in many instances where the results cannot be verified through satisfactory "correspondence" between all deduced consequences and observed facts.

The theoretical models designed for showing the effects of changes in tax rates, tariffs, wage rates, interest rates, and similar variables have been tested often enough to satisfy us concerning their general usefulness. To be sure, there have been numerous disappointments; but, when these occurred, acceptable reasons could usually be found. The most frequent reason for disappointment, that is, for a lack of correspondence between deduced consequences and observed facts, has been some unexpected change in conditions, some simultaneous event that had not been assumed to occur and, therefore, was not taken into account in the theoretical argument. In order to maintain our confidence, the "auxiliary hypotheses" employed to excuse failures and to reconcile expected with actual observations ought to be testable. This presupposes that the crucial constructs used in these hypotheses possess operational counterparts. Only then can one prove that the alleged disturbance has not only been "assumed" but that something of this sort has actually occurred according to available evidence.[10]

OPERATIONAL THEORIES, SO-CALLED

It is not easy to know what the economists who used the phrase "operational theory" really meant by this designation. They have not furnished any illustrations or examples for their designation. Technical jargon is usually not enough to make things clear. Thus, if I fail to understand them and misinterpret their intentions, they will have to forgive me.

What the economists could have meant when they called for "operational theory" is approximately what has been advanced in the preceding section, namely, that a theory ought to have sufficient links with the protocol domain, with data of observation. Links are "sufficient" if they allow us to choose intelligently the theoretical arguments that apply to particular "concrete" situations and, in addition, if they allow us to subject the theoretical system to occasional verification against empirical evidence.

The only good reason for calling such theories "operational" is because their links with empirical data require the availability of *operational counterparts* to some of the crucial theoretical constructs. Although the

---

[10] It has been said that a good economist is one who will be able to explain next year why his predictions of last year have not come true this year.

phrase has been used here almost constantly, it is well to repeat that by "operational counterpart" of a theoretical construct we mean an "operationally defined" term that can be accepted as a satisfactory empirical referent or proxy for the construct.

There is, however, the alternative meaning of "operational theory" as propositions containing exclusively operationally defined terms. This would be what has been called "empirical theory" or inductive generalizations. It usually correlates a small number of narrowly defined concepts, that is, *classes of data*, and since there is little or anything that can be deduced from it except that the same relations among these classes of data will probably recur in the future, it applies only to a very narrow choice of "cases." For example, an empirical generalization in the field of "taxes on imports" would presuppose that we have had many previous experiences with and observations of import taxes together with other things, such as prices and quantities of imports and amounts of foreign exchange sold by monetary authorities. We could, of course, never have anything like a "general price theory." And we would not be allowed to apply an empirical theory of the effects of sales or excise taxes to a case of import taxes, apart from the fact that such a theory would not include the variables relevant to the case of import taxes (such as imports, foreign exchange, etc.).

Thus, without a sufficient number of past observations in connection with import taxes we could not present, under the principles of empiricism and operationalism, an argument about the effects to be expected from the imposition of such a tax. These principles prohibit us from going beyond the specific empirical evidence, that is, beyond the established correlations among recorded data of a narrowly defined type. As soon as we go beyond these data and their correlations, we are in the domain of construction and have risen above inductive generalizations. Empiricists and operationalists may deplore it, but this is the only way of developing a general theoretical system fertile with useful inferences.

LAWRENCE NABERS

Lawrence Nabers, Ph.D., University of California at Berkeley, is Professor of Economics at the University of Utah. He has contributed a number of articles—in economic theory and the history of economic thought—to professional journals. He is the co-author of a series of monographs on regional population problems. Currently he is editor of the Western Economic Journal.

ESSAY

5

The

Positive

and

Genetic

Approaches

THE DISTINCTION BETWEEN POSITIVE AND normative economics has been implicit in the literature at least since the seventeenth century. Sir William Petty set as his goal the development of a method of analysis which would exclude the "mutable' minds, opinions, appetites and passions" of men in arriving at an assessment of the bases of England's prosperity.[1] This goal has been accepted by most of the writers responsible for the creation of the classical and neoclassical systems. The purpose of economic analysis, it has generally been held, is to work out the details of a set of propositions which are independent of the political, social, and psychological predispositions of their author. The analysis must be objective in the sense that anyone starting with the same data and using the same rules of logic must arrive at the same conclusions.

During the nineteenth century analysis of the desirability of alternative social or

[1] Charles Henry Hull, ed., *The Economic Writings of Sir William Petty* (Cambridge, 1899), p. 244.

individual ends was not excluded from economics; but such analysis was considered to be at a somewhat lower level—not "scientific" in the objective, value-free sense, but to be tolerated as the opinion of informed individuals who had proceeded as far as objective reasoning would carry them. It is in this spirit that, for example, John Elliot Cairnes and John Neville Keynes made the distinction between economics as a science and economics as an art, and Léon Walras was able to accept, though on quite different levels of abstraction, *économie sociale* and *économie appliquée* along with *économie pure*.

The feeling on the part of the neoclassical economists that value problems were not a part of economics was strengthened by many of Alfred Marshall's followers who were preoccupied with the logical details of the theory of allocation rather than with the classical problem of growth and accumulation. As almost any casual student of economics has noted, allocation theory lends itself to formal mathematical treatment and leads to many solutions under admittedly highly restrictive assumptions. The tendency to place a higher valuation or greater importance on products on which much labor has been bestowed has led to an implicit belief that the restrictions imposed by the underlying assumptions of neoclassical theory are not very important. In addition, the identification of many of the practitioners of neoclassical theory with the traditional social values leads them easily into the fallacy of misplaced concreteness when the results of their theoretical investigations were consistent with those values. The last statement is not meant as an *ad hominem;* it would be unfair to accuse someone such as, say, J. B. Clark of consciously falsifying reality to reach the conclusion that under competitive assumptions individuals received as income no more than what they contributed to the dividend. This result was socially justifiable in view of the work ethic strongly held by Clark and his contemporaries. But, nevertheless, his underlying social beliefs were strengthened by imputing scientific objectivity to his theoretical arguments.

Economists after Clark have been more sophisticated in avoiding explicit value positions. To some extent this attempt has been successful; and certainly the analysis of such important theoretical categories as production, cost, demand, consumption, investment, etc., does not necessarily involve value positions. The Marxist economist would find it difficult to disagree with a Western economist on the interpretation of input-output model. But when these theoretical building blocks are assembled into, say, a theory of economic development, then the fact that each part of the theory may be relatively value free (in the sense that its objective meaning does not depend upon a view of the good society) does not mean that the general theory is free from preconceived notions as to what the direction of development ought to be. The same observation holds true for other integrated approaches to such problems as the theory of employment or the theory of business cycles.

If the content of economic thought is held in principle to be composed solely of positive statements about the regularities which underlie economic data, then the proper approach is to examine the development and clarification of the techniques or building blocks which have been used to create theoretical systems. The use to which those theoretical systems may have been put is largely irrelevant because the success or failure of a social policy can only be determined in terms of the analysis of social or individual values—considerations excluded from the scope of economics. It may then be argued that one of the tasks of the history of economic thought is to expunge from the literature ideas which require value judgments at some point in the argument.

A more meaningful approach would be to use the history of economic thought as a basis for understanding the evolution of economic beliefs, values, and policy and in turn how these affect economic analysis. The proper context for this task is the sociology of knowledge, or more specifically, one of the primary techniques of the sociology of knowledge—the historico-genetic method. There is no reason why economics should eschew considerations of crucial historical and social problems simply because the method is not as satisfying and the results frequently require extensive qualification. The last statement contains two value judgments: some knowledge of important issues is at least as worthwhile as relatively complete knowledge of unimportant issues; and the historical, social, and political problems which can be approached through the history of economic thought are at least as important as the exploration of the implications of a set of economic postulates.

A CRITIQUE OF CURRENT TRENDS IN THE HISTORY OF ECONOMIC THOUGHT

Not too long after World War II Lionel Robbins remarked that the history of economic thought "has come to be regarded as a very important embellishment, as inessential to the economist as a knowledge of the history of chemistry is said to be inessential to the chemist." [2] Robbins thought this development unfortunate, though he must share a large measure of the blame. Twenty years earlier he had insisted that the proper concern of economics was with the calculus of the constrained maximum or—in those days of relative mathematical innocence—with "that aspect of behavior which arises from the scarcity of means to achieve given ends." [3] No economist in his professional capacity was qualified to select among those ends.

The purging from economics of a concern with ends led to an in-

---

[2] *The Theory of Economic Policy* (London: Macmillan, 1953), p. 1.
[3] *The Nature and Significance of Economic Science*, 2nd ed. (London: Macmillan, 1935), p. 24.

creased emphasis on the logical structure abstracted from questions of morality and policy, which have been the traditional concern of Western economics. Robbins merely began the modern phase of the discussion; it has continued more or less unremittantly through a depression, a great war, a series of minor wars and crises, and what appears uncertainly as the beginning of a new age or the end of an old one. It is impossible to detect any impact these contemporary events may have had on this discussion.

Tjalling C. Koopmans perhaps best represents the contemporary methodological position. He defines "postulates" as the premises of an economic argument; "terms" represent entities in the world of experience; and "interpretations" are the descriptions which connect the terms with observable phenomena. (As we shall subsequently see, interpretations arise out of the screening of experience through the axiological or value system.) In a crucial passage Koopmans then argues:

> Whether these interpretations are expressly provided or borrowed by tacit consent from the stream of literature, they lend relevance and economic meaning to the postulates. . . . However, from the point of view of the logic of the reasoning, the interpretations are detachable. Only the logical contents of the postulates matter.[4]

Koopmans does not deny the importance of interpretations, but their analysis is exceedingly difficult; and interpretations, unless one is very careful, will involve questions of ends. For a theory of choice to exist it is necessary to postulate that individuals have ends in the minimal sense of tendencies to conduct which can be defined and understood.[5]

If the definition or understanding is ambiguous, then interpretation in Koopmans' sense must depend upon the prior solution of the ambiguity, and one is led directly to the ends problem. Fortunately, however, for the economist who is concerned with pure theory, "the interpretations are detachable." And it has been precisely the acceptance of this detachability which has made the presumed neutrality with respect to ends and the exclusion of problems of morality and policy professionally acceptable.

A few examples of the tendency may make the point a little clearer. T. W. Hutchison is one of the more subtle representatives of positivism in economics. He would assert that the only meaningful statements which can be made about the subject matter of economics are those which are verifiable. In the world of the positivist these statements are inferences which are derived by observation of behavior.[6] Hutchinson implies that

---

[4] *Three Essays on the State of Economic Science* (New York: McGraw, 1957), pp. 132-133.
[5] Robbins, *The Nature and Significance*, p. 24.
[6] T. W. Hutchison, *The Significance and Basic Postulates of Economic Theory* (London: Macmillan, 1938), Chap. III *passim.*

the observer (economist) is separate and distinct from the object of observation even when the subject matter is his own reaction.

Hutchison in an appendix to his book examines "Some Postulates of Economic Liberalism."[7] His purpose is to explore the errors of the classical economists in arguing that "a *laissez-faire* economic policy leads to maximum returns for the community."[8] His conclusion is of interest for the thesis being developed here:

> It must always be remembered that *laissez-faire* and equilibrium doctrines had their origin in *rationalistic Utopia-building*. Because the postulates of economic theories were not always emphatically and unambiguously made clear, the Utopia, under the unique conditions of economic expansion in population, geographical area, and investment of the early nineteenth century somehow got mixed up with the mechanism of the economic world as it is, or as it approximately is, or even might be.[9]

Several comments should be made with respect to this conclusion and the methodology which makes it possible. First, there is an astonishing unawareness of the way ideology and logic are interrelated to argue that the Utopia "got mixed up in the mechanism of the economic world" because the postulates were not "unambiguously made clear." This point will be considered later. Second, to have avoided the mix-up the classical economists would have had to be able to act as objective observers after the fashion of Hutchison's model positivist economist. Hutchison's economist is a myth. In the social science any epistemology which separates subject and object or which requires a rigid separation between the observer and what is observed is scarcely a useful first approximation.[10]

Third, it is the problem of how the observer interacts with his environment which is of interest in the history of economic thought. Surely consideration of the relationship between economic liberalism and the theory of laissez-faire individualism is as important an issue as the purification of the postulates of the theory.

Another useful example of the bias towards analysis is to be found in Paul A. Samuelson's remarks to the effect that Marx from the point of view of economic theory was a minor Ricardian or at best a precursor of Wassily Leontief's input-output analysis.[11] Despite some doubt as to whether Samuelson's argument is as well-informed as it ought to be, the methodological point is that it is only possible to separate Marx's

---

[7] *Ibid.*, p. 137 ff.

[8] *Ibid.*, p. 177.

[9] *Ibid.*, p. 184.

[10] *Cf.* Edward Hallett Carr, *What is History?* (New York: Knopf, 1962), pp. 158-159.

[11] "Economists and the History of Ideas," *The American Economic Review*, 52 (March, 1962), 12 ff.

ideas from his "facade" of economics (Samuelson's term) if economics is solely economic analysis. The interesting and historically important problem (a value judgment if you wish) ought to be the relationship between that "facade" and the philosophical content of Marxian theory.

In the two examples given above the analytical bias has resulted in purging economics of much that is significant, granted that a crucial problem in economic thought is the explanation of the relationship between values and economic analysis. It is possible to take a much stronger position: As a practical matter the value problems cannot be avoided because the development of economic ideas involves a process which makes value judgments inevitable. The selection of the problem to be analyzed presumes an ability to discriminate between the important and the unimportant. The acceptance of a procedural method involves a similar type of value judgment. It is necessary to determine standards of factual relevance in the absence of the unlikely possibility that all facts may be considered. From a given theoretical analysis the content of the results may be presented differently, even though each possible presentation is in accordance with the accepted rules of logic. The selection of the contents of the conclusion is dependent ultimately upon the values of the theorist. Finally, of course, the assessment of the importance or significance of the results is based upon a kind of discrimination which has its roots in the value positions of the theorist.[12]

The same sources of value judgment occur at another level in the case of the historian of economic thought. For him the problem to be analyzed is why writers decided to analyze phenomena as they did. It is clear, then, that all of the sources for the intrusion of value judgment are operating at the level of the historian of economic thought as well as at the level of the creation of economic thought. There is no escaping the conclusion that an analysis of the value-theory complex is unavoidable.

SOME TYPICAL APPROACHES TO THE HISTORY
OF ECONOMIC THOUGHT

On one occasion Frank H. Knight provided the following reason for studying economic thought: "On the assumption that the primary interest in the 'ancients' in such a field as economics is to learn from their mistakes, the principal theme . . . will be the contrast between the 'classical' system and the 'correct system.' "[13] The clear implication is that progress is ever upward, that today is better than yesterday, and that the reason for looking at the past is to gain better insight into

---

[12] Ernest Nagel, *The Structure of Science* (New York: Harcourt, 1961), pp. 485 ff.
[13] "The Ricardian Theory of Production and Distribution," *History and Method of Economics* (Chicago: University of Chicago Press, 1956), pp. 37 ff.

ourselves by seeing how others erred. This attitude is rather good for the morale of present-day economists, but it does not seem to tell too much about how ideas are created. Nor does it give much insight into periods which judged by any standard are retrogressive. Consider the economics of the Third Reich.

In recent years the most vigorous defender of the bias toward analysis and certainly the most impressive has been Joseph A. Schumpeter. His *History of Economic Analysis* begins with the statement:

> By History of Economic Analysis I mean the history of the intellectual efforts that men have made in order to understand economic phenomena or, which comes to the same thing, the history of the analytic or scientific aspects of economic thought.[14]

Science is defined as "any kind of knowledge that has been the object of conscious efforts to improve it." [15] Schumpeter then continues:

> . . . our definition implies nothing about the motives that impel men to exert themselves in order to improve upon the existing knowledge in any field. In another connection we shall presently return to this subject. . . . Similarly, if an economist investigates the practices of speculation by methods that meet the scientific standards of his time and environment, the results will form part of the scientific fund of economic knowledge, irrespective of whether he wishes to use them for recommending regulatory legislation or to defend speculation against such legislation or merely to satisfy his intellectual curiosity. Unless he allows his purpose to distort his facts or his reasoning, there is no point in our refusing to accept his results or to deny their scientific character on the ground that we disapprove of his purpose.[16]

In other words, economic analysis is concerned with the development of analytical techniques which are of use in providing insights into economic phenomena. Schumpeter in his methodological remarks minimizes a consideration of the reasons why individuals select some phenomena, why their interests run in certain directions, why they make certain kinds of analytic errors, where the value judgments implicit in initial postulates come from, and so on.

M. Blaug has more persistently clung to the analysis approach. He does not deny that ideology may be of importance, but for him the task of the historian of economic thought is to find out "whether the analysis stands up when it is freed from its ideological foundation." [17] Blaug like Knight sees progress through time as the result of individual "conscious efforts to improve."

---

14 (New York: Oxford U. P., 1955), p. 3.
15 *Ibid.*, p. 7.
16 *Ibid.*, pp. 10-11.
17 *Economic Theory in Retrospect* (Homewood, Ill.: Irwin, 1962), p. 6.

Has there been progress in economic theory? Clearly, the answer is yes: analytical tools have been continuously improved and augmented; empirical data have been increasingly marshaled to verify economic hypotheses; extrascientific biases have been repeatedly exposed and separated from the core of testable propositions which they enmesh; the operations of the economic system are better understood than ever before.[18]

The defenders of the analysis approach rest their case largely on the judgment that the history of economics ought to be the history of positive economics. The difficulties of this limitation on the scope of economics have already been discussed. But the defenders of the positive approach have an important argument against those who believe that the development of economic theory can only be understood in the context of value positions.[19] All too often historians of economic thought fall into the trap of crude relativism, an indefensible position, and attacks against them have considerable merit whether the relativist argument is that all thought can be explained by class or individual interest or alternatively that thought is simply a reflection of historical exigencies. An example of the relativist type of argument may be found in Werner Stark's discussion of the sources of economic doctrine.

What is it that gave birth to the atomistic conception of society as the consequence of which the attempt to advance from individual psychology to market analysis must be understood?

It is easy to find the answer to this question. Never was society nearer to the state of perfect competition than in the years in which the utility theory of value arose—never, in fact, was it more a sum of independent individuals. There were as yet hardly protective tariffs for the peasants, hardly cartels for the entrepreneurs, hardly trade-unions for the workmen.[20]

And again he says, "but in all the phases through which it [political economy] has passed, it was a faithful reflection of the social reality." [21]

Another somewhat more sophisticated version of historical relativism is that of Eric Roll. His position is the more modest in simply arguing that "the economic structure of any given epoch and the changes which it undergoes are major influences on economic thinking." [22] In his methodological comments Roll emphasizes the difficulty of tracing out the causal link between thought and historical event, but in his interpretations of specific periods of economic thought he tends to make rather simple connections between the important historical occurrences and the type of economics developed.

---

[18] *Ibid.*, p. 7.
[19] For example, *ibid.*, pp. 2-3.
[20] *The History of Economics* (London: Routledge, 1944), pp. 55-56.
[21] *Ibid.*, p. 75.
[22] *A History of Economic Thought*, 3rd ed. (Englewood Cliffs, N.J.: Prentice-Hall, 1956), p. 14.

There are several objections to naïve relativism. First, either the view of history is too simple and uncomplicated or there is a tendency to select only those historical events which neatly fit the argument. Second, the naïve relativist fails to work out the specific process by which events influence thought. Third, too little attention is paid to the necessity to adapt the received knowledge to the new problems which changing events may have posed. And, finally, there is seldom a detailed analysis of the continuing feedback between thought and event.

These objections can be avoided if it is simply accepted that the purpose of the history of economic analysis is to determine the meaning and significance of a theoretical formulation. The meaning of a theoretical formulation is found in the use to which it is put. For example, the meaning in the classical analysis of the terms of trade is found in the rise of England as the center of a world market economy whose position required the free and efficient exchange of commodities. The significance of a theoretical formulation depends upon whether or not it is addressed to an issue which is crucial for the survival or well-being of a group of individuals defined by a context large enough to have some effect on the broad stage of history.

There is, of course, an inherent interest on the part of all intellectually honest theorists in creating more efficient tools of analysis. But the important question is the use which is made of these tools. How can it be possible to develop an explanation of the evolution of the tools of analysis without an explanation of the evolving purposes which the analysis purports to serve? In fact, the important figures in the creation of economic analysis have been those who were involved in the important issues of the day.[23]

Any economist necessarily operates with a received body of doctrine. It is a part of his stock in trade: he cannot dispose of it; he can only adapt it to the new problem. The fact that the theorist must adapt analysis which to some extent may be unsuitable for the problem at hand means that there will be continuing change in the form the theory takes. This is the dynamic factor which the positivist approach necessarily cannot take into account.

THE HISTORY OF ECONOMIC THOUGHT AS AN EXERCISE IN THE SOCIOLOGY OF KNOWLEDGE—THE GENETIC METHOD

The point has now been reached where an explicit alternative to the positivist approach should be suggested. The principles which have been

---

[23] *Cf.* The above leans heavily on Leo Rogin, *The Meaning and Validity of Economic Theory* (New York: Harper, 1956), especially Chap. 1.

advanced thus far are as follows: (a) the position that economics consists of sets of verifiable statements respecting a particular body of phenomena is unduly restrictive and subject to serious methodological objections; (b) an understanding of economic analysis in a meaningful context leads automatically to a consideration of policy and values; (c) an attempt to write a history of economic analysis (in the narrow sense) excludes the factors which are responsible for change and development—namely the way in which policy and values alter in response to historical change—and the historian of economic thought should be concerned with the meaning of economic theory, and the meaning of a theory is found in the use to which it is put.

In recent years a new methodology, the sociology of knowledge, has been evolving. It is an attempt to relate the ideas of individuals to the historical process and to identify the preconceptions which underlie the ideas. It further attempts to define the feedback path among individuals and ideas. Economic theory, after all, is simply a set of more or less abstract ideas. The sociology of knowledge is as adaptable to economic ideas as it is to political ideas.

Karl Mannheim, who first tried to establish the sociology of knowledge as an articulated system of analysis, described its development and purpose as follows:

> . . . as theory it seeks to analyze the relationship between knowledge and existence; as historical-sociological research it seeks to trade the forms which this relationship has taken in the intellectual development of mankind.
>
> It arose in the effort to develop as its own proper field of search those multiple interconnections which had become apparent in the crisis of modern thought, and especially the social ties between theories and modes of thought. On the one hand, it aims at discovering workable criteria for determining the interrelations between thought and action. On the other hand, by thinking this problem out from beginning to end in a radical, unprejudiced manner, it hopes to develop a theory, appropriate to the contemporary situation, concerning the significance of the non-theoretical conditioning factors in knowledge.
>
> Only in this way can we hope to overcome the vague, ill-considered, and sterile form of relativism with regard to scientific knowledge which is increasingly prevalent today. This discouraging condition will continue to exist as long as science does not adequately deal with the factors conditioning every product of thought which its most recent developments have made clearly visible. In view of this, the sociology of knowledge has set itself the task of solving the problem of the social conditioning of knowledge by boldly recognizing these relations and drawing them into the horizon of science itself and using them as checks in the conclusions of our research. Insofar as the anticipations concerning the influence of the social background have

remained vague, inexact, and exaggerated, the sociology of knowledge aims at reducing the conclusions derived to their most tenable truths and thereby to come closer to methodological mastery over the problems involved.[24]

Essentially, then, the position of the sociology of knowledge is that significant ideas do not evolve because of an inner dialectic, or because of the working out of logical possibilities, or because of historical laws. Rather, the source of ideas is to be found in the impact of existential factors on the formation of thought. These existential factors are relevant to the genesis of ideas as well as to the determination of the scope and content of experience.[25] There is no suggestion in the sociology of knowledge that existential factors determine in a direct and immediate way the form and content of ideas. Ideas cannot be explained merely by identifying the historical or class position of the individual responsible for those ideas. They must be carefully traced out in the context of social —or class—ideals, fears, aspirations, and objective possibilities. Frequently the existential factors give rise to inconsistencies which in turn result in theoretical configurations that falsify reality. This falsification of reality is what Mannheim calls false consciousness. If the theoretical configuration or set of ideas has implicit norms which result in an orientation of analysis or in the selection of data which lead to conclusions or courses of action which cannot be justified in the existing historical setting, then the configuration comes under the imputation of false consciousness. Examples of this phenomenon make up much of the history of economic thought—for example, the mercantilist attitude toward money, the classical analysis of the relationship between profits and wages, and the contemporary treatment of competition. It is surely one of the most important and significant tasks of the historian of economic thought to analyze such examples.

The sociology of knowledge should not be confused with the theory of ideology. Thought is said to be ideological when some factional or personal interest has implicitly entered into its formulation. The most frequent explanation of false consciousness is to be found in the existence of ideological elements somewhere in the system of thought.[26] But the falsification of reality need not come from ideological thinking. The sociology of knowledge is concerned with the total set of relationships, concrete or imagined, of a society.

To be sure, the development of a total sociology of knowledge is beyond

---

[24] *Ideology and Utopia* (New York: Harcourt, Harvest Books, N.D.), pp. 264-265.
[25] Robert K. Merton, *Social Theory and Social Structure* (New York: Free Press, 1949), Chap. VIII, esp. pp. 223 ff.
[26] Werner Stark, *The Sociology of Knowledge* (London: Routledge, 1958), pp. 50 ff. It should be pointed out that Stark's position in the present book is much broader and more defensible than in his earlier volume mentioned above.

the capability of anyone. But the attitude fostered by an acceptance of the principles of the sociology of knowledge would lead to a resolve on the part of the historian of economic thought to pursue the meaning of a theory wherever it might lead him. Alfred Marshall's advice is singularly applicable:

> If the matter is important, let us take account of it as far as we can. If it is one as to which there exist divergent opinions, such as cannot be brought to the test of exact and well-ascertained knowledge; if it is one on which the general machinery of economic analysis and reasoning cannot get any grip, then let us leave it aside in our purely economic studies. But let us do so simply because the attempt to include it would lessen the certainty and the exactness of our economic knowledge without any commensurate gain; and remembering always that some sort of account of it must be taken by our ethical instincts and our common sense. . . .[27]

The new understandings of social processes and the development of ideas will today permit one to go further than in Marshall's day; and one suspects that Marshall would be willing to go the greater distance today.

Stark has a useful paradigm which is helpful in understanding the particular concern of the sociology of knowledge.[28]

The subject and his approach	The Categorical Layer of the Mind	
	The Physical Apparatus of Perception	
	The Axiological Layer of the Mind	The concern of the sociology of knowledge
The objective world	The Objects of Knowledge	
	The Materials of Knowledge	

"Category" is used in a strict Kantian sense: all events, at least for *homo sapiens*, must be conceived of in terms of space, time, and cause.[29] Without becoming involved in the sticky questions of Kantian metaphysics, the reader is invited to try to think of some *event* of *datum* which is not located in space and time and which is unrelated to other events. The reference to the "physical apparatus of perception" is self-explanatory. By the "axiological layer of the mind" Stark means the prejudgments or value positions of the individual which lead him to select among the objects of knowledge those elements which he feels to be important. It is out of the relationship between the objects of knowledge and the axiological system of the individual that new ideas are created, which may in turn become a part of the axiological system of subsequent generations. As Stark points out, these prejudgments should not be considered prejudices in the narrow sense of the word. They "are the value-

---

[27] *Principles of Economics*, 8th ed. (New York: Macmillan, 1956), pp. 27-28.
[28] *Sociology of Knowledge*, p. 108.
[29] *Ibid.*

facts at the basis of the contemporary social set-up which enclose . . .
the individual and . . . [have] shaped his mind—shaped it, *uno actu*,
for practical conduct *and* for theoretical contemplation." [30] The "objects
of knowledge" are what is known by the individual out of the "materials
of knowledge" which contain everything which is knowable.

The concern of the sociology of knowledge is to explain the nature of
the axiological layer and how the objects of knowledge are selected for
emphasis and the creation of intellectual systems. The meanings of those
systems inhere in their affect on the environment of the individual. If
the historian of economic thought is considered a specialist within the
field of the sociology of knowledge, then it is his duty to explore in the
widest context available the prejudgments of the theorist with whom he
is concerned, the nature of objects of knowledge which may be quite
different from that of the historian, the logic of the theorist's system, and
its meaning in terms of the theorist's environment. He may also be interested in its meaning in his own environment.

At this point an important question arises: Can the theorist ever be
fully objective? If the individual is locked into a social class or into a
value position by the force of the axiological system with which he
operates, how is objectivity possible? In dealing with this problem
Mannheim was forced to posit the existence of a "socially unattached
intelligentsia," of an "unanchored *relatively* classless stratum" who were
capable of rising not only above ideology but of seeing their own
axiological systems from outside.[31] This view led with some justice to
Karl Popper's polemic:

> . . . the sociologists of knowledge hold that the "freely poised intelli-
> gence" of an intelligentsia which is only loosely anchored in social
> tradition may be able to avoid the pitfalls of the total ideologies; that
> it may even be able to see through, and to unveil, the various total
> ideologies and the hidden motives and other determinants which in-
> spire them. . . . The way to a true knowledge appears to be the
> unveiling of unconscious assumptions, a kind of psychotherapy, as it
> were, or if I may say so, a *sociotherapy*. Only he who has been
> socioanalyzed or who has socioanalyzed himself, and who is freed from
> this social complex, i.e., from his social ideology, can attain to the
> highest synthesis of objective knowledge.[32]

Popper's position is in strict logic unassailable, and it applied with
equal force against the positivist. This means that *absolute* understanding may never be available; but is intellectual endeavor motivated by a
desire for *absolute* understanding or simply by a desire to improve un-

---

[30] *Ibid.*, p. 107; Stark's italics.
[31] *Ideology and Utopia*, pp. 153 ff.
[32] *The Open Society and Its Enemies* (Princeton, N.J.: Princeton University Press,
1950), pp. 400-401.

derstanding? To the extent that it is possible for anyone to attain a degree of "objectivity," a presumption of objectivity should be granted to any serious worker—a presumption which is to be verified in a given instance by an appeal to the best canons of criticism. Those canons at any stage of development may have some ideological bias. But to the extent that they do, the charge of bias must be admitted; the ultimate solution to this difficulty depends upon the progress of knowledge.

To return to the main line of the argument: how should one proceed in attempting to understand the way a given intellectual configuration has developed? An appropriate answer is at hand. The most important revolution in science since Aristotle was the simple understanding that the present could only be understood in terms of history. The attempt to understand a phenomenon in terms of its origin or genesis and subsequent development was much richer than the other approaches—e.g., the natural law approach. In the nineteenth century the genetic method was swiftly applied in every field: Lyell in geology, Comte in sociology, Straus in biblical studies, Darwin in biology, Freud in psychology, etc. Only Marx consistently applied the method in economics. Marshall toyed with the idea, but his analysis remained essentially mechanistic. Veblen criticized economics for failing to appreciate the new methodology, but his own positive contributions were not systematic enough to provide a basis for the reconstruction of economic theory.

But if the position developed here is the proper one—viz., that the evolution of economic thought can only be understood in terms of the evolution of policy and individual values and in turn these assume meaning in the context of the historical milieu—then the genetic method seems the most applicable method of explanation. The cross-sectional, ahistorical approach is of little use; a full understanding of the formal relationship among elements of a system necessarily implies an understanding of how those relationships evolved. Bohm puts it rather neatly in the context of the natural and physical sciences:

> In order to understand just why and how the causal laws are so closely bound up with the definition of what things are, we must consider the processes in which things *have become,* what they are starting out from, what they once *were,* and in which they continue to change and to become something else again in the future. Generally speaking, such processes are studied in detail in a particular science only after it has reached a fairly advanced stage of development, while in the earlier stages the basic qualities and properties that define the modes of being of the things treated in that science are usually simply assumed without further analysis. Thus, in the earlier stages of the development of biology, the various classifications of living beings according to their basic properties and modes of life were simply accepted as eternal and inevitable categories, the reasons for the existence of which did not have to be studied any further. Later, however, there developed the theory of evolution, which explained

many of the fundamental traits that define the mode of being of each species in terms of the process of transformation. . . .[33]

The same considerations apply to the history of economic thought. The time has come when analysis should no longer concern itself with the classification of properties and modes; rather the concern should be with how those modes came about.

There are three points of departure to be distinguished in the genetic method: the psychogenetic, the logical and the historico-cultural.[34] The first, the psychogenetic, is concerned with the relationship between the individual and the form of the doctrine which he develops and to which he may add a particular element. The analysis of the origins and development of the set of propositions constituting the system is the second point of departure. The third point of departure emphasizes the relationship between the doctrine and the historical development of the relevant aspects of the culture.

These three approaches should not be separated from each other; they are more than interrelated; they are aspects of the genetic method. It is the task of the historian of economic thought to explain how the data collected under these various headings may be put together in a fashion which will expose the meaning of economic thought at a given point in time.

CONCLUSION

It would be absurd to deny that there has been a vast accumulation of knowledge. Every society approaches its problems with the received knowledge that it has at its disposal. But knowledge of events and the physical environment is not enough. It must be ordered, and the act of ordering implies a purpose or an end.

If the history of economic thought is to take its place alongside the other traditional studies in economics, it should accept the responsibility of analyzing those ends, discovering where they came from and what the achievement of those ends implies for society. It should try to make implicit values explicit. The positivist position would exclude such considerations from the subject matter of the history of economic thought. But, who can deny the importance of these issues and that an understanding of the relationship between economic analysis and social and individual values is prerequisite to an understanding of the social process at an historically meaningful level?

---

[33] *Causality and Chance in Modern Physics* (London: Routledge, 1957), p. 15.

[34] This classification is taken largely from two works of W. Windelband, *A History of Ancient Philosophy*, trans. Ernest Cushman (New York: Scribner, 1899), pp. 5 ff.; and *History of Philosophy*, 2nd ed., trans. James H. Tufts (London: Macmillan, 1923), pp. 7 ff.

PART 2

MATHEMATICS

AND

OBSERVATION

IN

ECONOMICS

INTRODUCTION

WE UNDERSTAND THROUGH CONCEPTS WHICH REFLECT THE EMPIRICAL WORLD in varying degrees. However, this understanding of phenomena is different from the phenomena themselves and economists hold different positions about the importance of the lack of correspondence. For some, highly abstract theories with a minimum of direct conformation are essential to science because they permit the greatest use of deductive methods. Others object that high abstraction, as in many of the mathematical formulations, reduces realism and relevance. A solution sometimes offered is that some problems require great simplification whereas others demand a richer empirical treatment. But this may merely beg the question unless the scientist can also specify why one can be effectively simplified and the other cannot. Moreover, there may be facets of a theory that elude empirical confrontation and fields of observation that resist orderly classification. Thus, in economics, as in all of science, this problem of an adequate balance between abstraction and realism forms a continuing dialectic.

Part 2 deals with the relationships between concepts and observation. It develops in greater depth some of the problems introduced in the earlier section, focusing more directly on the application of mathematics to economics and on the nature of the correspondence between concepts and their fields of application.

Mathematics provides a well developed machinery for deductive inference in the sciences, but its effective application requires substantial theoretical simplification and well-formulated empirical relationships. William Baumol and Eugene Rotwein discuss the application of mathematics to economics. Baumol accepts the validity of the mathematical form in economic reasoning, but points to some of the difficulties that may arise in application: mathematical models may be constructed for their own sake; trivial ideas may appear profound; preconceptions may be hidden even in the most explicit of axioms. But the limitations of mathematical formulation may be overwhelmed by its strengths: complex relationships can be simplified into manageable systems; unexpected connections and surprising results can be drawn in analysis; intuitive knowledge can be tightly formulated and subjected to procedures of verification; useful practical applications can be found. On the whole, Baumol's treatment is quite sympathetic, in contrast to the more skeptical approach of Eugene Rotwein.

Mathematical application in economics, according to Rotwein, is limited in its range. Consequently, the temptation to assign the non-mathematical areas to a "semi-limbo" within the field can be very harmful, especially where economics is identified mainly with the application of mathematical techniques. Even within its range of valid application, mathematical treatment frequently introduces excessive simplification. As a result, there is a lack of realism and a failure to predict. Rotwein, therefore, asks for greater restrictions in the application of mathematical technique. Sophisticated technique cannot substitute for breadth in the understanding of social and economic phenomena.

The correspondence between economic concepts and experience provides the focus for the essays by Gerhard Tintner and Kenneth Boulding. Tintner discusses the special problems of verification and empirical identification in econometrics, while Boulding outlines wide areas of human understanding which elude ordinary verification procedures.

Tintner defines econometrics as "the formal application of statistics to the mathematical models of economic theory." Although econometric models have focused on macro-economic relations and policy questions, they have drawn from the static assumptions of economic theory and have had only limited success in prediction and policy. Statistical techniques, on the other hand, are frequently not refined enough to organize data into forms that are theoretically meaningful. The identification problem—that of developing a consistent and close conformability between theories and their fields of observation—is a continual one.

Boulding discusses the problem of changing and refining our images of the world through verification. Verification is the process of confronting expectations, which our images create, with experience. However, this confrontation is sometimes very difficult to establish; indeed, many important things may be too costly or even impossible to test. How, for example, do we test for the existence of a state of economic equilibrium? How can predictions conform to theoretical expectations where random elements, such as changes in policy, alter the basic conditions of our prediction? Nonetheless, the improvement in human knowledge does require the continual confrontation of our images with experience. The sum of this knowledge reflects our ability to understand and change the world about us.

WILLIAM J. BAUMOL

*William J. Baumol, Ph.D., London University, is Professor
of Economics at Princeton University. He is the author of
a number of books including* Welfare Economics and
the Theory of the State; Business Behavior, Value, and
Growth; *and* Economic Theory and Operations Analysis.
*He is also Director of Economic Analysis at Mathematica
Incorporated, a consulting firm in Princeton, New Jersey, and
is currently completing a study on the economics of
the performing arts for the Twentieth Century Fund
and beginning on investigation of the mathematics of
corporation finance under a Ford Faculty Fellowship.*

ESSAY

6

Economic

Models

and

Mathematics

NOT SO VERY LONG AGO MATHEMATICAL
economists were among the most suspect
members of our profession. They were
generally considered to be more than a
little odd, caricature denizens of the most
ivory of towers, and sometimes there were
even hints of (harmless) fraud—deception
both of others and of themselves, with their
cabalistic symbols serving as tools of obfuscation to produce an air of spurious
profundity and rigor. Nor were these attitudes held only by those from whom
misunderstanding and hostility might most
readily be expected—from the practical
men and literary economists unequipped
to understand, much less to utilize, the
mathematical language. Critical views were
also aired by authorities as eminent as the
great Alfred Marshall and John Maynard
Keynes, whose fine mathematical training
and unquestionable theoretical bent placed
their motives beyond suspicion. Mathematical economists were then a small and
desperate band who produced their writings for extremely limited and inbred cir-

culation. Their works were frequently defensive in tone and were sometimes prefaced by an elaborate and passionate defense of the virtues of the mathematical method.

Today all this is changed, and though the new order was installed quietly and pacifically, the upheaval seems nevertheless to have swept almost all before it.

Today it is a rare issue of any professional journal whose pages are not pockmarked by formulae and symbols. Graduate students are, as a matter of course, and with few exceptions, required to learn to employ at least the more rudimentary mathematical tools. Few theorists of any repute write without fairly extensive use of algebra.

The new dignity of the mathematical economist is in no way better demonstrated than by the identity of his enemies and his friends. The former have been reduced to a small and little noted underworld group whose occasional outbursts are regarded more or less indulgently as expressions of harmless cranks. The mathematical economists still write answers to the charges proffered, but increasingly they grow embarrassed at having devoted any attention to their attackers and regret having dignified them by a reply.

Even more remarkable are the new friends of the mathematical economist. On the one hand he has found that even among the most eminent of pure mathematicians, there are those—such as Maurice Fréchet, and John von Neumann—who are willing to talk to him in a friendly and interested manner, and sometimes even to make their own contributions to the field. But, most surprising of all, the mathematical economist has suddenly found himself to have become the darling of many practical men. He is welcomed in Washington's inner councils, and businessmen vie with one another to pay him consulting fees and to obtain from him advice on many decisions which until now they guarded jealously for themselves.

As with any such radical rearrangement one may well wonder whether it has not gone a bit too far and whether the changes do not represent a shift in fashion rather than the consequence of a careful and well-reasoned decision.

But it is probably not very useful to pursue such grand evaluations in the abstract. Instead, this essay discusses the nature of the assistance offered to the model builder by the mathematical equipment and seeks to indicate some of the dangers of misuse by which it is accompanied. By reviewing and understanding these matters more clearly, one may be able to increase at least slightly the effectiveness of the tools. The discussion may incidentally be of some help to us in explaining and evaluating the new status of the mathematical economist.

MODELS AND THEIR ROLE

Before turning to an explicit discussion of the use of mathematics, it seems appropriate to review briefly the nature of a theoretical model, for the model is an indispensable instrument of mathematical economics, one which stamps its character on all of the writer's work.

A "model," as its name implies, is a less ambitious, scaled-down version of some situation or phenomenon which is the ultimate object of the analyst's concern. Because the problem with which he wishes to deal is too complex and too much beset by petty detail to permit effective analysis, he is forced to deal instead with a substitute problem, one which is sufficiently simple and orderly to be amenable to systematic study and yet which at the same time is close enough to the facts of the matter to permit the conclusions drawn from investigation of the model to retain some relevance for the more complicated phenomenon which the model is designed to represent. That sort of simplification and elimination of "extraneous matter" is an essential ingredient of any form of analysis.

As I have emphasized elsewhere, this leads us to two conclusions. First, all models inevitably are distortions of reality, and second, since increased realism always exacts a price—sometimes a high price—in reduced analytic tractability of a model, it is irrational to make willy-nilly demands for increased realism upon the model maker. Just as capital equipment can be too durable in terms of the cost of increased longevity or safety, stocks may exceed the optimal security level, it is perfectly possible for a model to be excessively realistic. In fact, one may well wonder, in examining some of the more extensive economic models, whether given our present analytic methods and resources, that they do not fall short of what we may perhaps call the optimal degree of artificiality.

Sometimes, indeed, models are designed to do no more than to present a relatively comprehensible *description* of some economic circumstances. The only limitation on the desirable degree of complication of such a model is the user's ability to follow its ramifications. The descriptive model serves a purpose analogous to a map which is a conventionalized representation of some geographic terrain. And because its purpose is purely descriptive, various scales and degrees of detail may be justified. The choice of scale is a matter of the use to which the map will be put, and the employment of a finer scale is only inhibited by the fact that it also exacts its price by imposing practical limitations on the extent of the territory which the map can cover.

A second type of model is one whose primary purpose is *prediction* in the most conventional and literal sense. A predictive model need require relatively little comprehension on the part of its users or even its designers. It is a machine which grinds out its forecasts more or less mechanically, and for such tasks, unreasoning, purely extrapolative techniques frequently still turn out the best results. Doubtless for some time to come the prognostications offered by our most sophisticated structural models will often be inferior (except in their identification of turning points) to those obtained by the assumption that trends which were observed yesterday will continue into tomorrow. Moreover, electronic computer technology has made it possible to utilize extrapolative models of astonishing size and detail. So long as the machine is capable of processing the model in all its ramifications, and of producing, with its aid, forecasts which conform reasonably well with subsequent developments, it does not matter that the model offers us little intellectual assistance.

It is, however, a third type of construct, the *analytic model*, which is of primary interest for our purposes and for those of the mathematical theorist. This sort of model is perhaps best described as a small-scale simple working mechanism, a piece of machinery which actually operates and whose mode of operation is observable either directly or with the help of some appropriate instruments. The analytic model is designed to tell us which gear meshes with which, to enable us to experiment and determine how the performance of the machine is affected when we press some one of its buttons, and to evaluate the magnitude of the effect of a given change in the setting of one of its knobs. The Keynesian models are among the most noteworthy members of this class. In such a model we attempt to reconstruct the relationship between consumption and investment decisions. We can use it to examine the effects of a change in some of our fiscal institutions and as a basis for evaluation of the influence of variables such as the rate of interest on the level of employment. This is the sort of model in which excessive realism can be extremely costly and may even debilitate analysis entirely.

These analytic models can usefully be grouped into two subcategories, the *general* and the *particular*, though the distinction is imperfect and can be hazy near the border line. Economic theory has focused on the more general model, trying to produce a widely applicable description of consumer behavior, of the monopolistic firm, or even of a growing economy. Because such a model is designed to be applicable to so wide a variety of circumstances, it must abstract from the details which make one consumer or one firm or one economy different from another. What then remains in such a model by way of empirical content may be very little. And from models which are highly restricted in their empirical content we cannot expect very startling or profound empirical conclusions. This is doubtless one of the main reasons there has so frequently been disappointment in what has come out of our theoretical models. But this disappointment is not entirely reasonable. Its source is our expectation from a piece of machinery of a variety of performance which it is, by its very design, incapable of delivering. The general models have, with some notable exceptions, delivered most effectively when they have been treated as machine tools rather than instruments capable of direct application.

More specifically, the general models have been extremely useful when employed as prototypes for the construction of the particular models which are necessary for the treatment of very specific questions. The general models provide the framework to be used in erecting the particular model and suggest the theorems which can be derived from it. But the particular model, while it can be extremely powerful, and is, in some ultimate sense, indispensable for systematic analysis of a specific issue, is extremely circumscribed in its domain of applicability. The relevant particular model must usually be different for each different set of circumstances which it is meant to represent—the Company *A* model must vary at least in detail from the model of Company *B*'s operations. Moreover, even the model of a specific economic entity must frequently be redesigned with changes in the problem under study. A model designed for the study of Company *A*'s inventory problem will not be the same as that which is most helpful in the selection of its advertising media.

These, then, are some of the basic types of models which arise in economic analysis and some of the broad considerations which are pertinent for their design.

CRITICISMS ARISING OUT OF MISUNDERSTANDING

Let us return now to the use of mathematics by the model builder. It must be emphasized from the very beginning that, like any other approach, the mathematical method has its shortcomings. As a matter of fact, most of these are widely recognized by mathematical economists, who have frequently taken pains to call them to the readers' attention.

But these difficulties are not quite the same as the crude and obvious charges which are sometimes leveled against mathematical theory. The kindergarten clichés that "Economics is not an exact science" or that "You can't put human nature into an equation" need hardly be considered in detail. No one pretends that the rich variety of human psychology can be captured by any set of simple models, nor does anyone deny that all empirical disciplines deal in approximations and that the degree of approximation achieved by the economist is poorer than most. These constitute a source of difficulty for all of economic analysis and do not represent a peculiar problem of mathematical economics. Mathematics can deal with partial information and with approximations, and not always less effectively than literary analysis. Nor need mathematical economics confine itself to problems for which psychology is of primary importance. There are many technical and technological questions in economics where mathematics can take us a good part of the way before human volition is introduced into the picture in a significant manner. Of course, mathematical analysis can deal more effectively with some economic problems than with others, and it is only good strategy to start off with those for which it is most promising. It is silly to berate a tool because it does not do Job X when it does Job Y very well. But we must not jump to the conclusion that mathematical economics can make absolutely no contribution to the areas of economics in which psychological elements are paramount. Utility theory is surely an area where the human psyche does matter, and, as is well known, some of the more suggestive and sophisticated bits of mathematical theory have inhabited this area.

SOME ABUSES OF MATHEMATICAL METHOD

What, then, are the more pertinent difficulties in the use of mathematics by the economist? A good proportion of these may be classified as the use of mathematics as an instrument for self-deception. No doubt the fault lies not with the instrument but with its user; yet it must be recognized that here is a tool which readily lends itself to such abuse.

One particular variant of this difficulty is the construction and manipulation of mathematical models for their own sake, where the ultimate criterion of success is the degree of entertainment provided to the model builder. Elaborate superstructures are erected to show off spectacular applications of esoteric theorems with little regard for relevance or illumination. The writer indulges himself in what has been described by a great economist as illicit intercourse with beautiful models. There is, of course, nothing intrinsically wrong with this sort of self-indulgence. As a matter of fact, it can provide diversion or even instructive ideas to other members of the profession. But one does have a right to ask that a product of this variety be labeled clearly and explicitly lest it be misused by the more gullible and inexperienced members of our profession. However, one cannot help suspecting that the inventors of such constructs are occasionally among those who are so beguiled. In such cases we can hardly expect warning labels to accompany the models. They then become all the more dangerous. An abstract and wonderfully complex model in search of application can pose a real danger to those who are induced to use it. In the long run it can only damage the reputation of mathematical economists as a class.

A second, and not unrelated, shortcoming of the mathematical tools arises out of the ease with which obscurity can be mistaken for pro-fundity. It is the noneconomist user of economics—the administrator in government, in the military, or in business—who, when he foregoes his excessive skepticism, characteristically runs into the opposite problem, the temptation to accept arguments as rigorous and "scientific" simply because mathematics was employed somewhere in their derivation. But, of course, no matter how sophisticated the mathematical method and how deep and difficult the steps between premises and conclusions, they can offer no protection against naïve and irrelevant models and against any misleading conclusions which may be derived from them.

The fact of the matter is that mathematics is devoid of empirical content. Mathematics can impart neither substance nor truth to a model in which these qualities are not present to begin with. This platitudinous observation can, nevertheless, help to explain a number of difficulties which have beset the economic theorist. The relatively limited empirical significance of his theoretical results can, in part, be ascribed to the generality of his models, as has already been argued. But, in addition, there are a number of cases where one is led to feel that writers have been distracted from an attempt to impart richer empirical content to their construct by sheer fascination with their formal mathematical structure. A related trap for those who overlook the empirical emptiness of mathematics is the temptation to criticize a theoretical construct which is largely mathematical in nature for its lack of veritable conclusions. Some of the more jaundiced views of the limited economic contribution of pure marginal analysis (differential calculus) or of pure linear pro-gramming theory, for example, can be ascribed to such an oversight.

Finally, let me call attention to a much more subtle snare which threatens the unwary theorist. It arises out of one of the virtues of sym-bolic analysis, which when imperfectly understood can be transformed into a dangerous pitfall.

EXPLICITNESS VS. TRANSPARENCY IN MATHEMATICAL STATEMENTS

One of the most widely recognized advantages of the mathematical methods is that their use requires the explicit listing of all premises em-ployed in the analysis. The rules of the game prevent us from switching assumptions in mid-argument or from the employment of a premise which is unstated and perhaps even unrecognized by us when we use it. It must be granted that here is a major weakness of literary analysis, into which it is often easy to sneak new assumptions as they become con-venient, and thereby to arrive at whatever conclusions are desired. A number of the standard logical fallacies are only variants of this maneuver.

The axiomatic method may be described as the very antithesis of such a procedure. The act of axiomatization consists in the very explicit formulation of the premises to be employed, and subsequent manipulations are only permitted if they can be justified by citations, chapter and verse, from among the listed axioms.

However, while the premises in an acceptable mathematical discussion must be *explicit*, it does not follow that they will be *transparent*. This distinction cannot be overemphasized. Even though the list of items which we have posited has been written out *in extenso*, the obscurity of their statement may leave us largely unaware of their full meaning. All too frequently an apparently innocuous assumption turns out to be a keg of dynamite whose explosion brings consternation or (perhaps more often) delight to its inventor.

The recent history of economics offers many illustrations of apparently straightforward premises whose serious implications were for some time seriously misunderstood. A case in point is the homogeneity postulate of mathematical general equilibrium theory which stated that the supply of or the demand for any commodity is a homogeneous function of zero degree *in prices alone*. The premise is deceptive, for it sounds like no more than an explicit restatement of the plausible assertion that the choice of unit of currency is of little real economic significance. Whether we describe the price of a pair of shoes as ten dollars or as twenty fifty-cent pieces may well be immaterial for rational decision making (unless too many careless shoppers are misled by the change and modify their behavior in a way which, in turn, affects us). But the homogeneity postulate really says more than this, and it does so in a manner which is hardly obvious. For it states that there will be no changes in decisions when all price quotations double (as they would if we were to transfer to a half-dollar currency unit), *even if the number of units of currency fails to double* (e.g., if there are now only as many half dollars as there formerly were dollars). Clearly, that is a far more implausible and more drastic premise; for if prices double and each of us has only as much cash as before, the purchasing power of our holdings will be cut in half, and it is likely that we shall react in some way. Failure to recognize this difficulty on the part of those who first formulated the analysis in mathematical terms led to a variety of difficulties which Don Patinkin has called to our attention, and whose resolution has required a long and painstaking discussion.

In this case mathematical statement seems initially to have been a major source of the difficulty. The assertion that the demand function $D_i = f_i(P_1, \ldots, P_n)$ is homogeneous of degree zero sounds so simple and attractive, and yet, what was concealed in this explicit statement was perhaps as significant as what it revealed.

Other illustrations are easily cited. Kenneth J. Arrow, one of the most sophisticated and skillful members of the profession, did not make clear the full implications of one of the crucial premises in his social choice analysis. His famous third condition was designed to preclude irrelevant alternatives from exercising a determining role in social choice (i.e., he asserted that an acceptable social decision machinery must not permit the candidacy of the prohibitionist standard bearer to determine whether the presidency would fall to the Republicans or the Democrats). But what was not clear in the formulation of this premise was that it also ruled out the use of anything but individuals' *rankings* as a basis for social choice, and thereby precluded relative strength of feeling from entering the calculation. If I want a lamp post to be erected before my house and my neighbor objects to it, sheer counting of rankings may leave us at an impasse. But if it transpires in discussion that I feel strongly about the matter while his concern is very slight, a decision may more easily be arrived at. It has subsequently been shown that the un-noticed proscription of anything but rankings by the mathematical state-ment of his third condition can be held responsible for the drastic out-come summarized by Arrow's possibility theorem—his conclusion that it is impossible to design a general social choice mechanism which satisfies a set of minimal acceptability criteria.

In the same way, lack of transparency in the earliest versions of the Von Neumann-Morgenstern utility axioms lured a number of us to our destruction. It led us to object to the analysis on grounds which involved basic misunderstanding of the assumptions.

It would be easy to provide other examples of the basic point—that the explicit mathematical statement of our premises should not delude us into believing that we understand just what we have postulated, nor does it relieve us of the obligation to attempt to make the contents of these premises clear to others and to ourselves.

The difficulty we have been discussing is not entirely accidental; it is intrinsic in our motivation that we prefer a mathematical process which derives startling and unexpected conclusions from premises which appear relatively innocuous and straightforward. The power of mathematics lies, at least partly, in its ability to accomplish just such feats—to offer us conclusions which are not obvious from direct inspection of a set of hypotheses. But, at the same time, it must be remembered that mathe-matics cannot derive anything which is not contained in its assumptions to begin with. Like good stage magic its operation consists in the subtle revelation of whatever was concealed, for it cannot cause things to materialize out of nothing. The very derivation of a surprising theorem then indicates that its premises must have been less innocent than they appeared.

Strong mathematical results must, therefore, be viewed by the practitioner with somewhat mixed feelings. At best they represent a relevant revelation about his problem; at worst they may cast doubt upon the appropriateness of his assumptions.

A clear example is the basic theorem of linear programming which, in economic terms, states that it is normally possible to determine a profit-maximizing product line for a firm in which the number of products does not exceed the number of inputs in short supply. Consider a firm which produces thousands of outputs but which is faced by only seventeen different types of bottlenecks (such as limited supply of some type of skilled labor). As this theorem shows, *regardless of market conditions* a linear program will usually claim that this company's profits can be increased by cutting the number of its products from the current level of several thousand down to no more than seventeen items!

When this theorem was first derived, it was greeted with delight by those whose primary interest is computational efficiency. For it permitted the calculation to confine itself to a trial-and-error procedure which considered only output combinations involving (in our example) no more than seventeen products, and to disregard all of the vast set of other possible combinations. As an economist however, I felt that the theorem was little less than a catastrophe because it showed conclusively how limited is the range of application of *linear* programming. We know that if a large company were to concentrate its vast resources and facilities on the production of so small a number of commodities, each of them would be produced in such large quantities that their marketing would become prohibitively expensive if not impossible. There are, in fact, almost always diminishing returns to expanded marketing outlays, and at least sometimes, nonconstant returns to large scale production.

The linearity assumption of a linear program, by precluding both increasing and diminishing returns, rules out these possibilities, and it can be shown that this is the foundation of the basic theorem. But by assuming away these possibilities it restricts materially the number of problems to which linear programming can safely be applied. Here, then, is a powerful and surprising theorem which may serve the economist primarily as a warning because it signals the drastic shortcomings of the premises of the model.

MATHEMATICAL TOOLS AS AN AID TO THE THEORIST

Thus far the discussion of mathematical methods has largely been negative, drawing attention to the dangers arising out of careless use of the techniques. But it must be re-emphasized that these problems are like those of any effective piece of equipment—if it is powerful, it is necessarily subject to abuse. There is no question in my mind that our analysis has, on balance, become far more effective and far more illuminating as a consequence of its use of the mathematical techniques. As we shall see, in some ways the strengths of these tools are merely the obverse sides of its pitfalls.

First, let us discuss how mathematics has helped in work involving the general models of the theorist, leaving until the next section its utility for the particular models of applied economics.

The most obvious use of mathematical analysis is in problems involving a very considerable level of complexity—a multiplicity of functions and a profusion of interrelationships. Most frequently such characteristics have been encountered in general equilibrium analysis. An example is the Slutsky theorem which asserts that if the real purchasing power of a utility-maximizing person is kept constant, a fall in the price of a commodity must lead him to buy more (or at least no less) of that item. Though the result seems intuitive enough, only under the simplest conditions can it be proved without recourse to some moderately sophisticated mathematics. The same holds true for the theorem that, in the absence of external economies and diseconomies, pure competition will lead to an optimal allocation of resources. Another illustration is provided by the existence theorems for general equilibrium systems which prove (under certain stated conditions) that those systems possess solutions. In each of these cases we deal with a multiplicity of variables, each potentially interacting with all of the others, and without the help of mathematical tools it is impossible to keep track of the results.

Another extremely important aspect of the utility of mathematics to the theorist is its ability to bring out unexpected connections and surprising results. As already noted, this is also closely related to one of the dangers of the mathematical method. But when employed carefully, this capacity of the analysis can be invaluable. An excellent example is the duality theory of linear programming which showed that implicit in the optimality calculations of linear programming are all the standard concepts of marginal analysis—the marginal profitability of each input and the opportunity cost of each output. As a further by-product, this theory shows that the variables of the dual program correspond to the Lagrange multipliers of the standard differential calculus and help to provide an economic interpretation of these Lagrange multipliers in terms of marginal analysis. As a curiosity it may be added that these implications of duality theory are sufficiently persuasive to have provided the basis for a restoration into favor of the marginal analysis in the Soviet Union where it had long been considered beyond the pale because of its doubtful relationship to the labor theory of value.

Other illustrations of surprising results in mathematical economics readily come to mind. A charming example of rather limited applicability is the Edgeworth taxation paradox where the analysis shows that in certain circumstances under price discrimination, an appropriate tax levied on the monopolist can make it profitable for him to reduce his prices simultaneously to all his customers!

A third way in which mathematics can assist the theorist is by helping him to verify results which he arrived at on the basis of intuition and to delineate the conditions under which the conjecture is valid. For example, it took mathematics to prove that a multiplier-accelerator system could lead to fluctuations in national income and to indicate circumstances under which other types of time path would result.

Similarly, in capital theory it has often been assumed, tacitly, that identical investment decisions will be arrived at if management maximizes the sum of the discounted present value of their anticipated future returns and if management chooses the investment whose marginal efficiency (internal rate of return) is highest.[1] It is by no means obvious that the discounted present value and marginal efficiency criteria are equivalent; as a matter of fact, it turns out that they are not. However, it has been proved that over a wide variety of relevant cases the two criteria do yield the same results, and either can be used in place of the other.

Perhaps equally important are the cases where intuitively derived hypotheses have been shown to hold only in very special circumstances, Mathematical models are often at their most effective in arriving at this sort of negative result. Since our models are, as has been emphasized, always oversimple and to some extent unrealistic, it is doubtful whether a result which holds for such a model will carry over to the messier and more complex world of reality. For this reason results like the ideal output theorem of perfect competition analysis have been treated with considerable skepticism as guides to policy.

But if it can be shown that an intuitively based proposition does *not* hold even in the simple economy of the model maker, there is very good reason to carry one's doubts about the validity of the alleged theorem over to other cases. Perhaps the most important example of such a negative proposition is the Lipsey Lancaster "second-best" theorem. It shows that where optimality requires a number of conditions to be satisfied simultaneously, then if one of these requirements is violated, it may not be desirable to have the others hold. An application is offered by a world where a number of industries are characterized by monopoly elements. Competitive pricing in other industries may then yield a poorer approximation to ideal output. This negative result casts severe doubts on some of the pricing policies which have been proposed for nationalized industries and which were designed to make them act rather like perfect competitors.

---

[1] To find the internal rate of return one determines a rate of interest which is just high enough to reduce the profitability of the investment to zero.

Another illustration is the work of Milton Friedman, A. W. Phillips and the author which shows that alleged stabilization policies can easily aggravate business fluctuations. Friedman and Phillips have demonstrated the presence of this danger for discretionary policies imposed by direct decision of the authorities, while Baumol's results apply to automatic "built-in" stabilizers. The warning to policy makers and to theorists alike may prove to be of some importance.

One of the conclusions which can be drawn from this and the discussions of the preceding sections is that intuition and mathematical analysis can serve as effective checks on one another. In the process one may be able to avoid a wide variety of errors—mistaken interpretation of inappropriate mathematical premises and straightforward errors of reasoning, both intuitive and mathematical. It is then frequently helpful, when possible, to formulate theoretical arguments twice, using both techniques. It is helpful to the reader, making it easier to evaluate and understand the discussion, and it is also helpful to the theorist in that it provides him with firmer grounds for confidence in his own work.

MATHEMATICAL TOOLS AND APPLIED ECONOMICS

The role of mathematics in applied analysis is only slightly different from its part in theoretical analysis. All of the things which mathematics can do for the theorist are also likely to be helpful in application. Several of the illustrations of the preceding section also have clear-cut practical applications. But there are several additional ways in which it can prove useful to the decision maker and which, in the present state of economics, are of comparatively little relevance for theoretical work.

Two major sources of such added utility are the relative availability of numerical values for the parameters of the applied economist's particularized models and the need for approximation in decision making.

Where we do have numbers to work with, sophisticated computational techniques may prove helpful or even indispensable. Decisions often involve "combinatorial" problems of astronomical magnitude (Which of the myriad possible product combinations or media combinations, or marketing outlay combinations will yield the largest profits?). Simpleminded direct attacks on such problems are likely to be totally valueless. Work is currently proceeding on a linear programming calculation involving over thirty thousand constraints and about a million variables; surely it is only with the aid of systematic mathematical procedures like the simplex method that one can even hope to begin the effective treatment of such a subject.

A second relevant feature of decision processes is the imperfect information on which they must be based and the limited time and budget which can be devoted to them. That being the case, these decisions must proceed by means of approximations and relatively simple rules of thumb. Mathematics can help us to determine better approximation procedures and more satisfactory rules of thumb. The formula of standard inventory theory which states that in certain circumstances inventory should increase only in proportion to the square root of sales is no more than a rough rule of thumb except in the context of the simplest models. Yet it was arrived at by mathematical analysis, and it has been shown time and time again to yield substantial savings when used in lieu of more traditional procedures.

Mathematical calculations can also help the practical man by providing him with confidence intervals and tests of sensitivity. If we are not sure of the estimated value of some parameter, we may be able to calculate the effects upon recommended policy of likely variations in the value of that parameter. Given a numerical model and some reason for believing that the value of parameter k lies between, say, 0.6 and 0.9, we can calculate two alternative optimal solutions using these two values in turn. If the calculated recommendation is not much affected by the result this can add considerably to our confidence in the analysis.

Enough has been said to suggest the types of assistance which applied economists can expect from mathematics. The fact that these only supplement the sorts of service described in the preceding section can help to account for the growing use of mathematical economics by business and government in recent years. Because the particular models of applied economics offer more for the mathematics to work on, it can yield more powerful and helpful results for such constructs. Several years ago when I once argued in conversation that mathematics may soon be more important for the applied economist than for the theorist, the assertion was taken to be facetious. It is becoming increasingly easy to take my view seriously.

CONCLUSION

This essay has sought to explain the role of mathematics in economic model building. It has emphasized that mathematics can play an important role in the construction and analysis of the abstract and general models of economic theory. For fairly straightforward reasons it can be at least equally helpful to the practitioner. But as with any powerful instrument, mathematics can be used excessively or inappropriately. I have tried to point out some of the ways in which such abuses have sometimes occurred. The discussion is, thus, designed to help explain the current success and popularity of the mathematical methods and to provide warnings against the sorts of misuse which can impede further increases in their appropriate utilization.

EUGENE ROTWEIN

Eugene Rotwein, Ph.D., University of Chicago, is Professor of Economics, Queens College of the City University of New York. He has written in several areas including the fields of methodology and economic philosophy. Among his writings in the latter field are the Introduction to his edition of David Hume, Economic Writings (1955), and "On 'The Methodology of Positive Economics,'" Quarterly Journal of Economics (November, 1959).

E S S A Y

7

Mathematical

Economics:

The Empirical View

and an Appeal

for Pluralism[1]

ONE OF THE MOST CONSPICUOUS POSTWAR developments in economics has been the growth in the use of mathematical techniques. This is amply evident in both the journal literature and in changes within the economics curriculum. Indeed, there are many, especially among the younger generation, who view the postwar trend as a major revolution heralding the beginning of a New Age in economics. There are several reasons for this development. An important one lies in the retrospective view concerning the growth of the discipline.

The view economists have taken of their field has varied considerably from one period to another. In John Stuart Mill's time there was a popular belief, apparently, that in various respects economics had already attained maturity as a science. Possibly another such wave of self-confidence, among

[1] This is a revised version of a talk given at the Midwest Economics Association Convention in April, 1962. The original talk appeared in the *Nebraska Journal of Economics & Business* (Autumn, 1962), pp. 15-25.

a sizeable segment of the profession, marked the period following the appearance of Alfred Marshall's *Principles*. In recent years the movement, I believe, has on the whole been in the reverse direction as older ideas have been questioned and the limitations of older doctrines and approaches have been exposed. This disappointment over the progress in the field—intensified by a seemingly inexorable widening of the gap between economics and the natural sciences—serves, I think, to explain much of the current support for mathematical economics. Since other approaches have not worked very well, why not invest more heavily in an area which has been exploited to a relatively limited degree up to now—especially when the techniques involved are so similar to those employed in the remarkable physical sciences? So the prevailing mood —or much of it—seems to say, with a note of hope and also, I think, not a little desperation.

The trend toward mathematical economics has, of course, not met with general approval. Many economists—particularly those of the older generation who have been trained in the "literary" or "nonsymbolic" tradition—are deeply suspicious of it. But it appears to have developed such momentum that many are inclined to yield to it simply because it seems pointless to oppose it. Vexing doubts, though expressed from time to time, have not been given a full airing nor have they received the attention they deserve.[2] Lest we are carried too far in further acquiescence, it is worthwhile, therefore, to pause and consider the basis of these doubts.

In adopting a critical view of the trend, I am not opposing the use of mathematical techniques as such. Mathematical economics has been with us for a long time. Individual economists have at various times found it helpful to rely heavily on mathematical techniques, and these techniques may be useful even to the predominantly "literary" economist because they enable him to perceive the implications of his line of analysis more rapidly and more fully. The central issue concerns the weight given such techniques; and the principal purpose of my discussion is to call attention to some of the major limitations on the fruitfulness of mathematical economics in the hope of contributing to a better perspective on the current trends in the field as a whole.

I

To turn to the most obvious limitation, there are many economic problems that do not lend themselves well to mathematical treatment.

---

[2] For examples of recent critical comment on mathematical economics, see George J. Stigler, "The Mathematical Method in Economics" in *Five Lectures on Economic Problems* (New York: Macmillan, 1950), pp. 37-45; the discussion on mathematical economics by D. Novick and others in *The Review of Economics and Statistics*, 36 (November, 1954), 357-368; Edwin E. Witte, "Economics and Public Policy," Presidential Address before the American Economic Association, *American Economic Review*, 47 (March, 1957), 12.

They resist fruitful analysis in terms of precise functional relations whose variables can be treated quantitatively. These problems cut across many of the subdivisions of the field. They may be found in the areas of industrial organization, public finance, economic history, labor, and so on. They may appear on the nonpolicy as well as the policy levels of analysis. And they are important problems.

Despite the obvious nature of this consideration, it is worth emphasizing because of a tendency within the field to claim priority for a particular approach while relegating others—including the problems they are concerned with—to a subordinate position. For decades up to the appearance of Keynes' *General Theory* price theory was treated as the "heart" of economics. This was the area that was especially worthy of the efforts of the "true" economist. Since the *General Theory* the pendulum has tended —though not in a blanket fashion—to swing in the other direction. Macroeconomics—especially when one includes its use in the analysis of economic growth—has not only come into its own in the postwar period, but there have been assertions concerning the field that are more than vaguely reminiscent of the claims once made for price theory. The importance of particular economic problems at specific times has much to do with such claims, but they are also attributable to the belief that economics should give predominant emphasis to material that can be well treated within an "analytical system." As the treatment of a particular problem area grows more systematic, priority claims on its behalf blossom. In the process the material with which it is concerned—because it can be handled within a given "system"—acquires a heightened measure of vividness. And by virtue of this it acquires a new degree of significance; often so much so that trivial matters within the area are given far more attention than important problems outside it.

Claims for mathematical economics reflect the sheer impact of the "systematic," and if the process should continue further, it may well lead to redefinitions of economics which consign nonmathematical approaches to a sort of semi-limbo within the field. It is already not uncommon to encounter assertions that the undergraduate major planning to continue with graduate work in economics ought to devote himself largely to mathematics. Other areas, if not read out of the field entirely, are considered to contain material that can be "picked up" subsequently *en passant*, should it become necessary to acquaint oneself more fully with the substantive content of such areas.

It, of course, cannot be assumed that material beyond the scope of a given "analytical system" does not contain analytical content of its own. Indeed, I would venture to say that even if the "systematic" is taken as the criterion for judging the "valuable," there is a good deal that falls outside mathematical systems that, in terms of "rigor" and the range of experience covered, would rival much that lies within them. However desirable as an ultimate objective of all inquiry, the systematic, in any event, cannot be identified with the "valuable." In the process of constructing "systems," observation and description are required; and careful attention to material that appears to be relevant to major problem areas is warranted regardless of whether at any particular time such material can be incorporated within a given "analytical scheme." Judged either in terms of the quality of the thought process or the nature of the material dealt with, there is no such creature as The Economist. The field of economics itself, as in the case of all other disciplines, has no "natural" content. It reflects the shifting nature of our problems and interests, the changing character of our knowledge and techniques, and simple convention. If we wish, we may—succumbing to the tendency to accord overriding importance to narrowly defined special "analytical" approaches in economics (whether mathematical, quantitative or otherwise)—exclude major areas of inquiry from our domain. But the outcome will only be the nominal gain in "prestige" associated with claims to interest exclusively in the purely "scientific." The problem areas excluded will remain. They will continue to require attention. And similarly requiring attention would be the relations between the findings in the exiled fields and the problems treated within the field of "economics."

II

The reference to the interrelations between problem areas raises the question of the interrelations between different levels of analysis generally, and this leads to a consideration of a second major limitation on the effectiveness of the mathematical approach in economics. Here I refer to the reliance, in constructing mathematical models, on highly simplified and distorted representations of reality. Since this is characteristic of much of the model building in economics generally, the point involved has applications beyond the area of mathematical economics. It may be presumed, however, to be particularly applicable to the latter area since the requirements of mathematical treatment may make oversimplification especially tempting.

The issue involved has a long history, and it has frequently been debated. But, despite the fact that it is essentially a simple issue and should by now have been entirely resolved, it repeatedly reappears. To state the central point, our ultimate objective in economics—as in any science—is to reduce the real phenomena of the field to regularities of coexistence and sequence, or to uniformities which enable us to state: "If A, then B." When we have such a uniformity, we have explained B by reference to A, or, alternatively, we may say that through such explanation we can predict B by reference to A. Where our models oversimplify and distort reality, they do not enable us to employ the entities of the model (as they stand) in establishing uniformities between "real" phenomena. In this respect, the reliance on such models is prima-facie evidence that the analysis is deficient.

The unwillingness to acknowledge the force of this simple position and the persistence with which various economists continue to attach exaggerated importance to a false model world is partly attributable, I believe, to the uncritical acceptance of certain arguments which gloss over or seek to circumvent the issue raised by "realism" itself. In view of the continuing appeal of "unrealism" and the unwarranted claims made in its behalf, it is well worth exploring these arguments—especially now, when model building is being further fed by the growth of mathematical economics.

One argument frequently brought against economics of the "descriptive" variety is that unless there is abstraction from much of the "descriptive" material, it will not be possible to arrive at propositions of high degrees of generality. This is, of course, correct. But rather than resolving the issue, the argument avoids it. The issue is not whether scientific generalization requires abstraction. Even on propositional levels commonly regarded as "descriptive" abstraction is involved. Otherwise in making any statement concerning reality we would be obliged to consider all the factors surrounding the phenomenon, including those contained in all historical experience. In some ultimate sense everything is related to everything else. Experience teaches us that many factors surrounding a phenomenon, however, can be safely disregarded in explaining that phenomenon, so that in making "descriptive" statements we are all engaged in model building.[3] The issue then, in arguing for higher degrees of abstraction than those involved in "descriptive economics," is whether the phenomena concerned are in fact explained on the higher levels of abstraction. This is a question of fact not of methodology, and it can only be resolved therefore by evidence. Indeed, the very existence of the disagreement which impels the resort to methodological disquisition concerning the necessity for "abstraction" itself indicates that satisfactory evidence for the abstractions has not been produced. With respect to their view of satisfactory evidence, economists are no different from others—including physicists and chemists. And, wanting evidence demonstrating the explanatory value of the more highly abstract treatment, there is no ground for rejecting attempts to find explanations on "lower" and more "descriptive" levels.

Nor does a resort to the principle of Occam's Razor—which is often invoked in such debate—help resolve the issue in favor of high levels of abstraction. Occam argued for the superiority of the "simple." Taken within the context of the methodology of science, where we are dealing with the "explanation" of experience, he must be construed as saying that when we are confronted with two equally satisfactory explanations

---

[3] In view of the pervasiveness of abstraction, it should perhaps be emphasized that when I speak of models which "distort" or "oversimplify" reality (or which are "unreal"), I mean that reality is falsified by what is *included* in the assumptions of the model.

of a given phenomenon, we ought to choose the simpler. The simpler of the two is to be regarded as the better explanation presumably on the ground that since it involves fewer assumptions, it is more likely to be correct. This supposition itself is questionable. To the Deity, in his infinite knowledge, everything is simple. But it does not follow that the human inquirer, approaching experience with his finite perspective will (in choosing the simpler explanation) happen upon the one that is correct. In a given case, the more complicated may be the more correct, even though, given fuller knowledge, this itself may be subsumable under more simple general principles. When one considers inquiry into experience as a whole, it is difficult to see any basis for assigning a greater likelihood of validity to "simple" explanations. In any event, we are dealing with a case involving a choice between two *equally satisfactory explanations,* and in economics this is hardly the common case. More typically we are faced with a general hypothesis that fails to explain crucial aspects of the phenomenon in question, and the problem is to secure a better and fuller explanation. This may require reference to material at lower or more "descriptive" levels of analysis either as a supplement to or as a substitute for the more general hypothesis. In any case, the handling of the problem requires judgment and cannot be resolved by an appeal to methodological principles.

Another defense of highly abstract model building rests on the distinction between the world of models and the world of reality. This distinction has been characterized in numerous ways. Models have been termed parts of "deductive" or "logical" or "analytical" systems, while statements concerning reality are designated as "inductive" or "empirical" or "descriptive" propositions. Sometimes so much attention is given this distinction that the argument suggests that the taxonomy alone suffices to justify the scientific value of models. It is almost as though, representing a separate universe of discourse, the world of models was thought to have a self-sufficient justification of its own; and sometimes one gets the impression that there is a reluctance to leave this world at all. The distinction in question can be granted without argument. With impeccable logic we can construct a highly elaborate analytical system based on premises that flagrantly falsify reality.

If, however, it is to be shown that the analytical system has scientific value, then at some juncture it becomes essential to demonstrate the relationship between the entities of the system and the empirical world. It is here that the difficulty emerges since frequently such a relationship cannot be established. At this point the argument is sometimes dropped entirely, and we are left to conclude that, to the extent that the assumptions of an analytical system falsify reality, the system does not in fact meet the standards of science.

More recently this conclusion has been challenged. It has been argued that the scientific value of an analytical system is not undermined when its assumptions (as contained in the models) falsify reality. What matters, rather, is solely the nature of the predictions that can be drawn from these assumptions. The assumptions may be valid and yet falsify experience, provided it can be shown that the predictions derived from these assumptions (within the "model" world) are accurate in the real world.[4]

There are several ways of showing that this position is untenable.[5] All matter of fact propositions concerning the external world, as indicated, can be stated in the hypothetical form "If A, then B." As such, these propositions are statements of association between entities or events—here between A and B. The statement is shown to be valid when we have demonstrated that the relationship posited is one of a constancy of association. This is the uniformity which, in the world of observables, science seeks. And it is through a demonstration of such uniformity that science, in the face of disagreement, can compel belief. We come to "believe" that B will appear when A is present when it can be shown that this is in fact regularly the case. The view that A (the assumption) may falsify reality and still be part of an entirely valid hypothesis provided B (the prediction) holds thus runs directly counter to what is meant by validation of an empirical proposition, i.e., an entity (that of the model) which in the real world is found to be disassociated from another is held to be part of a scientifically validated association.

Stated in a somewhat different way, the view in question fails to deal with the meaning of "explanation." As noted, we say—when the hypothesis "If A, then B" is confirmed—that A "explains" B. A constancy of association is required for scientific explanation. A disassociation between A and B in the real world thus leaves B unexplained; and this is in no way altered by the fact that within the "model" world B is logically derivable from A. Should a price-output prediction logically requiring the assumption of perfect competition be found to hold true in a case of monopoly, we could not say that the prediction here was "explained" by perfect competition. For this reason we would be suspicious of the prediction. Since the prediction is unexplained—or apparently contradicts what we had reason to believe would be true in the given case—we would, for any given level of confidence, require a larger number of successful predictions in such cases. Predictions arrived at through this crystal ball technique (which, as long as we disregard the realism of the assumptions, gives us no inkling of where the predictions are to be found in reality) are not likely to evoke much confidence; and, raising as many questions as they appear to answer, they will certainly not resolve fundamental

---

[4] See, Milton Friedman, "The Methodology of Positive Economics," in *Essays in Positive Economics* (Chicago: University of Chicago Press, 1953), pp. 3-43.

[5] A detailed discussion of Friedman's position is contained in my article "On 'The Methodology of Positive Economics,'" *Quarterly Journal of Economics*, 73 (November, 1959), 554 ff.

disagreements among economists. The fact is that in the natural sciences
an hypothesis is treated as "invalid" (or as wanting in confidence) as
soon as, and to the extent that, any part of the hypothesis is found to
contradict experience. This must be the case since it is the objective of
all science to make experience intelligible or to predict through explanation. In the world of science there can be no distinction between the
"true" and the "valid."

If we wish, we may state the deficiency of the view under consideration wholly in terms of the meaning of "prediction." It can be shown
more specifically, that on the basis of this view "prediction" itself vanishes.
In any meaningful hypothesis the association involved is reducible to
subsets of associations. In the hypostatized association "If A, then B"
the terms A and B are themselves reducible to associations, and this
will be true as long as the hypothesis remains meaningful. For example,
in the proposition "If firms are perfectly competitive, then price equals
marginal cost," the assumption "firms are perfectly competitive" specifies
a relationship between a "firm" and certain properties of the environment
in which the firm operates (large numbers in the industry and so on).
Similarly, the prediction "price equals marginal cost" specifies a relationship between the entity "price" and the entity "marginal cost." The
prediction itself then can be couched in the hypothetical form "If this is
a price, it will be equal to marginal cost"; and this is reducible in turn to
an assumption ("this is a price") and a prediction ("it is equal to marginal
cost"). To say, then, that we should not concern ourselves with the
"realism" of "assumptions" but only with the realism of "predictions" is
internally contradictory since predictions themselves always involve
assumptions.

It should be noted that the view here under criticism deals with models
whose assumptions falsify experience. This implies that the entities
denoted by these assumptions are observable or that they can be tested
directly by observation. If they are not so testable—if, for example, we
were dealing with the "germ theory" of disease before germs could be
observed—the tests of the theory could only be indirect or could be
performed only on the implications of the theory, say, with respect to
the treatment of disease. In the philosophy of science the term "theory"
is sometimes exclusively confined to the hypothesis whose assumptions
are unobservable in order to distinguish it from the hypothesis with observable entities (termed a "law hypothesis"). In economics I would
venture to assert that most of the assumptions we deal with contain at
least some observable entities, or to this extent are parts of "law
hypotheses." This holds true even of many of the assumptions which
refer to human motivation or are, to this degree, "subjective," since
frequently these can at least be partially checked through "introspection"
and "communication."

III

The discussion thus far has been concerned with the limitations on the fruitfulness of mathematical economics in particular and, in connection with this, the shortcomings of oversimplified and false models in general. Models of this nature are of course not necessarily sterile; and in the interests of preserving an undistorted perspective on the issue, their potential value ought to be explicitly recognized.

I have argued that there is no basis for the view that the falsity of the assumptions of an hypothesis is irrelevant in a test of the validity of the hypothesis. This should be distinguished from the view that hypotheses (or models) with false assumptions may, as a stage in the reasoning process, be "useful." This latter is a commonly held position. In this view, assumptions that are false (or oversimplify reality) are helpful in analysis because they serve as a first approximation, or as a convenient point of departure, in dealing with a reality that is too complex to be grasped all at once. By altering the assumptions as we go along, we can—through successive approximations—come closer to the real dimensions of the problem at hand; and in the process, of course, we likewise alter the predictions to allow for the changes in the assumptions (or conditions). No claim is here made for the validity of the false or oversimplified model. The latter is, rather, treated wholly as an aid (necessitated by the complexity of experience) in the process of arriving at valid conclusions.

No formal objection can be brought against this view. We can well use any and all aids in the analysis of experience, and the one in question has been employed by many. In practice, however, it often does not prove to be as helpful as anticipated; for, in addition to the difficulty in securing the data required for testing the "final approximation," in the course of setting up the model with a view to constructing a theoretically determinate system it may be necessary to do considerable violence to important elements in reality. In such cases as we relax the assumptions of our first approximation in approaching reality, the very foundations of the determinate system crumble; our capacity to handle the problem analytically begins to vanish, and we are left with not much more understanding of the phenomenon than we would have attained had we not used the model at all. The method of successive approximation via highly abstract models cannot be treated as *the* indicated method for all problems. In many areas it works poorly, while in others the matter is not so clear as to preclude the indulgence of one's own intellectual predispositions in the choice of method.

Especially at the present time—when the physical sciences seem to play so important a role as the paradigm for methodology in economics —it ought to be emphasized that in constructing highly refined theoretical models the physical sciences can make use of innumerable confirmed laws. Much of the material encompassed by the models has been reduced to uniformities. Under these circumstances the model building is likely to prove far more fruitful than in a field such as economics where many hypotheses on relatively low levels of abstraction continue, and after decades of disagreement, to remain subjects of heated controversy.

Despite their limitations, the potential uses of highly abstract "unreal" models in economics should not be lost from view. In providing a point of departure in the treatment of a problem, they may help carry the analysis further than would otherwise be the case; and at their best they may yield highly promising hypotheses—of the sort that are worthy of painstaking empirical testing. The development of econometrics together with improvements in data, moreover, may not only make more effective tests feasible, but may contribute to more fruitful model building as well —though the use of quantitative data is not an open-sesame to broad-scale scientific progress in economics. Especially when one considers the whole range of economic problems, the question of whether the subject matter can be measured quantitatively bulks large, as does the more basic question of the effectiveness of mathematical functions in the handling of human behavior.[6]

We have been discussing the use of models as an aid in the process of arriving at valid hypotheses. Even when they fall short of yielding such hypotheses, models may be of value. For when they enable us to carry the analysis of a problem substantially further than would otherwise be the case, they may yield important insights. The term "insight" is difficult to define since the light it sheds on experience falls somewhere between complete ignorance on the one hand and the kind of knowledge embodied in a validated hypothesis on the other. As propositions arrived at through "insight" do not compel belief, they remain controversial; and "subjective" factors play an important role in determining the position taken by different inquirers. Moreover, because they are wanting by scientific standards, the fruits of insight are not likely to command attention unless—compensating for their uncertain status—they deal with fundamental issues and illuminate broad aspects of human experience. But such insights have played an important role in the most significant analytical systems in economics—for example, those of Marshall, Marx, and Schumpeter. Considering these systems as a whole, each rests very largely on propositions that leave much to be desired in the analysis of experience. Beyond the gross levels of analysis and then only

---

6 In his Presidential Address before the American Economic Association (entitled "The Economist and the State"), George Stigler emphasized the contribution quantitativism can make to the development of economics, but nowhere does he deal with the limitations of this approach. See *American Economic Review*, 55 (March, 1965), especially pp. 16-17.

in certain cases, these propositions do not lead us to accurate prediction. More often than not they yield only "hindsight prediction"—or tell us, after the event, that a given phenomenon was attributable to specific factors. Nonetheless, they provide a measure of understanding of experience which otherwise could not have been attained. Approaching experience via "pure" or "ideal" types, they manage to distill elements in their problem areas that we believe to be important; and because the models are simple and lend themselves to manipulation, they enable us to trace through their major implications. The systems moreover involve policy prescriptions. And, as they deal with basic issues, the prescriptions (if often misleading half-truths) cannot be readily dismissed.

The durability of systems of this nature testifies to the grip of their insights. But in this context it is their deficiencies that require emphasis. Perhaps if these were more fully recognized—if it were explicitly acknowledged that these systems fell significantly short of the requirements of a "predictive system"—much of the controversy concerning their usefulness would disappear. Then too, realizing that we are here dwelling in a sort of epistemological twilight zone, we might be more willing to accept rival systems. Since none has an exclusive claim to scientific validity, each may well be accepted for its own special insights. As an argument for pluralism, this leaves model systems in an ambiguous position. But, if it is difficult to carry several buckets on one's shoulders, the evidence to date does not indicate any more adequate procedure. Similarly, it serves as a special ground for guarding against the excesses of overrefinement which so often flow from a preoccupation with elaborating the implications of an analytical system.

IV

My comments with respect to mathematical economics—and more generally with regard to model building and analytical systems—have terminated in an appeal for pluralism because I believe the subject matter of economics demands it. Considered in the light of the many facets of a given economic problem area as well as the wide variety of problems economists encounter, the field (concerned as it is with conscious, purposive agents operating in a historical context and with capacities to reshape their behavior in the course of experience) is far more complex than the material dealt with in the physical sciences. Economists, moreover, cannot segment their problems through recourse to laboratory experiment, and the alternative conceptual and statistical procedures employed for this purpose are imperfect substitutes. Under these circumstances a respect for realism in economic analysis (without which we can have neither "science" nor any measure of "insight") argues for considerable flexibility in the approach to problems, and it argues as well for the crucial importance of "judgment" in the field—or a sense of proportion and a full awareness of potentially relevant factors in the problems we encounter. Allowing for the necessity of specialization within a discipline, the pursuit of any approach—such as the mathematical—at the expense of a substantial decline of interest in other major avenues of inquiry is thus particularly undesirable.

In this connection, the effects of the current trend on the education of future economists are especially worthy of note. Theoretical work— mathematical and literary—is an important part of the economics curriculum. But the breadth of perspective required for developing judgment in the field cannot be achieved simply through such work supplemented by forays into other areas "on the wing." It is, after all, a matter of experience. The experience that can be gained by grappling with complex substantive problems in a wide variety of areas while in school, the habit patterns that are so formed—all this is not easily attained subsequently when perspectives are more largely set and one is to no small extent emotionally as well as intellectually conditioned. There is much that we absorb in roundabout ways or by the process of osmosis. The absorption comes from a total environment. As in the case of all learning processes of significance, it takes time, and at no period is it more appropriate to begin than when in school, where the material can be handled in an organized and disciplined way. I suspect that the tendency to overlook this on the part of some is attributable to the fact that "judgment" at best appears to be something nebulous and, in any event, cannot be cultivated directly in a clearly defined way. By comparison, models are nothing if not systematic. They have the appeal of the rigorous and the stamp of the "professional" on their face, while work that does not fit within the mold of models seems unexciting and unheroic as well as more difficult to present in an impressively systematic fashion. I suspect, too, that some among the older generation who enthusiastically support the increasing emphasis on mathematical economics forget that, since they were reared in a different tradition, their students will not have the same breadth of perspective as their own. They seem to assume that a heavy concentration on mathematical economics and an education for breadth and judgment are entirely compatible. The cumulative impact of a narrow training over successive generations should be apparent.

Disciplines generally do not develop in an orderly way. Swings and cycles, vogues and fashions are to some extent unavoidable. They are particularly difficult to avoid where the stabilizing influence of laboratory experiment is lacking. The development of mathematical economics, moreover, may well accelerate progress in the field, and progress is usually attended with an increase in waste. Whatever the progress, it is to be hoped that—with a view toward the interests of the field as a whole—the waste can be minimized.

GERHARD TINTNER

Dr. Gerhard Tintner, Ph.D., University of Vienna, is Distinguished Professor of Economics and Mathematics at the University of Southern California. He has served as consultant to a number of government agencies and his academic awards and honors are many. His writings include a number of books—the most recent being Econometrics (1961)—and approximately one hundred articles for professional journals.

ESSAY

8

Some Thoughts About the State of Econometrics [1]

ECONOMICS MAY BE DEFINED AS THE SCIENCE that studies the administration of scarce resources. Economic theory derives deductive systems in terms of which we hope to explain empirical economic phenomena. Some economists, for example, members of the German historical school and American institutionalists, pretend that economic theory is superfluous and ought to be replaced by historical or institutional studies.

Without depreciating the study of economic history and of economic institutions (e.g., banks, trade unions), it seems obvious that a successful study of these phenomena must involve some theoretical concepts, if only in the selection of the historical and institutional features studied. Hence, economic theory seems indispensable.

In the past economic theory has been frequently developed in nonmathematical

[1] I am much obliged to the editor and to M. Bronfenbrenner and E. Fels for advice and criticism. Research supported by The National Science Foundation in Washington, D.C.

terms. The magnificent systems of Smith, Ricardo, and Marx are good examples. But mathematics can contribute to the clarification of the fundamental economic concepts and elucidate the method of economic reasoning. Economic theory might even be developed axiomatically. There seems to be a great advantage in mathematical economic theory, and economics has in recent times tended to use more and better mathematical methods.

But economics is an empirical science. The development of theoretical and mathematical structures, however refined, is not sufficient. We desire the verification of economic hypotheses and also the numerical evaluation of certain economic magnitudes for the purposes of economic policy. This involves the utilization of statistical methods in order to deal with empirical economic data. But economic statistics is not yet econometrics. Economic theory must be utilized in order to construct the mathematical models which we shall try to verify and use in order to evaluate numerically certain parameters which might be of some use in applications to policy. Economic statistics, e.g., sampling surveys, national income statistics, etc. provide only the raw material for econometricians, who will employ the statistical methods in order to verify mathematical economic models.

The statistical methods used in econometrics, however, should not blindly be copied from the biological or agricultural statistician. In contrast to biology, in economics we cannot make experiments. Hence, it is more difficult to disentangle the complex economic relations existing in the empirical world.

ECONOMETRIC MODELS

Econometrics [2] is the application of mathematical statistics to models constructed with the help of mathematical economic theory. Mathematical economics is the mathematical formulation and analysis of economic theories. However, the purpose of econometric models is often claimed to be application to policy. Since large scale models have had very limited success, their impact is very doubtful, as is their usefulness. Exceptions are perhaps: input-output models, linear programming models, demand functions, supply functions, and inventory models.

Before we proceed further it is advisable to delineate these areas so that there will be no misunderstanding in our discussion.

Input-output models: [3] Assuming static, i.e., timeless, conditions the

---

[2] G. Tintner, "The Definition of Econometrics," *Econometrica,* 21 (1953), 31 ff.
[3] W. W. Leontief, *Structure of the American Economy 1919–39,* 2nd ed. (New York: Oxford, 1951). *Studies in the Structure of the American Economy* (New York: Oxford, 1951).

total economy is divided into a number of sectors and the flow of commodities and services between the sectors is studied. Customarily one makes rather unrealistic assumptions about the conditions of production. One assumes constant coefficients of production, i.e., the output of a given sector is strictly proportional to the inputs from the other sectors of the economy. One also assumes free and perfect competition, so that in equilibrium the price of a commodity equals exactly the average cost necessary to produce it. This model enables the economist to study relationships between net outputs of the sectors, prices, employment, and so forth.

Linear programming models: [4] From a mathematical point of view they treat the maximization or minimization of a linear form (called the objective function) under conditions which are linear inequalities, and also under the condition that none of the solutions is permitted to become negative. These methods have a wide application in modern economics and operations research. The maximization of profit of an enterprise in the short run, where production takes place under conditions of constant coefficients of production and the amounts of the factors of production (various types of land, labor, and capital) are given. The transportation problem, where for instance the total sum of shipping cost is minimized if the demand and supply in various places is known, etc.

Demand functions: [5] We study the quantity of a commodity demanded on a given market as depending upon certain other variables, for instance the price of the commodity, the prices of other complementary or competing commodities, disposable income, and so forth. The relationships are not necessarily linear and the results of the analysis might be used in market research.

Supply functions: [6] We investigate the quantity of a commodity or service supplied as it is influenced by other economic variables, for instance, the price of this commodity, various cost factors involved in producing the commodity, technical progress, and so forth. Again the relationships need not be linear.

Inventory models: [7] Assume that a probability distribution of the quantity of a commodity demanded is known, also production and storing cost are available. Then we might determine the optimal

---

[4] R. Dorfman, *Applications of Linear Programming to the Theory of the Firm* (Berkeley: University of California Press, 1951). S. Vajda, *Mathematical Programming* (Reading, Mass.: Addison Wesley, 1961).

[5] H. Wold and L. Juréen, *Demand Analysis* (New York: Wiley, 1952).

[6] E. O. Heady and John L. Dillon, *Agricultural Production Functions* (Ames, Iowa: Iowa State University Press, 1961). J. Johnston, *Statistical Cost Analysis* (New York: McGraw, 1960).

[7] T. L. Saaty, *Mathematical Models of Operations Research* (New York: McGraw, 1959).

inventory policy which minimizes in a certain sense the total cost involved in production and storage. These methods are widely used in operations research.

Note that the really important questions of policy (unemployment, economic development) cannot be handled with the models which have had a moderate amount of success.

ECONOMIC THEORY AND ECONOMETRIC MODELS

Economic theory, which precedes econometrics by decennia (really centuries, if we start as we should with Aristotle), has had a deep effect on the construction of econometric models. Mathematical economics has made very rapid progress in recent years,[8] but this progress, very interesting from a purely mathematical point of view and satisfying aesthetically, has been limited almost entirely to economic statics. In economic statics the variables are not dated, time does not intervene. Even here it should be noted that we move almost entirely in the field of pure competition. In free competition we deal with a very large number of economic units which do not influence each other. Mathematical economics, however, has made virtually no progress on the fundamental problem of oligopoly (i.e., markets with a few sellers) and oligopsony (i.e., markets with a few buyers), so important for mature economies like that of the United States. The assumption that the individual units are independent cannot be maintained in the case of oligopoly or oligopsony. The promises of application of game theory in this field have not been fulfilled.[9] In economic dynamics, where economic variables are dated and individuals have certain (single-valued) expectations, according to J. R. Hicks [10] we have also made very little progress. Theories of stability of equilibria cannot be considered true dynamics, and it is not easy to see which purpose they are supposed to serve. Note that dynamic theories developed in the 1930's (G. C. Evans,[11] C. F. Roos [12]) which now have been forgotten were more satisfying. However, with very few exceptions, these theories were never empirically verified.

Economic dynamics, as defined—certain (single valued) expectations of all individuals in an economy—neglects, however, the most realistic models of risk [13] (the existence of known probability functions) and un-

---

[8] R. G. D. Allen, *Mathematical Economics* (London: Macmillan, 1956).
[9] M. Shubik, *Strategy and Market Structure* (New York: Wiley, 1959).
[10] *Value and Capital*, 2nd ed. (Oxford: Clarendon, 1946).
[11] *Mathematical Introduction to Economics* (New York: 1930).
[12] *Dynamic Economics* (Bloomington, Ind.: Principia, 1934).
[13] G. Tintner, "The Pure Theory of Production Under Technological Risk and Uncertainty," *Econometrica*, 9 (1941), 305 ff. "A Contribution to the Nonstatic Theory of Production," in *Studies in Mathematical Economics and Econometrics*, ed. O. Lange et al. (Chicago: University of Chicago Press, 1942), 92 ff. "A Note on Stochastic Linear Programming," *Econometrica*, 28 (1960), 490 ff.

certainty [14] (the case of unknown probability functions). Some progress has been made in this direction by the statisticians (A. Wald,[15] L. J. Savage [16]) but it seems doubtful if these ideas are relevant for economics. Some tentative applications of risk and uncertainty in inventory theory may be helpful, but empirical verification is again lacking.

All these models are micro-economic, i.e., deal with the individual household and the competitive firm. There has been moderate success in the empirical derivation of demand and supply functions, Engel curves, production functions, and so forth.[17] An Engel curve is a relationship between the expenditure for a given commodity and total expenditure or income. A production function describes the relationship between the amount of a commodity produced and the amounts of various factors of production (different types of labor, land, and capital) used in the process of production.

For dealing with really crucial problems of policy we need, however, macro-economic models. Macro-economic models investigate economic relationships in a total economy. This implies, first, aggregation (the construction of index numbers).

AGGREGATION PROBLEM

The construction of a single index from individual economic data is an aggregation—e.g., the construction of an index of industrial or agricultural production from data on the production of individual commodities. Unfortunately, not much progress has been made in this field. The mathematically fascinating work of U.S. econometricians,[18] French mathematicians [19] and recently that of the Dutch econometric school [20] has only pointed out the almost impossible task of defining (let alone

---

[14] G. Tintner, "Eine Anwendung der Wahrscheinlichkeitstheorie von Carnap auf ein Problem der Unternehmungsforschung," *Unternehmungsforschung*, 4 (1960), 164 ff.

[15] *Statistical Decision Functions* (New York: Wiley, 1950).

[16] *The Foundations of Statistics* (New York: 1954).

[17] Heady and Dillon, *Agricultural Production Functions;* S. J. Prais and H. S. Houthakker, *The Analysis of Household Budgets* (Cambridge: Cambridge U. P., 1955).

[18] L. R. Klein, "Macroeconomics and the Theory of Rational Behavior," *Econometrica*, 14 (1946), 93 ff. "Remarks on the Theory of Aggregation," *Econometrica*, 14 (1946), 93 ff. K. May, "The Aggregation Problems in a One Industry Model," *Econometrica*, 14 (1946), 285 ff.

[19] A. Nataf, "Sur la Possibilité de la Construction de certains Macromodéles," *Econometrica*, 16 (1948), 232 ff. R. Roy, "Les Elasticitiés de la Demande Relative Aux Biens de la Consommation et Aux Groups Des Biens," *Econometrica*, 20 (1952), 391 ff. E. Malinvaud, "L'aggregation dans les Modéles Economiques," *Cahiers Du-Seminaire Econometrique*, 4 (1956), 69 ff.

[20] H. Theil, *Linear Aggregation in Economic Relations* (Amsterdam: North-Holland, 1954).

computing) an "ideal" index. The approach proposed by the author,[21] based upon H. Hotelling's principal components,[22] is not very satisfying from an economic point of view nor has it found many applications. Perhaps the attempts to utilize the lognormal [23] distribution in this connection are a little more promising. We assume that the money spent on a given commodity by an individual consumer (or family) depends upon the logarithm of total expenditure on all commodities. But this total expenditure follows the lognormal distribution, i.e., its logarithm has the well-known bell-shaped normal or Gaussian distribution. These assumptions permit a simple estimation of the relationship between average expenditure on a given commodity and average total expenditure on all commodities (Engel curve).

MACRO-ECONOMIC MODELS

In my opinion as previously indicated, static open Leontief (input-output) models have had a certain success.[24] We might use them for forecasting a few years in the future. These models have a very simple structure, but in spite of this (or because of it) they seem to work reasonably well in terms of predictive power. We know that the fundamental assumptions (linearity, constant returns to scale, fixed technology, etc.) are not true, even in the short run. Nevertheless, it seems that they are reasonably good approximations, again valid only for the short run. Similar models have been used with some success for short-run planning in India.[25] It should be noted, however, that these models cannot easily be made dynamic,[26] and used to study the development of the economy over time. Also, they are unable to deal with monetary phenomena and serious problems involving long-term economic development.

Related to these models are linear programs. Again, there has been limited success here. A linear program may, for instance, be used to determine the optimal production pattern of a competitive firm in the short run. In the short run all costs are assumed to be fixed, prices are given, and production conditions are represented by inequalities which involve the constant input-output coefficients, i.e., we assume a fixed and

---

[21] G. Tintner, *Econometrics* (New York: Wiley, 1952), 102 ff.

[22] "Analysis of a Complex of Statistical Variables into Principal Components," *Journal of Educational Psychology,* 24 (1933), 417 ff.

[23] J. Aitchison and J. A. C. Brown, *The Lognormal Distribution* (Cambridge: Cambridge U. P., 1957).

[24] O. Morgenstern, ed., *Economic Activity Analysis* (New York: Wiley, 1954). O. Lange, *Introduction to Econometrics* (London: Pergamon, 1959).

[25] P. C. Mahalanobis, "The Approach of Operational Research to Planning," *Sankhya,* 16 (1955), 3 ff.

[26] R. Dorfman, P. A. Samuelson, R. M. Solow, *Linear Programming and Economic Analysis* (New York: McGraw, 1958), 265 ff.

invariable relationship between the inputs of various factors of production (different types of land, labor and capital) and the quantities produced. The greatest success has been with static models. In dynamic programming the same assumptions are employed for programming over several time periods (e.g., years).[27] Integer programming [28] makes the further, more realistic assumtpions, that some or all of the solutions must be integers. This is an attempt to deal with the problem of indivisibilities, so important and so much neglected in much of economic theory. Stochastic programming [29] is based upon the assumption that the coefficients of production, the availabilities of the factors of production, and also perhaps the prices of the commodities are not given numbers but random variables, whose joint probability distribution is known.

But by far the most important econometric models for dealing with some burning economic policy problems (unemployment, inflation) are the Keynesian models—potentially at least. That the ideas of Lord Keynes have revolutionized economic thinking cannot be denied. However, there are some considerations about the original (and very fruitful) ideas in the General Theory [30] which are usually neglected:

A. The original Keynesian model is static (or stationary) and is an effort to explain permanent excess supply of factors of production (unemployment) under static conditions. Time is not involved in the analysis.

B. One of the fundamental assumptions of the models is that under equilibrium conditions the supply of labor depends upon money wages and not real wages (i.e., money wages divided by a price index or cost of living index). This queer kind of universal money illusion does not seem to exist in any real economy and was to a certain extent falsified by investigations of the supply of industrial labor in England [31] and the U.S.[32]

L. R. Klein must be credited with the most persistent and interesting efforts to apply the Keynesian models to the U.S.[33] and recently to the

[27] R. Bellmann, *Dynamic Programming* (Princeton, N.J.: Princeton University Press, 1957).

[28] W. J. Baumol, *Economic Theory and Operations Analysis* (Englewood Cliffs, N.J.: Prentice-Hall, 1961).

[29] G. Tintner, "A Note on Stochastic Linear Programming," *Econometrica*, 28 (1960), 490 ff. "The Use of Stochastic Linear Programming in Planning," *Indian Economic Review*, 5 (1960), 159 ff.

[30] J. M. Keynes, *The General Theory of Employment, Interest and Money* (London: Macmillan, 1936).

[31] G. Tintner, *Econometrics*, pp. 143 ff.

[32] E. Mosback, "Fitting a Static Supply and Demand Function for Labor," *Weltwirtschaftliches Archiv*, 82 (1959), 133 ff.

[33] L. R. Klein, "The Use of Econometric Models as a Guide to Economic Policy," *Econometrica*, 15 (1947), 111 ff. *Economic Fluctuations in the United States 1921-41* (New York: Wiley, 1950). L. R. Klein and R. S. Goldberger, *An Econometric Model of the United States, 1929-1952* (Amsterdam: North-Holland, 1955).

British economy [34] It should be noted, however, that in order to apply the Keynesian models to actual economic data Klein is forced to make them dynamic, i.e., he must introduce time lags. Also, he limits himself to linear models (see below). Whereas great theoretical interest cannot be denied to these empirical verifications, it cannot easily be claimed that these models can actually be applied to the solution of concrete problems of economic policy.

The main shortcomings of these models are as follows:

1) *Linearity.* Although there is no objection to approximate complex nonlinear relations by linear equations, the danger of the neglect of nonlinearity for long term prediction (and really for any prediction outside the range of the data) is very great. Also, in the field of Engel curves and production functions we know that nonlinear models seem to work reasonably well.

2) *Free competition.* The models seem to be based essentially upon the simple assumption of free competition. But we know that in the developed countries free competition is not really the prevailing market form. Until the problem of oligopoly and oligopsony is solved, it is difficult to see what alternative models should be employed.

3) *Casual dynamisation.* Essentially static models are made dynamic by the somewhat arbitrary introduction of time lags. There is no theoretical justification for this procedure. In the theory of distributed lags [35] we make the (somewhat arbitrary) assumption that the influence of the past values of certain economic variables (e.g., prices) decreases like the terms of a geometric series with longer and longer lags. This may be a step in the right direction, but seems to be a very inflexible scheme of handling dynamic problems and its employment must still be tested more extensively in empirical applications.

STOCHASTIC MODELS: A PROPOSAL

If we look at economics from the point of view of history of ideas— as, for example, in Joseph Schumpeter [36]—then we must be impressed by the deep influence exerted on theoretical economic models by the ideas of classical mechanics. This is already true for the physiocrats

---

[34] L. R. Klein, R. J. Ball, A. Hazlewood, P. Vandome, *An Economic Model of the U. K.* (Oxford: Oxford University Press, 1961).

[35] L. M. Koyck, *Distributed Lags and Investment Analysis* (Amsterdam: North-Holland, 1954). M. Nerlove, *The Dynamics of Supply* (Baltimore: Johns Hopkins, 1958).

[36] *History of Economic Analysis* (New York: Oxford, 1954).

(*tableau economique*)[37] but becomes most apparent in the magnificent mathematical model of a competitive static economy derived by Léon Walras,[38] a model of clearness and consistency and unsurpassed in its achievement.

But physics itself has changed. The deterministic system of nineteenth-century physics has been replaced by the ideas of modern physics, based on quantum mechanics and involving from the beginning the much less satisfactory ideas of probability. (Relativity may in this connection be considered as the crowning achievement of classical physical ideas.)

There seems to be a cultural lag between physics and economics. Is it not time that we might try to model our economic theory after modern statistical physics, instead of elaborating stubbornly new (but not much more satisfactory) models after the ideas of classical physical statics and dynamics?

The magnificent new theory of games of strategy [39] was designed to deal, especially under static conditions, with the economic problems of oligopoly, bilateral monopoly, etc. Bilateral monopoly exists if a monopolist faces a monopsonist, i.e., there is exactly one buyer and one seller in the market. This type of market organization is especially important in the field of labor economics. Unfortunately, great as the impact of these ideas has been in other related fields (utility theory,[40] linear programming,[41] static competitive equilibrium systems [42]) there is not as yet any evidence that much progress can be made with the help of these ideas in dealing with noncompetitive market structures which are not simple monopolies or monopsonies, i.e., where there are a few buyers or sellers in the market.

The theory of stochastic processes [43] has made a lot of progress. A stochastic process is a family of random variables, i.e., variables associated with given probability distributions, which depends upon a parameter, e.g., time. There are interesting applications especially in physics and biology, and also in the field of operations research, which is really the econometrics of the enterprise. This encourages one to hope that similar methods may also be used in economics. It would have the advantage of introducing stochastic, i.e., probability considerations in a

[37] F. Quesnay, *Tableau Economique* (London: 1894).

[38] *Elements d'économie Politique Pure* (Lausanne: 1877).

[39] J. von Neumann and O. Morgenstern, *Theory of Games and Economic Behavior* (Princeton, N.J.: Princeton University Press, 1944).

[40] M. Friedman and L. J. Savage, "The Utility Analysis of Choices Involving Risk," *Journal of Political Economy*, 56 (1948), 279 ff.

[41] R. Dorfman, P. A. Samuelson, R. M. Solow, *Linear Programming and Economic Analysis* (New York: McGraw, 1958).

[42] G. Debreu, *Theory of Value* (New York: Wiley, 1959).

[43] M. Fisz, *Probability Theory and Mathematical Statistics*, 3rd ed. (New York: Wiley, 1963), 250 ff. A. T. Bharucha-Reid, *Elements of the Theory of Markov Processes and Their Applications* (New York: McGraw, 1960).

more fundamental way directly into economic models.[44] It is suggested that the utilization of the theory of stochastic processes might enable us to deal more efficiently with chance factors, which play a great part in many economic phenomena.

STATISTICAL PROBLEMS CONNECTED WITH THE VERIFICATION OF ECONOMETRIC MODELS

It cannot be denied that the statistical methods used in the empirical verifications of econometric models have greatly advanced in recent years. Since the path-breaking work of T. Haavelmo [45] a lot of progress has been made. However, there are still some outstanding unsolved problems, and we would be deceiving ourselves in claiming that all is well in this connection.

A. *Simultaneity.*[46] Since Haavelmo all econometricians have recognized that there must be a close interrelationship between the theoretical model constructed (including stochastic assumptions) and the statistical methods used. This has given rise to a clear recognition of the problem of identification [47] and its implication for statistical estimation methods.[48] The identification problem comes before questions of statistical estimation. It deals with the possibility of disentangling the individual and economically meaningful equations (e.g., demand functions, production functions, etc.) from each other, given the nature of the assumed model which consists of a system of equations with errors in the equations only (shocks). These errors are assumed to result

---

[44] T. Haavelmo, *A Study in the Theory of Economic Evolution* (Amsterdam: 1954). G. Tintner, "A Stochastic Theory of Economic Development and Fluctuations," in *Money, Growth and Methodology,* ed. H. Hegeland (Lund: Gleerup, 1961), 59 ff. V. Mukerjee, G. Tintner, and R. Narayanan, "A Generalized Poisson Process With Applications to Indian Data," *Arthaniti,* 7 (1964), pp. 156 ff.

[45] T. Haavelmo, "The Probability Approach in Econometrics," *Econometrica,* 12 (1944), Suppl.

[46] L. R. Klein, *A Textbook in Econometrics* (Evanston, Ill.: Row, Peterson, 1953). *An Introduction to Econometrics* (Englewood Cliffs, N.J.: Prentice-Hall, 1962). J. Johnston, *Econometric Methods* (New York: McGraw, 1963). J. Marschak, "Economic Measurement for Policy and Prediction," in ed. W. C. Hood and T. Koopmans, *Studies in Econometric Method* (New York: Wiley, 1953). R. H. Strotz and H. O. H. Wold, "Recursive vs. Nonrecursive Systems," *Econometrica,* 28 (1960), 417 ff. T. C. Liu, "Underidentification, Structural Estimation and Forecasting," *Econometrica,* 28 (1960), 855 ff. F. M. Fisher, *A Priori Information and Time Series Analysis* (Amsterdam: North-Holland, 1962). A. S. Goldberger, *Econometric Theory* (New York: Wiley, 1964).

[47] T. C. Koopmans, "Identification Problems in Economic Model Construction," *Econometrica,* 17 (1949), 125 ff.

[48] T. C. Koopmans, H. Rubin, and R. B. Leipnik, "Measuring the Equation System in Dynamic Economics," in ed. T. C. Koopmans, *Statistical Inference in Dynamic Economic Models* (New York: Wiley, 1950), 50 ff.

from the effect of variables which actually influence the given relationship but have been neglected in the model. However, there are also some ambiguities here:

1) The classification of variables into current endogenous variables (economic variables simultaneously determined in the model) and predetermined variables (exogenous variables, which are essentially noneconomic and given from the outside; and past values of endogenous and exogenous variables) is all right theoretically, but it is not always easy to perform in practice. For example, if we study a small market, we may consider income as exogenous, which it surely is not. Can population really be assumed to be exogenous, in contradiction to a large part of classical economic theory (Malthus, Ricardo)? Also, past values of endogenous variables cannot really be taken as fixed and given as postulated in the methods proposed for the estimation of econometric relations. An honest treatment of our systems as a set of stochastic difference equations would be preferable, if such a usable theory existed.

2) Assumptions made for the purpose of identification consist typically in assumptions that certain variables are absent in some equations. But these assumptions are frequently ad hoc, and it is difficult to justify them theoretically and to test them statistically. It is often forgotten that the conclusions reached are derived under the assumption that the theoretical model assumed holds, and hence give us conditional probabilities.

3) Many ingenious statistical methods are now available which enable us to get statistical estimates. The full maximum likelihood method,[49] however, seems to be rather impractical. Maximum likelihood estimates a given relationship by maximizing the probability of obtaining the given sample of observations. Since the equations involved are nonlinear, we have to use numerical methods. Numerical methods have been derived, but even they do not guarantee the achievement of the maximum maximorum of likelihood, rather than a local maximum. The limited information method has been very popular. In the limited information method we estimate a single equation or a group of equations in a total system of simultaneous equations while neglecting certain information

---

[49] H. Chernoff and N. Divinsky, "The Computation of Maximum Likelihood Estimates of Linear Structural Equations," in ed. W. C. Hood and T. Koopmans, *Studies in Econometric Method* (New York: Wiley, 1953).

about the part of the system which is not estimated. But it may lead to contradictions if all equations of a given system are estimated in this manner. The two-stage least-squares method of H. Theil [50] and R. L. Basmann [51] has the advantage of cheapness and simplicity. With the two-stage least-squares method, we estimate first by the method of least squares the reduced form equation, i.e., the relationship between each endogenous variable and all predetermined variables. These estimates are then used for an estimation of the original relationship in the system of simultaneous equations again by the method of least squares. It has not yet been used very extensively in practical applications. The derivation of small sample distributions of the estimates of econometric structures is still in its infancy.[52]

However, the methods used in estimating simultaneous econometric systems are based upon the existence of errors in the equations (shocks) *alone*. Also, we assume that the shocks are free of autocorrelations and serial correlations. Autocorrelation describes the relationship of subsequent errors in time. If the errors at a given point in time are independent from errors at another point in time, we have no autocorrelation, and the errors are said to be independent if they follow the normal distribution. Serial correlation describes the relationship between the values of a given series and the lagged values of another variable. Again, if we assume normal distributions, absence of serial correlation implies independence over time. The presence of autocorrelation and serial correlation creates very difficult estimation problems. In this fashion, we also neglect the existence of errors in the variables (akin to observation errors) and especially the time series nature of our data. No wonder that we frequently in practical applications encounter problems of multicollinearity [53] (i.e., the existence of strong relations between independent variables) and that the computed deviations from our structural relations very frequently show discernible autocorrelative properties. This should indicate to us that perhaps not all is well.

[50] H. Theil, *Economic Forecasts and Policy* (Amsterdam: North-Holland, 1958), 225 ff.

[51] R. L. Basmann, "A Generalized Classical Method of Linear Estimation of Coefficients in a Structural Equation," *Econometrica*, 25 (1957), 77 ff.

[52] R. L. Basmann, "A Note on the Exact Finite Sample Frequency Functions of Generalized Classical Linear Estimators in Two Leading Overidentified Cases," *Journal of the American Statistical Association*, 56 (1961), 575 ff.

[53] G. Tintner, *Econometrics*, 121 ff.

B. *Errors in the variables.*[54] It has been pointed out by Morgenstern that our data are frequently affected by large errors in the variables. Some result from the difficulty of defining economic concepts (e.g., national income) in a sensible empirical fashion. But apart from this, we cannot pretend that in general economic data are free from plain observation errors.[55] For instance, prices in the big commodity markets and stock market prices may be established with reasonable accuracy, but this is much less true with the quantities consumed, produced and stored. Models based upon errors in the variables alone have not been very popular recently. But the complete neglect of the possibility that our empirical data may not possess complete accuracy will lead us into large errors.

C. *Multicollinearity.* If we compute the unrestricted reduced-form equations, we find the least-square regression of all endogenous variables on all predetermined variables, both the truly exogenous variables (noneconomic variables) and the past values of endogenous and exogenous variables. If exact linear relations exist between the predetermined variables, the reduced form equations cannot be computed. But if linear relations hold only approximately, perhaps because of the existence of errors in the variables, the reduced form equations can be computed but the coefficients become (in the limiting case) solely the effect of errors and are meaningless.

The multicollinearity will often exist because of the strong and positive autocorrelative of economic time series, which has been observed frequently. Economic variables tend to move together; price rises are rarely confined to a single sector of the economy. A boom in the quantities produced tends to spread through the whole economy, so does a slump. In short, economic phenomena are largely interdependent and the complicated relationship between them can be approximated by linear equations. Hence, multicollinearity.

If we know the variances and covariances of the errors in the variables, we are able to test for multicollinearity and to estimate (in a fashion) the number of independent linear relations actually existing between the error free variables in the population. I have proposed to estimate the error variances and covariances by the Variate Difference Method,[56] but this is probably not a very good

---

[54] G. Tintner, *loc. cit.*
[55] O. Morgenstern, *On the Accuracy of Economic Observations* (Princeton, N.J.: Princeton U. P., 1950).
[56] G. Tintner, *The Variate Difference Method* (Bloomington, Ind.: Principia, 1940).

procedure. If the data come from sample surveys, we might have an idea of the sampling error and this could serve as an estimate for the error variances.

In case our model is a model with errors in the variables (but not in the equations) weighted regression might be used in order to establish the structural relationships.

D. *Time series nature of our observations.* All the statistical methods discused above assume explicitly that consecutive error terms are independent in the probability sense. But statistical tests [57] show very frequently that this is not the case with empirical economic time series.

Ideally, we would like to have at our disposal a valid statistical treatment of multiple time series or vector statistical processes.[58] Unfortunately, there are only the merest rudimentary beginnings of such a theory available. One particular difficulty arises because our empirical time series are by necessity not stationary (e.g., frequently involve trends) and not ergodic.

Until these problems are solved, we have to use methods which are certainly inferior substitutes to an honest statistical treatment of multiple evolutionary time series. Some of these methods are:

1) *Computation and elimination of trends.* The convenient polynomial trends are not really suitable, especially for long series. A polynomial will by necessity tend to infinity. The same holds for exponential trends. The logistic trend,[59] which has desirable properties from an economic point of view, is difficult to fit. The logistic function possesses an upper asymptote.

2) *Introduction of time explicitly into the economic relationships.*[60] This method frequently diminishes autocorrelation of the residuals, but it is not really satisfactory since trends as such cannot be easily interpreted in economic terms.

3) *Estimation of the error variance by the Variate Difference Method.*[61] This idea is based upon the assumption that our series consist of a smooth deterministic component and a superimposed error term which has finite variance and is not autocorrelated. The scheme is probably much too simple for serious applicants.

---

[57] R. L. Anderson, "Distribution of the Serial Correlation Coefficient," *Annals of Mathematical Statistics,* 13 (1942), 1 ff.

[58] M. H. Quenouille, *The Analysis of Multiple Time Series* (New York: Hafner, 1957).

[59] G. Tintner, *Handbuch Der Oekonometrie* (Berlin: Springer, 1960), 273 ff.

[60] R. Frisch and F. V. Waugh, "Partial Time Regression as Compared With Individual Trends," *Econometrica,* 1 (1933), 387 ff.

[61] G. Tintner, *The Variate Difference Method.*

4) *Methods for testing correlations between autocorrelated time series.*[62] For large samples these methods show that autocorrelation diminishes in a certain sense the number of degrees of freedom. The number of effective degrees of freedom is less than the number of observations. These methods are only rough approximations.

5) *Modification of standard errors of regression coefficients in the presence of autocorrelation.*[63] Here the results are large sample results and presuppose the knowledge of the nature of the autocorrelation scheme assumed.

6) *Autoregressive transformations.*[64] If we know the nature of the autocorrelation of the deviations involved (i.e., the correlogram which is constructed from all the autocorrelation coefficients), we might make certain linear transformations which will eliminate autocorrelation of the residuals. Of course, the theoretical correlogram is never known, but approximation methods are available.

7) *Difference transformations.*[65] Since in short economic time series most of the autocorrelation can be approximated by a linear trend, working with first differences will frequently eliminate or at least greatly reduce autocorrelation of the residuals.

None of these methods are really very satisfactory. The exact statistical treatment of multiple time series for small samples involves, however, formidable mathematical difficulties. Hence, we can only expect slow progress.[66]

---

[62] G. H. Orcutt and S. F. James, "Testing the Significance of Correlations Between Time Series," *Biometrika*, 35 (1948), 397 ff.

[63] H. Wold and L. Juréen, *Demand Analysis* (New York: Wiley, 1952), 209 ff.

[64] D. Cochrane and G. H. Orcutt, "Application of Least Squares Regression to Relationships Containing Autocorrelated Error Terms," *Journal of the American Statistical Association*, 44 (1949), 32 ff.

[65] R. Stone, D. A. Rowe, W. J. Corlett, R. Hurstfield, M. Potter, *The Measurement of Consumers' Expenditure and Behaviour in the United Kingdom* (Cambridge: Cambridge U. P., 1954).

[66] S. Alexander, "Price Movements in Speculative Markets; Trends or Random Walk," *Industrial Management Review*, 2 (1961), 7 ff. J. S. De Cani, "On the Construction of Stochastic Models of Population and Migration," *Journal of Regional Science*, 3 (1961), 1 ff. C. W. J. Granger and O. Morgenstern, "Spectral Analysis of New York Stock Market Data," *Kyklos*, 16 (1963), 1 ff. R. Henn, "Markowsche Ketten bei Wirtschaftsprozessen," *Metrika*, 3 (1960), 61 ff. J. G. Kemeny, J. L. Snell, G. L. Thompson, *Introduction to Finite Mathematics* (Englewood Cliffs, N.J.: Prentice-Hall, 1957). B. Mandelbrot, "The Pareto Law and the Distribution of Income," *International Economic Review*, 1 (1960), 79 ff. J. K. Sengupta and G. Tintner, "On Some Aspects of Trend in Aggregative Models of Economic Growth," *Kyklos*, 14 (1963), 47 ff. H. A. Simon, "On a Class of Skew Distribution Functions," *Biometrika*, 42 (1955), 425 ff. J. Steindl, *Random Processes and the Growth of Firms* (New York: Hafner, 1965).

KENNETH E. BOULDING

Kenneth E. Boulding, educated at Oxford and Chicago, is Professor of Economics at the University of Michigan. His published works include a dozen books and numerous articles covering a wide range of fields, including most notably—in addition to economics—the fields of peace research and international systems. From its beginning, he has been associated with the Center for Research on Conflict Resolution at the University of Michigan, currently serving as its Director.

ESSAY

9

The Verifiability of Economic Images

THE FIRST TASK OF THIS PAPER IS CLEARLY to take a brief look at the concept of "verifiability" itself. It is a concept which may appear fairly obvious on the surface; nevertheless, there is hardly any other concept around which so many philosophical banshees howl. It has been the subject of a still unresolved argument among philosophers almost as long as there have been philosophers. The problem, stated very simply, is this: Every human being has an image of a world of time and space, causality, value, and so on in his mind. This we might call the "subjective world." Part of this image consists of a conviction that corresponding to the subjective world inside him there is an objective world outside him to which his subjective image corresponds. If he is a normal person, he can distinguish quite readily between those parts of his image which he regards as "real," that is, corresponding to something outside, and those parts of his image which he regards as unreal or fantasy. The image which he has of his home, his street, his town, his place of work, he regards as real. The image which he has of Santa Claus or fairies, or little green people from outer space, he usually regards as fantasies.

It now seems pretty clear, especially from what we now know about the development of sense perception, that this distinction within the image between the real and the unreal is developed by a process of testing. Testing is a complicated process, and there are many things about it which are still very puzzling. There can be no doubt, however, that such a process in fact goes on. It involves a number of elements. The first is an expectation or prediction, that is, an image of what we expect the "real" part of our image to be like at a certain date in the future. Because of the sheer passage of time, the date in the future eventually arrives, and then we are faced either with confirmation or with disappointment. Confirmation means that the image of reality as we experience it in the present corresponds with our expectation, that is, with the image as we conceived it in the past. For instance, I may have an image of going out to the mail box to pick up the mail. This is an image of the future, even though a very near future. Then when the future "arrives," I in fact go out to the mailbox to pick up the mail, and if there is mail in the mailbox, my image is confirmed. If there is no mail in the box, then my image is disappointed. On a more elaborate scale, the scientist may set up an experiment in which he expects a certain result. The result may be confirmed, or it may be disappointed.

The learning process is the process by which images are changed, presumably in the direction of reality. Crucial in this process is the nature of our reaction to disappointment. If our expectations are confirmed, there is practically no pressure to change the image, even though confirmation is no proof of the correctness of the image on which the expectation was based. Confirmation might be an accident, but if it is, there is no way of discovering this. It is only as we are disappointed that we are placed under any pressure whatsoever to readjust our images of the world or to change our distribution between reality and fantasy. There may, however, be three reactions to disappointment. The first is the rejection of the message which informed us regarding the reality of our present image. Thus, if I open the mailbox and find no mail, my first reaction may be to open it wider and look further inside, thinking that the message which first informed me that there was no mail was inaccurate and was to be rejected. The illustration points out that this is by no means always a stupid reaction. It is just as rational to do this, however, when messages are confirmed as when they are not, for there is nothing in the nature of things which says that confirming messages are more reliable than disappointing messages. The fact is, however, that we are much less likely to take a second look if the message confirms our expectation than if it disappoints it. This is why disappointment is a much more powerful source of change than is fulfillment.

Suppose, however, that in spite of the second look the message remains that there is no mail. I may then reject the inference which gave rise to the expectation in the first place. An inference is a derivation of an expectation from an image of the world. My image of the world says that there is a mail service and that mail is delivered regularly in my mail box at a certain time each day. The inference is that on this particular day there will be mail in the mail box at a certain time. If I go out and find there is no mail, I may simply reject the inference. I may say, for instance, that even though there is a mail service on this particular day, nobody has sent me any mail. The inference here is a probabilistic one— that there is a certain probability of there being mail in the mail box at a certain time, and that if there is no mail, this merely means that the slightly improbable has occurred (which, of course, it always may). If our expectation is probabilistic, that is, if we expect something with a certain probability, then disappointment is probabilistic too. In other words, we do not really know whether we have been disappointed or not. Even if I have a 99 per cent chance of finding mail in the mail box, it is certainly not unreasonable to suppose that if there is no mail in the box the 1 per cent chance has come off. At some point, indeed, it is likely that a very low probability is equated psychologically with zero probability; that is, there is some just-noticeable-difference of probabilities, as psychologists say, and if a probability is below this, this will be equated with zero. Under these circumstances, failure of expectations will inevitably produce sharper impact than if the failure is within the recognizable range of probability.

Rejecting the inference is also sometimes a perfectly rational thing to do, especially where the expectation is probabilistic. It may even be rational where the probability of the expectation is 1, that is, the expectation is certain, because, like messages, inferences on re-examination may prove to have been false. It is one of the virtues of mathematical inference that if it is false, there are strong rewards for somebody finding this out, and hence, false inferences are likely to be discovered. In the case of more vague verbal inferences, however, the rewards may go the other way. That is, the person who points out that the inference is wrong may be received with something considerably less than joy, especially by people who have taken a firm stand on their inferences.

The third possible reaction to disappointment is a reorganization of the basic image of the world itself. If, for example, I find there is no mail in the box, I may suddenly remember that it is a public holiday and that there is no mail delivery. If I had recalled this earlier, I would not have made the inference that there would be mail in the box. It is a peculiar virtue of the method of science that it protects itself very carefully against rejection either of the message or of the inference; hence, when scientific experiments result in the disappointment of expectations, there is hardly anything to do but to reorganize the basic image of the world. This, indeed, is what we mean by scientific testing.

Images of the world may be classified roughly in the order of the ease or of the difficulty with which they may be tested. In general, it may be asserted that narrow and relatively unimportant images are fairly easy to test but that the wider, the more extensive, and the more fundamental the image under consideration, the harder it is to test. It is fairly easy to test whether there is any mail in the box. It is harder to test whether the absence of mail is due to the fact that nobody has written or whether it is due to a breakdown in the mail truck. It is still harder to test whether the postal system in general is efficient, and it is extremely hard to test whether, for instance, a postal service run by a privately owned but regulated utility would be more or less efficient than the present state-owned and state-run operation. It is fairly easy to test the existence of chemical elements; it is very hard to test the existence of God.

In economics, it is not difficult to make a rough classification, finally, of economic images in the order of the difficulty of testing them—that is, in the order of verifiability. A good starting point might be to discuss first what we mean by economic images and how we distinguish these from other parts of our image of the world. This, however, should emerge in the course of the discussion, and for the moment I will simply suggest that economic images are those which revolve around the concept of exchange as a central focus. It is not easy, and indeed probably is fruitless, to try to define the boundaries of economics, for it merges indistinguishably into its related disciplines. Economic theory, however, abstracts from the social system those aspects of it which are closely related to the phenomenon of exchange. Economic institutions, such as banks, insurance companies, and corporations, are those in which exchange is a dominant aspect of the institution's history and behavior; and economic behavior, if it is indeed to be distinguished from rational behavior in general, is that behavior which is particularly associated with exchange and with objects of exchange, that is, commodities. An economic image then is some image of the world related to exchange, or to the whole system of exchanges, or to the production and consumption of those things which are or which may be exchanged. The problem here, therefore, is that of the testing of images of this kind. I shall use four very rough categories which will be described as: (1) easy to test, (2) hard to test, (3) very hard to test, and (4) impossible to test.

Among the images which are easy to test are images of prices and of commodities offered for sale or for purchase. Suppose, for instance, I read an advertisement in the paper that a certain store is advertising shirts for sale at five dollars. I have an image that if I go to the store and place five dollars on the counter, I will get a shirt in return. It is very easy to test this image by simply trying it out. If the store is in fact selling shirts for ten dollars, I would not only be disappointed, I would be indignant, for the disappointment of easily tested images usually creates emotional stress.

Every time we make a purchase or sale we are in fact testing out an image of the price system. This is done frequently in the case of ordinary commodities. For those commodities which are frequently bought and sold, then, our image of the price system is likely to be highly realistic, simply because if it is not, we will be rapidly disappointed.

What this means is that for any seller or buyer who is operating under conditions approximating perfect competition, it is very easy to test the nature of his market environment. If he can buy or sell an indefinite amount of a commodity at a given price, all he has to do is to look at the price tag and he has a great deal of confidence that his image of the market is correct. Similarly, if production functions are fairly simple, it is quite easy to find out what they are, especially when they are linear. The cookbook is a good example of a set of rather simple production functions. If we follow its instructions correctly, we would certainly be quite surprised if things did not turn out as expected. This, however, is only because we are operating within a fairly narrow range of quantities. The cook who is cooking for a thousand people certainly has to use a different kind of a cookbook than one who is cooking for a family. The more complex the process, the more difficult it is to test. Nevertheless, the image which most firms have of their production functions—that is, of how much of what inputs produce how much of what outputs—is likely to be fairly accurate, here again, because the process is going on all the time. Where there is much repetition, testing is easy.

Testing becomes harder as the systems get more complex. A buyer or seller with imperfect markets has a much more difficult time finding out what is the nature of his market environment. If, for example, the quantity which the buyer can buy or the seller can sell is a function of the price itself, it is by no means easy to find out the parameters of this function. In the case of perfect competition all we need to know is the price; in the case of imperfect markets we need to know a function relating the price and the quantity. Here we encounter the difficulty that often recurs, which is that testing becomes difficult because the act of testing alters the thing that is tested. We can test whether a pie is good by eating it, but then we do not have a pie. A firm often is unwilling to test the nature of the demand curve which faces it because if, for instance, it lowers its price and is disappointed, it fears it may not be able to raise the price again to its previous level without suffering a loss of sales. The act of lowering the price itself alters the nature of the market.

At this point the problem of the cost of testing, that is, the cost of search (as it is sometimes called), may have to be taken into consideration. The problem may be summed up in the dilemma that there is sometimes, indeed frequently, a better way of doing something, but it costs so much to discover the better way that the reward is not worth the trouble. This problem frequently bedevils large and complex organizations of any kind. In·the case of a large business organization, it is very common. There is a good deal of evidence that the search process is not very well organized and that the search for better alternatives either tends to be done in a rather random fashion or else is unduly influenced by spectacular or noticeable phenomena. Thus, as Richard M. Cyert and James G. March have indicated,[1] a particularly spectacular industrial accident may set in motion a very substantial process of search that may have quite unintended consequences for an organization far beyond the search for greater safety that gave rise to it. This again points up the proposition noted earlier—that disappointments are more likely than confirmations to result in revision of images. We can perhaps extend this to the proposition that when things are going well, little search is likely to be made for methods or decisions which would make things go even better. It is only when things go badly that the process of search is brought into play. Perhaps the greatest danger to the advance of knowledge or even to the survival of organizations is when things are going well for reasons which are not properly understood. Under these circumstances the search for better ways of doing things will probably not be made, and if circumstances change and things do not go well, the organization will be quite unprepared because it did not understand why things went well in the first place. Nothing fails like success, especially a misunderstood success.

From the point of view of the system as a whole, the process of competition, especially insofar as it results in bankruptcies and reorganizations, can be thought of as a rather rough but effective method of testing the validity of images according to which economic decisions are made. The testing is quite expensive, insofar as it represesents loss of capital invested, both in physical resources and in human time and commitment. However, perhaps one of the most fundamental principles of economics is that knowledge cannot be acquired for free, and that any testing process involves some sort of expense. Indeed, the expense of testing can be taken as a rough measure of the ease or difficulty of testing.

What is very hard to test is the method of testing itself. In fact, a good deal of present-day history can be interpreted in terms of a search for cheaper methods of testing. Much of the emotional drive behind socialism, for instance, is a result of dissatisfaction with the perceived costs of the kind of testing of economic decisions which characterizes a system of private enterprise and free capitalism. It can be argued, of

---

[1] *A Behavorial Theory of the Firm* (Englewood Cliffs, N.J.: Prentice-Hall, 1963), pp. 48 ff.

course, and very convincingly, that the socialists have not proved their case that the testing of economic decisions in a centrally planned economy is any cheaper than in the competitive market economy. Indeed, one of the major criticisms of socialism is that centrally planned economies are singularly deficient in any kind of process by which the decisions of the central planners can be tested. The mistakes of capitalists are very easily discovered. For example, the Ford Motor Company produces an Edsel. The fact that a mistaken decision has been made is very rapidly found out, simply because not enough people buy Edsels. Consequently, there is very rapid feedback into the organization. An attempt is made to correct the mistake, and the Edsel is discontinued. If a centrally planned economy makes a similar mistake, there is very little feedback. There is, indeed, a powerful tendency for the information system itself to be corrupted by the exercise of political power. We saw this, for instance, under Stalin, when some disastrous mistakes in agricultural policy were made, for instance in the first collectivization and even subsequently, and yet no one really dared to tell Stalin of this. Those who did try to tell him were sent to Siberia or worse. In an atmosphere of universal fear and purges, extraordinarily little information could get through. In a market society the cost of testing economic decisions consists of the losses of bankruptcy and of bad investments, which after all are not very severe, whereas in a totalitarian socialist society the losses due to bad decisions could add up to millions of deaths and disastrous losses of capital.

Nevertheless, the experiences of the past do not dispose of the future, which is why I would place the problem of the comparative economic systems in the "very difficult" category of testing. The Great Depression certainly taught Western capitalism that it could not rely on the unregulated processes of the market, in the kind of society it had, to insure full employment. Here again was a process of very costly testing; on the other hand, it does seem to have resulted in some expansion of knowledge which makes the probability of severe depressions in the future much less than it has been in the past. It may equally be argued that Stalinism also taught the socialist countries a good deal, even though the Chinese do not seem to have learned this lesson yet. We cannot categorically assert that a centrally planned economy is impossible in which there are extensive feedbacks of information from the society into the planners and in which therefore, mistakes can be tested fairly easily and corrected. I would not venture to predict, therefore, what the argument between centrally planned and market economies will look like in a hundred years, after we have had a continued modification of both systems.

Democratic election in a two-party system can likewise be regarded as a testing process. We may assume that there is a certain difference in the image of the economic system in the two parties, even though there may be a great deal of overlap. If the election of one party is followed by a period of prosperity and successful government, the ideas of the unsuccessful party are likely to converge toward those of the successful one. If, on the other hand, the election of one party is followed by a depression, or a disastrous war, or some sort of social failure, the ideas and image of the world of the party in power will be discredited, the other party will move even further away from it and is likely to be elected in the next election. This process of testing can be very costly, especially if the process by which one party or the other gets elected has strong random elements in it. The election of a party which has an unrealistic view of the world, hence, may be quite disastrous and involve a very high cost.

However, a workable two-party democracy can be defended by contrast with any totalitarian system on the grounds that the cost of testing social images and ideas in a democratic system is much less than it is in a totalitarian system. Certainly the mistakes of democracy seem to have been much less disastrous than the mistakes of a totalitarian dictatorship, whether Hitler, Stalin, or even Sukarno. Once again, we have to be on the lookout for the dangers of partial success. The very success of democracy in the Western countries perhaps inhibits them from conducting further search for political and constitutional change. It is conceivable, therefore, that the totalitarian countries of today, simply because of the glaringly high cost of totalitarian government, have a pressure for search for better solutions to the political problem, and it is not impossible that this search might result in something which is superior to the solution of two-party democracy—superior in the sense that it is able to test competing images of the social system at less cost.

Finally, the discussion turns to things which are impossible to test by their very nature. Many such images are held with great tenacity and have enough importance for the people who hold them so that they cannot be dismissed out of hand, despite all the protests of the logical positivists. The Roman Catholic doctrine of the transubstantiation of the elements in the Mass is one such image, for transubstantiation takes place by definition in aspects of the elements which are not testable. The Marxist doctrine of surplus value is not very different. The amount of socially necessary labor embodied in a commodity is not to be detected by anything so crass as its price. The man who says "My country, right or wrong" or the ardent Communist who thinks that whatever the Soviet Union does is for peace is likewise inhibited by definition from testing his belief. It may be that there is a deep need in mankind for a belief in something that is untestable and that therefore cannot be shaken. Perhaps we should recognize such a need rather than attack it and seek to provide for it in ways that are least harmful.

Another situation where testing is impossible is where the universe itself is random and subject to no law. The movements of stock prices, for instance, have so strong a random element in them, especially in regard to relative stock prices, that anyone who detects a law in their behavior is probably as much under illusion as he who detects a law in the fall of the dice. Under these circumstances neither experience nor disappointment can be a teacher simply because there is nothing to learn. The human mind, however, seems to have an extraordinary distaste for randomness, and experiments have shown that even when subjects are presented with totally random data, individuals will always seek to interpret it in terms of a law, that is, "superstition." The psychologist B. F. Skinner has demonstrated how superstition may be produced even in pigeons. This problem becomes particularly difficult when the system is mixed, in the sense that it contains both random and nonrandom elements. Predictions can then only be made with a certain degree of probability, and if they are not fulfilled, we are never quite certain whether this is because of a random event or whether it is because the image or inference upon which the prediction is based is faulty. It is only through many repeated experiments and predictions that we can ascertain what are the random and what are the nonrandom elements of such a system. Unfortunately, social systems are nearly all of this type, which is one reason why it is so hard to be sure what the essential nonrandom elements of such systems are.

The previous section was concerned primarily with the testing of common, or folk images, of economic life. This section is concerned with the problem of testing the sophisticated images of economic theory. These images are the result of many generations of reflection and debate among economists.

Economic models fall roughly into two categories—static or equilibrium models, which comprise by far the largest body of economic theory, and genuinely dynamic models, which are expressed in terms of difference or differential equations. In the former category are supply and demand analysis, a large portion of the theory of the firm, much of the theory of imperfect competition, and the Keynesian analysis of underemployment equilibrium. These models almost without exception consist of a set of equations, one or more of which is an identity and the others of which express certain propositions about human behavior. The identities, of course, do not have to be tested, as they are true by definition; thus it is not necessary to test the proposition that in an exchange the quantity bought is equal to the quantity sold, these being exactly the same thing, or the proposition that saving, defined as income minus consumption, is equal to investment, which is also defined as income minus consumption.

The testing of the behavior equations is more difficult since they are supposed to represent properties of the empirical world and hence may or may not be true. The testing of equilibrium theory is particularly difficult because equilibrium is never actually observed in nature. All that can ever be observed is an approximation to it or perhaps a tendency toward it, but it would be extremely unlikely to find that at any one moment there would be an actual state of equilibrium. It is particularly hard to test equilibrium theory if there are no major divergences from the equilibrium position, for then any tendencies observed are almost by definition small and barely noticeable.

The best tests of the equilibrium theory occur when there are wide divergences from the equilibrium position—for example, during price control or in a time of severe inflation or depression. Thus we predict that if we interfere with the price system in order to raise certain prices, as for instance in agricultural price supports, surpluses are likely to result; whereas if we interfere, as in wartime price control, in order to lower prices, shortages are likely to result. The impact of rent control on housing is a classic case in point. In depressions, when investment is low and there are no offsets in the way of increased consumption, there is unemployment. When investment or government expenditure is high, as in a war, there is full employment. These might be described as qualitative tests of the theoretical system. The predictions are in terms only of direction, not in terms of the magnitude of change. It is both easier to predict and to detect changes in direction than it is to predict and detect changes in magnitude.

In order to predict changes in the magnitude of the various variables of the economy, we would have to know the exact parameters of our system of equations. Econometrics attempts to discover these, but its success can only be regarded as modest. The classic example of failure in this respect was the prediction of large-scale unemployment after the end of World War II, which almost all economists made for very good reasons, but which fortunately, were totally disappointed. These predictions were made on the assumption that certain parameters, such as those defining the consumption function which had been characteristic of the economy in the 1930's would persist into the 1940's. In fact they did not; the consumption function was much higher. Hence, the postwar disarmament in 1945-1946 was accomplished with astonishingly little difficulty and completely failed to fulfill the gloomy predictions of the economists. The failure of prediction here can be regarded either as a difficulty which is inherent in the system where the magnitude of the parameters is subject to certain random shifts, or it can be regarded as a failure to develop an adequate model with a sufficient number of equations and unknowns. It may not be enough, for instance, simply to postulate consumption as a function of income; it may be necessary to postulate it as a function of a number of other variables as well. The difficulty here is that it is virtually impossible to find out what the parameters of these systems are unless in the first place the parameters are reasonably constant and in the second place the system itself exhibits variation. Without change, knowledge is impossible. The consumption function is a good case in point. We might have made much better predictions of the postwar level of output and employment if we had used a consumption function which included not only income but also stocks of liquid assets. In the 1930's, however, though there was enough variation in income to permit the development of an empirical consumption function relating consumption to income, the variation in liquid assets was not large enough to permit the development of any secure relationship to consumption. Consequently, economists were quite unprepared for the effects of the enormous accumulation of liquid assets that took place during the war.

The predictability of dynamic models fares little better than that of the equilibrium models. The only dynamic model with which we have achieved any success at all in prediction is in the projection of movements of population, and even this has been subject to massive failures in prediction, again in the 1940's. Population projections rest on a simple set of difference equations, the principal one being that any group of members of the population who are x years old in a particular year will either be $x + 1$ years old next year or dead. Our ability to predict, as opposed to project, populations depends upon the assumption either of stable specific birth and death rates or birth and death rates which are subject to a dynamic law expressed as a function of time. The failure of population predictions, especially again in the 1940's, was a result of a sudden and unexpected change in these parameters. In the advanced countries there was a sudden unpredicted increase in the birth rate; in the countries of the tropics in the late 1940's there was a dramatic decline in the death rate as a result of the introduction of chemical insecticides. These changes made all the predictions of the 1940's completely worthless. Perhaps one should say that they were false rather than worthless, for at least one understands why they were falsified.

All predictions, even in the physical sciences, are really conditional predictions. They say that if the system remains unchanged and the parameters of the system remain unchanged, then such and such will be the state of the system at certain times in the future. If the system does change, of course the prediction will be falsified, and this is what happens in social systems all the time. In astronomy, however, we have now reached the situation where predictions are highly successful, except in the case of the incidence of artificial satellites. Prediction is successful in astronomy because we have discovered a system which has extremely stable parameters. In social systems, up to this point at any rate, no such stable systems have been uncovered. It may be, indeed, that in social systems there are no stable systems to be discovered because stable systems do not exist in reality. That is, social systems may contain essentially random elements, which impose as it were a generalized Heisenberg Principle on the social scientist in his search for knowledge.

What this means is that the failure of prediction in social systems does not lead to the improvement of our knowledge of these systems, simply because there is nothing there to know. This may seem like an unduly pessimistic conclusion, and I do not doubt that we are capable of developing models of society with parameters much more stable than those we now use. The development of social science is by no means at an end; indeed, perhaps it is only just at its beginning. Nevertheless, the possibility that our knowledge of society is sharply limited by the unknowable is something that must be taken into consideration. The boundary of the unknowable may still be some distance off, but the fact that it exists is indisputable.

A factor in the testing of economic images, especially economic models of the system as a whole, which has become of great importance in recent years is the development of improved data collection and processing. The development of national income statistics since 1929, for instance, has made an enormous difference in our ability to test certain images of the economy. I remember Professor Schumpeter once saying to me as a student, "How nice economics was before anybody knew anything," meaning of course that in the old days before the development of data collection, anybody could spin any theories he liked, whereas now the development of improved information made it possible at least to check the wilder absurdities. Karl Marx's theory of "immiserization" finds rough going in the face of national income statistics which reveal that the proportion of a constantly increasing national income which goes to labor also almost constantly tends to increase.

The development of scientific sampling as a means of getting information of a degree of accuracy from a large universe has enormously increased the capacity for getting information out of the social system. A good example of the kind of testing process which modern methods of data collection and processing permit is to be found in the effects of the 1964 tax cut. It is now possible to follow the effects of such a cut quite closely through the economic system. Even though the prediction of the effect of such a move is always subject to a certain degree of ignorance about the possible parameters of the system, within what are now fairly narrow limits there can be a good degree of confidence in a prediction for at least short-run movements. It is much harder, of course, to predict the impact of policies which have long-run effects, simply because the long run has such a long waiting period for it to take effect. It is a general problem of science, indeed, that systems which exhibit lags between causes and effects which are longer than the life of a single investigator are extremely hard to investigate. Social systems may have a good many relationships of this kind, and the testing of propositions involving long-run effect needs a research organization which extends beyond the lifetime of a single investigator. In a way this holds true, for example, for national income statistics, the annual survey of consumer finances, and so on, which build up cumulative data. In astronomy the building up of records beyond the lifetime of a single individual was of great importance in permitting the development of highly predictable systems; a similar pattern can be anticipated in the social sciences. In economics the fact that we have had national income series since 1929 is beginning to make a real impact on our image of the economy.

One may conclude, therefore, on a note of cautious optimism. Economists do know something. They do have a certain amount of testable knowledge, and indeed they know a great deal more than they did fifty years ago. This in itself has a marked impact on the operation of the economy. One need only contrast the operations of the economy of the Western world in the twenty years following the end of World War I with the twenty years following the end of World War II. The contrast is striking indeed. The first period saw laggard growth and the Great Depression and an almost total failure to deal with major economic problems. The second period has seen relatively rapid growth, indeed spectacular growth in some countries, and there has been no great depression. This relative success can be attributed in part to the increase of economic knowledge, and how it affected the policies of governments.

The record is much less encouraging for the poor countries, and it may look even worse in many parts of the world in the next twenty years. In a way the transition from a stagnant traditional society to a developing one is a social system of greater complexity even than that of the operation of the advanced economies. We cannot pretend to understand it very well, and we certainly cannot claim any great successes for predictions concerning its behavior patterns. On the other hand, the same kind of process of ferment of thought in regard to this problem seems to be occurring that took place in the 1920's and 1930's regarding unemployment and depression. It may well be that as a result of this ferment a new body of testable knowledge will arise, the fruits of which may not be seen for the next fifty years, but which will eventually produce enormous benefits for mankind. The stakes here are obviously very high, and the payoffs for genuine knowledge are enormous.

I have suggested that it is impossible to know everything about social systems or even about economic systems because of some very fundamental obstacles which these systems themselves place in the way of advancing knowledge. To state that we cannot know everything, however, is not to state that we cannot know anything. We can know a great deal, and virtually everything that we know can be of use. The difficulties of the task should inspire us not to despair, but to renewed effort.

PART 3

THE
BOUNDARIES
OF
ECONOMIC
THEORY

INTRODUCTION

IT MIGHT SEEM SIMPLE TO LOCATE WHERE ONE AREA OF INQUIRY LEAVES off and the next begins; however, this is not an easy task. It is possible to decide what economics is by proclamation, by presenting a rule, "economics *is*. . . ." But such definitions are not especially useful because social theories take the form of open systems requiring relatively large numbers of variables and limiting conditions. This means, on the one hand, that if economics ignores cultural and institutional change it may be unable, within itself, to explain important classes of phenomena, while, on the other hand, if economics includes too many variables it runs the danger of becoming unmanageable. Substantively, the question of open and closed systems concerns the relationships among economics and its neighboring disciplines: the sociological or political assumptions introduced in what seem to be purely economic formulations; the restrictions introduced on behavior by assuming maximization; the applicability of marginal analysis to other disciplines.

Moreover, the problematic boundaries are not merely those between economics and other disciplines. There are also within economics uncertain relationships between micro- and macro-explanations. To what extent can the aggregative terms of macro-theory be reduced to assumptions about behavior in the smaller units? What restrictions must be imposed when behavior observed in the micro-units is aggregated? Within conventional economics the gap between micro- and macro-theory can be as difficult to bridge as that between economics and other disciplines.

If systems cannot be closed, they cannot have distinct boundaries.

Emile Grunberg develops the reasons for and the implications of open systems. Because large numbers of relevant variables must always be omitted, predictions will always be hedged with qualifiers, and verification will be uncertain. Predictions depend on how the omitted variables and relations influence results. Definitions necessarily omit important variables, hence they must have an *ad hoc* quality. While this is true of the number of variables, it is also a characteristic of the level of abstraction in a given social theory. In the hierarchy of theoretical levels, the place of any particular hypothesis is frequently unclear. Therefore the social sciences, including economics, must work within ill-defined boundaries.

While boundaries are indeterminate, there are also important points of overlap and borrowing among the disciplines. James Buchanan clarifies the kind of borrowing and lending that is possible between disciplines, that is, the "spillins" and the "spillouts." Buchanan summarizes some of the main exchanges between economics and other fields. Economics can, for example, offer reality to the humanist, theory to the political scientist, problems to the statistician. In turn, it can borrow from other disciplines variables omitted from its own framework. Such exchange reduces the parochialism which results from a rigid definition of field.

Economics is bounded by rules, customs, and institutions as well. Ben Ward discusses linkages between behavioral and institutional rules and some of the main branches of economic thought. For example, rational behavior, the basic axiom of economic reasoning, is limited by rules. The criteria for individual decisions, the frameworks for group behavior, the structures of institutions, and the legal environment of behavior impose different kinds of rules. Ward explains that general equilibrium analysis and macro-dynamics neglect rules and rule making. On the other hand, theories where rules and rule making are explicit, such as game theory, are not broadly useful. However, inclusion of rule phenomena has been increasing. In contexts dominated by market-determined relations, rules are introduced among the givens. But when such problems as external effects, monopoly, political decision making, and social contexts are considered, rule making must become a part of the basic reasoning process. Consequently, there is always some risk in developing theories which do not provide for rules in their structure.

Rule making calls attention to the boundaries between economics and neighboring disciplines. The problem of aggregation concerns the consistency of internal relations within a discipline. It is the problem of linking through addition and deduction our generalizations about the small into analyses about the large. Kelvin Lancaster discusses the logical and operational difficulties of forging such relationships. At the heart of aggregation is a summation, theoretical or statistical. Is it fruitful in a given context to assume that individuals have identical marginal propensities to save or that the distribution of income is constant? Under what conditions can the capital to labor ratio be assumed the same for all firms? Units can always be summated to yield an aggregate by making postulates about their homogeneous behavior or by averaging out their differences through statistical weighting or index procedures. But the fundamental difficulty is that differences in the small yield in their sum substantial and unpredictable consequences for the large.

The problem of aggregation is a universal one in the sciences. Besides constructing functions that are consistent one to another in the micro- and macro-frameworks, there is another fundamental issue. The problems which a micro-theory has been designed to solve may be of a different logical order than those of the macro-theory. Consequently, a meaningful macro-theory may be constructed with a minimum of linkage to the world of micro-variables and relations. In effect, a micro- and a macro-theory may present two distinct lines of inquiry, theoretical as well as empirical.

EMILE GRUNBERG

*Emile Grunberg, Dr. rer. pol., Frankfurt am Main, is
Professor of Economics and Head of the Economics Department at the University of Akron. He was Ford Foundation Research Fellow in 1958. He has published two books
(in German) and contributed to learned journals in the
United States and in Europe. In recent years his work has
been concerned, chiefly, with the predictability of
social events and the verification of economic hypotheses.
Currently, he is engaged in a research project on
rationality and bargaining behavior.*

ESSAY

10

The Meaning of Scope and External Boundaries of Economics

IT IS QUITE USUAL FOR LAYMAN AND SCIENTIST to look upon the social sciences as inferior to the natural sciences. This attitude arises from the comparative lack of success on the part of the social sciences in controlling the course of those events with which they are concerned. The most cursory survey of the history of modern science, say since the fifteenth century, shows that there has been in the social science not one major breakthrough of the kind and nature of those which mark the development of physics, chemistry, biology, medicine. No doubt there have been advances in the social sciences too during the last five centuries. But these have been weak and indecisive in one crucial aspect: old theories here are not definitively superseded by new ones in the way in which, for example, the famous phlogiston hypothesis has been superseded by a better one. In fact, the history of the social sciences shows no clearcut case in which a theory has been disconfirmed by contradictory evidence.

Now, if the layman is chiefly concerned with the power of science to control events, the scientist is rather concerned with its power to explain and predict correctly, for the power to control events is a by-product of successful explanation. It may be a psychological motive, and it may serve as the social justification for engaging in the pursuit of science. It is, however, itself neither an aspect of science nor a methodological standard by which to judge it. A hypothesis is verified by using it in making predictions. Thus, the reason for our inability to control social events better than we do, is to be found in the generally acknowledged predictive weakness of the social sciences. Although much of the argument of this paper is applicable to all the social sciences, it deals explicitly only with economics, which today possesses the most elaborate theoretical structure among the social sciences.

Explanation and prediction require (1) observation statements describing an *explanans* and an *explanandum;* those describing the *explanans* are called initial conditions; and (2) at least one but normally more general laws logically connecting both sets of observation statements so that with their help the *explanandum* can be inferred from the *explanans*. In an explanation both sets of observation statements describe events which have already actually occurred. In a prediction the statements describing the *explanandum* refer to an event which has not yet occurred but which according to the prediction should occur in a specified space-time region. Explanation and prediction are logically symmetrical.[1]

By the standard of reliability applied to predictions in the natural sciences, economics makes a poor showing.[2] Now, with one notable exception, predictions in the natural sciences are made under controlled laboratory conditions, that is, in effectively closed systems. The exception is astronomy. But although laboratory experiments are not possible in astronomy, predictions, at least those referring to events within the

---

[1] C. G. Hempel and P. Oppenheim, "The Logic of Explanation," *Philosophy of Science,* 15 (1948), reprinted in *Readings in the Philosophy of Science,* ed. H. Feigl and M. Brodbeck (New York: Appleton, 1953); C. G. Hempel, "Deductive-Nomological vs. Statistical Explanation," *Minnesota Studies in the Philosophy of Science* (Minneapolis: University of Minnesota Press, 1962), Vol. III; Adolf Grünbaum, "Temporal-Asymmetric Principles, Parity Between Explanation and Prediction, and Mechanism Versus Teleology," *Philosophy of Science,* 29 (1962), 146-170, and the literature quoted there.

[2] The degree of accuracy required to consider a prediction to be correct is dictated by the standards of the particular discipline but ultimately contains an element of subjective judgment. Let x_{t+1} be the value of a variable x. Then x_{t+1} will be accepted as a correct prediction if: $x_t - e \leq x_{t+1} \leq x_t + e$, where x_t is the prediction made at time t, and e is an arbitrary variable chosen by the predictor. Kepler is reported to have been deeply disappointed because an astronomical event occurred a few hours later than he had predicted. The economist, on the other hand, would be highly gratified if he could reliably predict turning points of the business cycle within two weeks or so.

solar system, are also made within effectively closed systems. A closed system is one in which all relevant variables are refered to in the *explanans* set so that no factor which potentially could have a measurable effect on the predicted event is left unaccounted for.[3] The emphasis is on "relevant" and "measurable." The predictive success of astronomy indicates that the role of laboratory experiments is that of achieving artificially closed systems, that is, in isolating arbitrarily selected variables where in the uncontrolled world these variables can be observed only embedded in the context of nonclosed systems. In closed systems hypotheses are disconfirmable: if a prediction turns out to be wrong, part or all of the general laws used in making it are considered to be thereby falsified.

The economist, on the other hand, can neither—like the astronomer—find closed systems sufficiently approximated in the real world, nor can he approximate them—like other natural scientists—in the laboratory.[4] No matter how many variables he includes in an *explanans* set, an indefinitely large number of potentially relevant variables are known to be left out. Thus, the *explanans* set is incomplete and the explanation in Carl G. Hempel's terms remains an "explanation sketch." [5] Predictions made in such a context are subject to an unspecified *ceteris-paribus* condition. Therefore, the general laws used in making them cannot be disconfirmed: if a prediction in these circumstances is found to be false, either the theory used in making it is defective or else the numerical values of some of the variables covered by the *ceteris-paribus* condition have changed between the making of the prediction and the time specified for the predicted event to occur, or both may be the case.[6] Note, however, that this does not exclude the possibility of successful prediction in economics. The *ceteris-paribus* condition may well be effectively fulfilled

---

[3] Variables thought to be irrelevant at one time may, of course, be recognized to be measurably relevant later in the light of increased knowledge and with the help of improved measuring techniques.

[4] It is no longer quite true that the economist cannot perform controlled laboratory experiments. In recent years techniques have been perfected which at least permit one to make a start in the systematic testing of behavioral economic hypotheses. See S. Siegel and L. E. Fouraker, *Bargaining and Group Decision Making, Experiments on Bilateral Monopoly* (New York: McGraw, 1960); L. E. Fouraker and S. Siegel, *Bargaining Behavior* (New York: McGraw, 1963); K. J. Cohen, *Computer Models of the Shoe, Leather, Hide Sequence,* Ford Foundation Doctoral Dissertation Series (Englewood Cliffs, N.J.: Prentice-Hall, 1960); G. P. E. Clarkson, *Portfolio Selection: A Simulation of Trust Investment,* Ford Foundation Doctoral Dissertation Series (Englewood Cliffs, N.J.: Prentice-Hall, 1962).

[5] "The Function of General Laws in History," *Journal of Philosophy,* 39 (1942), reprinted in *Readings in Philosophical Analysis,* ed. H. Feigl and W. Sellers (New York: Appleton, 1949), pp. 465-466.

[6] See E. Grunberg, "Notes on the Verifiability of Economic Laws," *Philosophy of Science,* 24 (1957), 337-348, reprinted in *Theorie Und Realität,* ed. Hans Albert (Tübingen: J. C. B. Mohr, 1964).

during a given time interval.[7] Obviously, in this case correct predictions can be made provided that the general laws used in making them satisfy the standards of acceptance. The chances that the *ceteris-paribus* condition is fulfilled are the better the shorter the interval between making the prediction and thè time specified for the predicted event to occur. This is why economists are by and large more successful in making short-run predictions than in making long-run predictions. It is, however, when the prediction is false that the full effect of the *ceteris-paribus* condition becomes apparent. Its most serious effects are felt in the construction of higher-level theories because false predictions do not result in the disconfirmation of hypotheses, and thus hypotheses cannot be verified.

A comparison of economics with meteorology is instructive. This comparison is, indeed, often made because, like the economist, the meteorologist must operate in nonclosed systems. There is, however, a fundamental difference between the two situations. The general laws used by the meteorologist in his predictions are chiefly those of physics and chemistry. He cannot verify these laws since his predictions too are subject to the *ceteris-paribus* condition. But these laws have been verified before the meteorologist used them and quite independently from the use he makes of them. They are supported by a great deal of evidence and, therefore, command the confidence of the meteorologist. If his prediction turns out to be false, he is justified in concluding that the *ceteris-paribus* condition was not fulfilled.

On the other hand, the general laws of economics have not been verified independently from the use the economist makes of them in the explanation and prediction of economic events. Therefore, when a prediction turns out to be false, the situation as regards the general laws used in making it is indeterminate: it cannot be known with certainty whether one or all of the general laws have been disconfirmed or whether the *ceteris-paribus* condition has not been fulfilled.

In the following pages the consequences of this state of affairs are explored: (1) for the definition and the determination of the external boundaries of economics; and (2) for the formulation of economic hypotheses. The first section deals with the definition and the external boundaries of economics in general. The next two sections very briefly consider two particular aspects of the determination of the external boundaries. We then discuss two concepts of "generality" of a theory which

---

[7] Let P_t be the value of the variable P predicted at time t; P_{t+1} the value actually observed at the specified time, $t+1$; x_i the ith variable in the indefinitely large set of relevant variables covered by the *ceteris-paribus* condition. Then "effective
$$(\delta P_{t+1}/\delta x_1) \ dx_1 + (\delta P_{t+1}/\delta x_2) \ dx_2 + \ldots + (\delta P_{t+1}/\delta x_n) \ dx_n \leqq e$$
fulfillment" of this condition means:
where e is an arbitrary variable such that if
$$P_t - e \leqq P_{t+1} \leqq P_t + e$$
the prediction is accepted as correct.

are called respectively "generality₁" and "generality₂." In the concluding
section the chief points of the argument are summed up.

MICRO-ECONOMIC THEORY AND THE FREE ENTERPRISE SYSTEM

The concepts to which the terms in scientific propositions refer must
be defined as unambiguously and precisely as possible because otherwise
the propositions themselves have no, or at least no precise, meaning and
cannot be tested. Thus, definition of its concepts belongs to the task of a
given scientific discipline.

On the other hand, definitions of scientific disciplines and the determination of the boundaries between them are not needed for the formulation of verifiable hypotheses. Whether a hypothesis, H, is to be accepted
or rejected depends solely upon its consistency with the already accepted
body of theory and on the direct and indirect evidence by which it is
supported. The statement, however, that H belongs to some particular
scientific discipline is either consistent or inconsistent with accepted
linguistic usage, but in either case irrelevant to the status of H. Neither
is it itself a hypothesis making an assertion which could be found to be
false or true.

Especially in the older economic literature we encounter occasionally
prescriptive statements to the effect that certain phenomena are and others
are not the proper concern of the economist. Such statements imply some
definition of economics and are at best awkwardkly formulated descriptions of a given situation. Since the content and concern of scientific
disciplines change constantly, such statements—even on the most charitable
interpretation—are valid only at the time at which they are made. As a
rule, prescriptive statements presented in methodological garb are
suspect.

Sometimes what appears in the form of definitions of economics and
dogmatic prescriptions actually are statements reflecting substantive
disagreement. Clearly, something more than definitions is involved, for
example, in the disagreement among neoclassical writers whether economics is a part of psychology or whether it merely uses psychological
laws as premises just as it uses physical laws without, however, being
responsible for their formulation and their verification.[8]

---

[8] J. N. Keynes, for example, argues that economics ". . . presupposes psychology
just as it presupposes the natural sciences . . . but the science is not therefore a
branch of psychology." *The Scope and Method of Political Economy* (London: Macmillan, 1891), p. 85.

V. Pareto, on the other hand, asserts that: "Psychology is evidently at the base of
political economy as it is at the base of all social sciences. Perhaps the day will
come when we will be able to deduce the social laws from the principles of psychology. . . ." *Manuel d'Economie Politique*, trans. from the Italian by A. Bonnet
(Paris: Marcel Giard, 1927), p. 40. (English translation mine.)

In the end, however, we do use definitions of scientific disciplines. The word "economics" has a meaning, or else it would not be retained in the language. As our knowledge of the world increases, the referents of such terms as "physics," "biology," "psychology," "economics" change and therefore, the meaning of the words themselves and the definitions of the scientific disciplines keep changing too. But at any given time these words refer to a given body of knowledge concerned with a more or less rigorously determined set, S, of observed phenomena and a set, S', of postulated concepts; usually a class of unsolved problems involving S, S' are included. Thus, P. W. Bridgeman suggests that the concept of "temperature" is characteristic of thermodynamic systems.[9] In the same way, the concepts of "utility" and "price" are characteristic of micro-economic systems, those of, say "consumption," "saving," "investment" of macro-economic systems.

Now, because the natural sciences operate in effectively closed systems, the classes of phenomena with which each of their various disciplines are concerned, are—at any given moment—relatively small and can be considered to be exhaustive. On the other hand, economics which operates, as we saw, in a system not amenable to effective closure, is necessarily concerned with an indefinitely large class of phenomena. This greatly increases the difficulties of formulating a descriptive definition of economics.

The concept of "natural law" is itself surrounded by a penumbra of vagueness and is the subject of continued discussion.[10] However, in ordinary usage it seems to be required of any statement qualifying as a law-like statement that it make explicit mention of all the conditions under which a particular effect is expected to occur. Thus, all the phenomena with which a discipline is concerned should find explicit mention in the laws of which its theoretical structure is composed. No phenomena not so mentioned are supposed to have any effect on the events which the laws predict. In this respect, economics is notably defective because all its predictions are subject to an unspecified *ceteris-paribus* condition. Since (a) every phenomenon represented explicitly by a variable in a law is considered to belong to the class of phenomena with which the discipline is concerned, and (b) there is at least conceptually no limit to the num-

See also Philip H. Wicksteed, "Political Economy and Psychology," and "The Scope and Method of Political Economy in the Light of the 'Marginal' Theory of Value and Distribution" (especially p. 780), both in *The Common Sense of Political Economy and Selected Papers and Reviews*, ed. L. Robbins (London: Routledge, 1944), Vol. II; Friedrich von Wieser, *Theorie Der Gesellschaftlichen Wirtschaft*, 2nd ed. (Tübingen: 1924), p. 9.

[9] *The Nature of Thermodynamics*, Harper Torchbooks (New York: Harper, 1961), p. 10.

[10] See, for example, E. Nagel, *The Structure of Science* (New York: Harcourt, 1961), especially Chap. V.

ber of variables to be explicitly mentioned in economic laws, i.e., to be included in S, it follows that membership in the class of economic phenomena does not rest on objective criteria alone but to a large measure on arbitrary *ad hoc* decision. Descriptive definitions of economics are, therefore, more vague than those of the natural sciences and less able to indicate the boundaries of the discipline at any given point in time. It is significant and characteristic of this unsatisfactory state of affairs that the definition of economics and the determination of its scope have for more than sixty years been the subject of an often controversial discussion which still continues, while at the same time the natural sciences have shown very little concern with the definitions of the various natural disciplines and their respective scopes. The customary definition of economics as the discipline of the rational allocation of scarce resources to practically unlimited wants reflects this weakness. Quite apart from the difficulties surrounding the concept of rationality, this definition covers the whole spectrum of purposive human action.

Most of the body of economic theory has been developed since the rise of the capitalistic system. This, of course, is true of scientific knowledge in general. The natural sciences, however, from their beginnings have striven for universality. So, among the social sciences, have sociology and political science. On the other hand, with perhaps the exception of the German Historical School, economics, and especially micro-economic theory, have been and still are concerned apparently with only one economic system—namely, the capitalistic free enterprise system. Economists speak of the phenomena characteristic of this system as if they were the economic phenomena *par excellence*. Discussion of other economic systems, past or now in existence, usually is restricted to economic policy and possibly the underlying social and political thought. Micro-economics deals explicitly with the interaction of individual buyers' and sellers' decisions in the market. Howard S. Ellis, for example, in his criticism of Lionel Robbins asserts that

> Alternatively, one may express the same idea by saying that Robbins' definition errs in accepting any and all "given ends"; one must be stipulated by economics itself, and that is the freedom of the individual to make the best of his situation as producer or consumer, so far as this does not entail greater loss of freedom upon other individuals.[11]

This passage seems to convey the idea that economic theory deals only with very narrowly defined socio-economic organizations. In a critical vein the same point has been made by Karl Marx and his followers in asserting that traditional economic theory is essentially the theory of capitalism.

---

[11] "The Economic Way of Thinking," *American Economic Review*, 40 (1950), 3.

Marx himself has never provided a general theory of a socialistic economy. Such attempts as, for example, Karl Ballod's view of a socialistic state of the future belong in the category of blueprints and are not explanatory theories at all.[12] Soviet Russian economic literature largely ignores micro-economics. It is, moreover, concerned predominantly with issues of planning, that is, with "engineering" and development rather than with explanation proper. Enrico Barone's [13] and Oskar Lange's [14] famous papers merely show that it is not conceptually impossible for a planned economy to allocate scarce resources as rationally as an ideal free market economy could do. Important as these two contributions are to economic thinking, they do not refer to observable phenomena and do not constitute explanatory theories. Lange's argument by setting forth decision-rules which enable a planned economy to allocate its scarce resources rationally also has a normative flavor. This aspect of economic theorizing is discussed in the next section.

Now, the hypotheses of micro-theory are those implications of the behavioral assumptions which follow if the economic agents are divided into entrepreneurs (sellers) and consumers (buyers) and if the individuals in both groups are essentially free to act so as to maximize their utility or their profits. This limitation, however, leaves the theory in an unsatisfactory situation because (a) we know very well from observation that other economic systems have existed in the past and do currently exist and (b) micro-theory as it stands today has, therefore, the character of a special theory which aims to apply to a specific historical class of phenomena. Since it would be altogether absurd to consider economic explanation as being conceptually possible only under the conditions of capitalism, there exists the need for a more general theory from which micro-economic theory can be derived. Such a theory does not exist yet, but the obvious candidates for the status of propositions in it are the basic behavioral assumptions of economic theory.[15]

THE NORMATIVE AMBIGUITY IN MICRO-ECONOMIC THEORY

Since economic theory is concerned with the way in which the economic agents achieve certain ends, these ends are explicitly mentioned in economic theory.[16] This is especially the case in micro-economics which

---

[12] *Der Zukunftsstaat. Produktion und Konsum in Sozialstaat,* 3rd ed. (Stuttgart: J. H. W. Dietz, 1920).

[13] "The Ministry of Production in the Collectivist State," in *Collectivist Economic Planning,* ed. F. A. V. Hayek (London: Routledge, 1950).

[14] "On the Economic Theory of Socialism," in the volume of the same title ed. Benjamin Lippincott (Minneapolis: University of Minnesota Press, 1948).

[15] See, for example, G. P. E. Clarkson, *The Theory of Consumer Demand: A Critical Appraisal* (Englewood Cliffs, N.J.: Prentice-Hall, 1963), especially Chaps. 6, 7, 8.

[16] See the quotation from H. S. Ellis on page 154.

deals immediately with the producing, selling, investing, buying decisions of the agents rather than, like macro-economics, with the observed aggregate results of these activities. And here lies the danger that what originally were meant to be objective propositions about the agents' directly or indirectly observable desire to maximize their utility and their profits change almost imperceptibly into value-judgments about what the agent should achieve or what he is entitled to achieve.[17] Our inability strictly to verify economic hypotheses greatly enhances this danger and has, indeed, permitted a disturbing ambiguity to persist in economic theorizing. We find that the hypotheses of micro-economics have at times been presented as norms which—*if observed by the agents*—will enable them to reach their ends. For example Stephen Enke gives the theory of the firm deliberately or unintentionally a clearly normative twist:

> As a matter of fact, a corporation economist, but not a government economist, should use marginal analysis. . . . Once he has decided what future values to assume, for important variables and functions, he should introduce them into the formulae dictated by marginal analysis. Having made his assumptions, he needs marginal analysis to show what policies can yield what is hoped will be maximum profits. . . . Marginal analysis, given a set of expectations, will tend to give the greatest possible profits if the future confirms the expectations. In so far as the future can be dimly sensed, the use of marginal analysis should increase firm profits more often than not.[18]

Less clear than Enke, H. T. Koplin too arrives at a normative interpretation of micro-theory. It is irrelevant here that he seems to feel that the government economist rather than the business economist should use price theory. He argues:

> The chief advantage of the formulation of the profit maximization assumption in this paper is not that it is logically consistent with the rest of price theory, but rather that it is consistent with the *efficiency norm*. It provides a base for empirical studies of the ways and extent to which businessmen *in fact fail to maximize profits, and for consideration of the policy implications of such divergences*.[19]

It would be easy to extend the list of examples of this ambiguous attitude which pervades much of economic literature. For our purposes the two quotations given here may suffice. More than most other scientific

---

[17] The statement in the text is independent of the current controversy about the methodological nature of the behavioral assumptions in economics. Even if we admit (which I do not) that these assumptions need not be "realistic," they still are considered to be propositions which are at least indirectly verifiable.

[18] "On Maximizing Profits," *American Economic Review*, 41 (1951), 578.

[19] "The Profit Maximization Assumption," *Oxford Economic Papers*, N. F., 15 (1963), 139 (italics mine). See also: E. Grunberg, "The Profit Maximization Assumption: Comment," *Oxford Economic Papers*, N. F., 16 (1964), 285-290.

disciplines, economic theory is still rooted in the desire to control rather than simply to explain. It is significant in the present context that the principle of profit maximization and, in general, the principle of optimization are today securely established as ends in the applied disciplines of scientific management and in the context of important areas of economic policy. On the other hand, as fundamental behavioral hypotheses of micro-economics, they have been under heavy attack since the 1940's.[20]

Profit maximization conceived as a norm guiding the behavior of the economic agent belongs evidently to the rules of management whose purpose, like that of engineering, is not to explain but to control. True, in order to be effective at all, policy and engineering must be based on theoretical knowledge, but they are not theory themselves. Consequently, if micro-theory is interpreted as a set of norms, it ceases thereby to be a set of lawlike statements, for it cannot be both at the same time.[21] In the physical and biological sciences such ambiguities are not encountered. Consider, for example, the generalizing description of the life cycle of some parasite. It would assert what happens when the parasite meets its host(s) and describe the successive stages of its development in one or more hosts. It would also include a listing of the environmental circumstances, such as climate, availability of hosts, etc., required for survival of the parasite. This set of statements cannot be interpreted as norms for the parasite's behavior nor be used to measure any observable discrepancy between its actual behavior and that stipulated by the norms. If the parasite's behavior is observed to be different from the one described in the hypothesis, the hypothesis must be amended accordingly or possibly abandoned altogether.[22]

---

[20] See, for example, the "marginalist debate" of the 1940's: R. A. Lester, "Shortcomings of Marginal Analysis for Wage-Employment Problems," *American Economic Review,* 36 (1946), 63-82; "Marginalism and Labor Markets," *American Economic Review,* 37 (1947), 135-148; F. Machlup, "Marginal Analysis and Empirical Research," *American Economic Review,* 36 (1946), 519-554; "Rejoinder to an Antimarginalist," *American Economic Review,* 37 (1947), 148-154; H. M. Oliver, Jr., "Marginal Theory and Business Behavior," *American Economic Review,* 37 (1947), 375-383; R. A. Gordon, "Short Period Price Determination," *American Economic Review,* 38 (1948), 265-288; also K. Rothschild, "Price Theory and Oligopoly," *The Economic Journal,* 57 (1947), 290-320, reprinted in *Readings in Price Theory,* eds. G. J. Stigler and K. E. Boulding (Chicago: Irwin, 1952).

[21] The argument in the text neglects the potential reflexivity of public statements in general and thus also of publicly known theories. See E. Grunberg and F. Modigliani on the narrower issue of the reflexivity of public predictions: "The Predictability of Social Events," *Journal of Political Economy,* 62 (1954), 465-478. However, there is for the time being no empirical evidence available which would indicate that publicly known economic theories are actually reflexive.

[22] It is possible, of course, that the parasite changes its behavior under the influence of changes in its environment, e.g., encroachment of human civilization and the like. Then the original hypothesis continues to describe adequately the parasite's past behavior. But a new hypothesis is required to describe and predict his changed behavior.

The methodological consequence of interpreting any part of a theory as a norm for behavior, is to remove it from the theory and to leave unexplained the class of phenomena which it was designed to explain. To admit the interpretation of, for example, the profit maximization assumption as a norm would leave without systematic explanation the observed behavior of economic agents.

Thus, the norm-hypothesis ambiguity constitutes a serious weakness of micro-theory. If this ambiguity has its origins in the concern of economic theory with the purposes and goals of human beings and the resulting value connotations of such terms as maximization of utility and optimization, its persistence is due to our inability to verify strictly the behavioral assumptions of the theory. If we could verify whether the economic agents actually act so as to maximize the value of some variables, it would be impossible to interpret the same statement simultaneously as a hypothesis stating what will happen given certain conditions and as a norm which, of course, need never be fulfilled.

Our argument would be incomplete if we failed to make at least some mention of the recent attempts to verify systematically the fundamental behavioral hypotheses of micro-economics. Foremost among these new approaches are experiments performed under controlled laboratory conditions and computer simulation. Perhaps the most notable among these experiments are those on bargaining decision making under conditions of bilateral monopoly and oligopoly first designed and carried out by S. Siegel and L. Fouraker, and now continued by Lawrence E. Fouraker.[23] The experimental techniques and the interpretation of the results so far obtained are still highly tentative. If, however, they are successful, it might become possible to formulate disconfirmable hypotheses about the behavior pattern of the economic agent from which further micro-economic theorems could then be deduced. In this process the economist himself may undergo profound change as he becomes increasingly involved in the formulation of explicitly behavioral hypotheses. But what of it?

GENERALITY$_1$

When a lowest-level hypothesis, e.g., an empirical generalization, has been formulated, it is possible to ask why things are the way this hypothesis asserts them to be. The answer to this question is a new hypothesis of higher level which explains the empirical generalization. Although it is often possible to do so, it is not necessary that this new higher-level hypothesis be itself directly verifiable through confrontation with observations. As we know, it is sufficient that it be verified indirectly

---

[23] See footnote 4 on page 150.

through the verification of the lowest-level hypothesis which it explains.[24] In developed theoretical systems the higher-level hypothesis will serve to explain more than one empirical generalization.

More than one such higher-level hypothesis may be required to explain the empirical generalization. At any rate, as soon as these higher-level hypotheses have been formulated, we may, of course, again ask why things are the way that they assert them to be. The answer will take the form of new hypotheses on a still higher level. In a developed theoretical system these new hypotheses will explain a number of lower-level hypotheses which, in turn, will explain a possibly large number of empirical generalizations.

Evidently, this process can be continued indefinitely. At any given time, every theoretical system, no matter how developed, includes a set of temporarily highest-level hypotheses from which the other hypotheses in the system can be deduced, but which themselves are not explained and thus not deduced from other hypotheses.[25] The question why things are the way these highest-level hypotheses of a system assert them to be can always be meaningfully asked. To assume otherwise would either imply absolute limits to human knowledge or some notion of knowing already all there is to be known. Neither assumption is justifiable within the framework of scientific explanation. A developed theoretical system constitutes a hierarchy of hypotheses. The base is formed by the empirical generalizations which may be and often are established quite independently from each other. On these, by successive explanation, is erected the pyramid of hypotheses of higher and higher-levels whose apex is always formed by those hypotheses from which the other ones are deducible in the system but which themselves for the time being are not yet explained.[26] Thus, in the empirical sciences the process of explanation proceeds from the empirical generalizations at the base upward to hypotheses of higher and higher levels.

A higher-level hypothesis is said to be more general than the hypothesis it explains. In a first approximation this means that the lower-level hypothesis which is to be explained (the *explanandum*) can be logically deduced from the explaining higher-level hypothesis (the *explanans*), but not the other way around. Generality in this sense is a relation between statements and will be referred to as "generality$_1$."

Ernest Nagel has given the elements of a more rigorous definition of

---

24 Higher-level hypotheses not only need not but cannot be directly verified whenever they do not contain terms referring to observable events or phenomena but contain only terms referring to postulated concepts, such as *positron* or *utility*.

25 See R. B. Braithwaite, *Scientific Explanation* (Cambridge: Cambridge U. P., 1955), pp. 342-354.

26 The argument made in the text is not affected by the fact that high-level propositions which in one context appear as basic assumptions or postulates, may in another context be derived from other propositions.

"generality$_1$."[27] In bare outline this definition is as follows: Consider two universal conditionals of the simplest form, H_1 and H_2. Let H_1 be the hypothesis "All A is B"; and H_2 be the hypothesis "All C is D." Then H_1 is said to be more general than H_2 if and only if "All C is A" is logically true, while "All A is C" is not. If "All C is A" and "All A is C" are both logically true, then H_2 is said to be as general as H_1. If neither "All C is A" nor "All A is C" are logically true, then H_1 and H_2 are said to be not comparable with respect to their generality$_1$.

For example, of the two universal conditionals

H_1: "All warm-blooded animals are vertebrates"
H_2: "All birds are vertebrates"

H_1 is more general than H_2 because "All birds are warm-blooded animals" is logically true, while "All warm-blooded animals are birds" is not.

Note, however, that the relationship depends upon the form in which the hypotheses are presented. If H_2 is replaced by H'_2 "All not-vertebrates are not birds," the relationship no longer holds. Although H_2 and H'_2 are logically equivalent, H_1 is not more general than H'_2. If we replace also H_1 by H'_1, the relationship of generality$_1$ is reversed:

H'_1: "All not-vertebrates are not-warm-blooded animals"
H'_2: "All not-vertebrates are not-birds."

The complement of the class of birds, namely the class of all the things which are not-birds, includes the complement of the class of warm-blooded animals, namely the class of things which are not-warm-blooded animals; "All not-warm-blooded animals are not-birds" is logically true, while "All not-birds are not-warm-blooded animals" is not. Similar difficulties arise if either or both hypotheses are replaced by other logical equivalents.

Nagel argues that:

> These difficulties are not necessarily fatal to the proposed explication of the notion of greater generality. But to avoid them one must drop the . . . requirement that logically equivalent statements must be equally general, and adopt the position that the comparative generality of laws is relative to the way they are formulated.[28]

As far as the hierarchical structure of theoretical systems is concerned, this seems to be an innocuous restriction. The choice among the logical equivalents of a statement is not entirely arbitrary, nor are hypotheses once formulated arbitrarily replaced by their logical equivalents. It is not accepted practice to assert that whatever does not fall in a vacuum with

---

[27] The following argument is entirely based on E. Nagel's explication of generality in *The Structure of Science*, pp. 37-39.

[28] *Structure of Science*, n. 27. Nagel goes on to give an explication of "more general" as used in reference to scientific disciplines. This meaning of "more general" is, however, not relevant to my argument.

equal velocity is not an object, although this statement is logically equivalent to the hypothesis that in a vacuum all objects fall with equal velocity. This is so because in formulating hypotheses we take care that the referents of the terms appearing in them are the events and phenomena about which assertions are made. We conceive of generality$_1$ as a relation between those specific attributes by which in a given context classes of events are defined.

GENERALITY$_2$

In the meta-language of economics the terms "generality" and "more (or less) general" appear also in a second sense which will here be designated by generality$_2$ and more (or less) general$_2$. In this sense the terms do not refer to the locus of the hypothesis within the hierarchical structure of a theoretical system. They refer rather to the number of variables explicitly mentioned in a hypothesis or a combination of hypotheses on the same hierarchical level. Usually the hypotheses to which the terms are applied are on or close to the lowest level, i.e., that of empirical generalization. Thus, an hypothesis, H_r, is called more general$_2$ than an hypothesis, H_s, if in addition to the variables explicitly mentioned in H_s, it mentions one or more variables not mentioned in H_s. The variables mentioned in H_r but not in H_s are considered by the latter as covered by an unspecified ceteris-paribus condition. Therefore, it may be said that H_r releases more variables from the ceteris-paribus condition than H_s.

The following illustration may help to clarify the point. Consider the Marshallian demand function

$$q = f(p), \tag{1}$$

where q stands for the quantity bought of some commodity and p for its unit price. The hypothesis further states that:

$$- \infty \leqq dq/dp \leqq 0$$

If it is found, for example, that more of the commodity is bought even though its price has increased or less even though its price has decreased, we usually argue that some or all of the following variables must have changed: prices of substitutes, prices of complementary goods, buyers' incomes, buyers' tastes, and buyers' habits. However, none of these variables is mentioned in (1).

Mentioning explicitly the prices of substitutes and of complementary commodities as well as buyer's incomes, the demand function is rewritten:

$$q_i = D_i \ (p_1; \ p_2; \ \cdots \ p_i; \ \cdots \ p_n; \ y), \tag{2}$$

where p_i and q_i stand for the price and quantity bought of the ith commodity, respectively; the other p's stand for the prices of substitutes and complementary commodities; and y stands for buyers' incomes.

Writing (1) in the form

$$q_i = D_i \; (\bar{p}_1; \; \bar{p}_2; \; \cdots \; p_i; \; \cdots \; \bar{p}_n; \; \bar{y}) \qquad \qquad (1a)$$

where the bars indicate that the value of a variable is considered to remain constant, shows that the formulation $q = f(p)$ is asserted to hold provided that none of the other variables known to be relevant changes its value; that is, it holds subject to an unspecified *ceteris-paribus* condition. Formulation (2) is said to be more *general₂* than (1) and (1a) because it explicitly mentions more relevant variables or—what is the same thing—releases them from the hold of the *ceteris-paribus* condition.

Note that here no notion of hierarchy, no difference in the level of explanation is involved. Formulation (2) is not considered the *explanans* of (1) and (1a). In fact, they are all three on the same level of *generality₁*, namely that of empirical generalization.

We know that the relationship described by (1) cannot be observed even in approximate isolation, i.e., in an effectively closed system, because of the potential effect of the other relevant variables.[29] But by releasing more and more of these variables from the hold of the *ceteris-paribus* condition we seem to be able to make (2) apparently as complete as we please. Thus, because economics must operate in nonclosed systems, it strives in the formulation of its laws for *generality₂* which, on the other hand, is of comparatively minor importance in the formulation of physical laws.

Consider, for example, a statement about the boiling point of water. In order to achieve a high degree of *generality₂* such a statement would have to take explicitly into account all the chemical compounds which might occur in water in solution or suspension, vibrations and shocks to which the water could be exposed, and, in fact, an indefinitely large number of other variables. But this is not done. Indeed, no attempt is made to formulate such an inclusive statement about the boiling point of water. Instead a statement is made about the boiling point of an ideal water, free of all impurities, at various levels of atmospheric pressure. Similarly, the effect of each of the other variables can be stated by a separate hypothesis. These hypotheses are used as needed, e.g., in order to explain an observed discrepancy between the boiling point of ideal water and the actually observed boiling point of a particular sample of

---

[29] This does not imply that there is no justification for the formulation (1). After all, sellers have acted on the assumption that buyers will take more of some good or service at a lower rather than at a higher price for at least 2500 years. The point is not that there is no confirmatory evidence but that this law cannot be disconfirmed by any contradictory evidence.

water containing known impurities, or in order to predict the boiling point of a concrete sample of water with known impurities. This is so because each of these separate hypotheses can be verified individually in effectively closed systems, which in the case of our example means under controlled laboratory conditions. Therefore, it is far less damaging here than it is in economics that in the end every prediction about a concrete sample of water in a specified space-time region—and in general every prediction of a unique event—remains subject to an unspecified *ceteris-paribus* condition.

Now, supposing for a moment that it were feasible to take explicitly into account all relevant variables in the statement of an economic law and thus to achieve effective closure of the system, would the law thereby become strictly disconfirmable? If by "law" we mean a statement of the form (2) or, in general, of the form

$$X = \phi \ (x_1; \ x_2; \ \ldots \ x_n) \tag{3}$$

then the answer is negative, since such a statement merely asserts that there exists some functional relationship between the dependent variable, X, and some number of independent variables. If, on the other hand, we mean a statement which specifies the shape of the functional relationship between X and the independent variables, then the answer is in principle affirmative. The simplest form of such a statement would be

$$X = a_1 x_1 + a_2 x_2 + \ldots + a_n x_n \tag{4}$$

where all the a_i's are known.

However, even if it were possible to formulate laws of the form of (4) in economics, they would rapidly become unmanageably complicated as we increase the number of independent variables explicitly taken into account. Thus, the striving for greater and greater *generality*$_2$ may be self-limiting and self-defeating. This is all the more so as our assumption that it may be feasible to take into account all the relevant variables is patently false, the number of these variables being indefinitely large.

A word must be said here about statistically estimated economic relationships, such as statistical demand, supply, and cost functions. Superficially they resemble empirical generalizations in the natural sciences. But they are fundamentally unlike these in that they are at best known to hold for the particular space-time region from which the data used in computing them have been taken. The parameters appearing in them are themselves functions of other, "exogenous" variables. Viewed as empirical hypotheses, the statistical functions are also subject to the *ceteris-paribus* condition. A discussion of the thorny problem to what extent these functions may provide confirmatory evidence for theoretical laws transcends the scope of this paper.[30] But since they cannot disconfirm economic theories, their use in the verification of such theories is for the time being limited. Actually, these statistical functions are description sketches of unique events and thus individual observations rather than empirical generalizations.

SUMMARY AND CONCLUSION

Economics operates in nonclosed systems. Predictions in economics are therefore subject to an unspecified *ceteris-paribus* condition. In this paper we have explored some consequences of this state of affairs.

(1) Because the number of variables which affect the events with which economic theory deals is indefinitely large, descriptive definitions of economics are more vague than those of the natural sciences and less able to indicate the boundaries of the discipline at any given moment. The very concern with a definition of economics in the literature of the last sixty years seems to reflect these difficulties.

(2) Because economics explicitly mentions the ends of economic activity and because, moreover, the fundamental behavioral hypotheses have so far not been rigorously verified, there exists, especially in microeconomics, a disturbing ambiguity in the interpretation of parts of the theory. Thus, profit-maximization and optimization and marginal analysis are sometimes considered to be behavioral hypotheses subject at least in principle to direct or indirect verification and sometimes considered to be norms for the behavior of the economic agents. This norm-hypothesis ambiguity is a serious weakness since a statement interpreted as a norm thereby ceases to be an explanatory hypothesis.

(3) Economics has so far not developed an imposing hierarchical structure of theory and its deductive chains are short compared to those of other theoretical systems. On the other hand, *generality$_2$* which plays a minor if any role in the formulation of hypotheses in the natural sciences, is much in evidence in economics. However, no matter how many variables are explicitly mentioned in an economic hypothesis, the predictions in the making of which it is used, remain subject to the *ceteris-paribus* condition.

It is important to remember, in the end, that from the formal statement that all economic predictions are subject to this *ceteris-paribus*

---

[30] See F. Machlup, "On Operational Concepts and Mental Constructs," *Giornale Degli Economisti E Annali di Economia* (September-October 1960), p. 24: "The so-called statistical supply and demand functions have not really been 'observed'; they are the result of highly imaginative computations with data recorded at different times under different conditions and manipulated on the basis of unverifiable assumptions which range from 'plausible' to 'contrary to fact.' "

condition, it does, however, not follow that correct prediction in economics is not possible. It only follows that false predictions do not disconfirm hypotheses and thus neither compel nor justify their rejection. Whenever the *ceteris-paribus* condition is effectively fulfilled, correct predictions can be made. There is no reason to assume that it never can be fulfilled. But the chances that it is fulfilled are the greater the shorter the time interval between the making of the prediction and the date specified in the prediction.

The difficulties encountered by the economist as a result of the fact that he must operate in systems defying effective closure are sometimes expressed by the statement that there are no constants in economics. This assertion is no doubt adequately descriptive of the past and present situation in economics. But if "there are no . . ." is interpreted as itself an economic law, then the assertion is of highly dubious character. In the unqualified form in which it is frequently made, the statement asserts, indeed, far more than just the past and current predicament of economic theory. It asserts that there are no invariant relationships to be found in the domain of phenomena with which economic theory is concerned. If we grant that it does not seem very likely that strictly invariant relationships will be found to exist between the variables of traditional economic theory, this in itself would only mean that we have to look elsewhere for them. In doing economic research we have committed ourselves to the search for invariant relationships. Unless we choose to believe that economic events are entirely erratic so as to defy even the formulation of probabilistic laws, we must accept that somewhere underlying these events there must be invariant relationships and constants. It is conceivable that these invariant relationships cannot be expressed in the language of traditional economics but perhaps in those of psychology or even physiology. Thus, the statement that there are no constants in economics should be understood to refer only to the current formulation of economic theory.

JAMES M. BUCHANAN

James M. Buchanan, Ph.D., University of Chicago, is Paul G. McIntire Professor of Economics, and Director, Thomas Jefferson Center for Studies in Political Economy, University of Virginia. His published works include: Public Principles of Public Debt (1958); Fiscal Theory and Political Economy (1960): The Calculus of Consent with Gordon Tullock (1962): and Public Finance in Democratic Process (1966). His research interest is the intersection of private choice and public choice through the fiscal process.

ESSAY

11

Economics

and

its

Scientific

Neighbors

THERE EXISTS SOMETHING THAT IS CALLED "economics."[1] Courses in this something are offered in most universities; departmental faculties exist as separate administrative units. Specialized professional positions, in both private and public industry, are held by "economists." Professional journals and many books are written, printed, and presumably read, which libraries and bookshops catalogue under

[1] In a recent paper, labeled explicitly as an "essay in persuasion," I called for some shift of emphasis in the attention of economists, and by implication for a somewhat modified conception of "economics" as a scientific discipline. My criticism was directed primarily at the post-Robbins concentration on the allocation problem independently of the institutional-organizational setting. In essence, my plea was for a re-emphasis on the central role of human behavior in the exchange relationship, or the theory of markets, broadly conceived. I shall not repeat here the arguments therein presented, and I shall limit to the maximum extent that is possible normative judgments about the appropriate boundary lines for the discipline that we variously define as "economics." See my "What Should Economists Do?," *Southern Economic Journal*, 30 (January, 1964), 213-222.

"economics." All of this creates the presumption that there is some widely shared common language, some special communication network among those who qualify as professionals, which makes for efficiency in discourse. Such a language is a necessary condition for science, but it is not a sufficient one. The efficiency in discourse must be measured also against the standards of science, which are those of understanding, not utility, of predictive ability, not platitudes, of objectively detached interpretation, not reasoned justification.

To an extent at least, "economics" qualifies as a science under these criteria. I propose to begin with this "economics" as empirical fact and to examine in some detail the relations of this science with its neighbors. Preliminary to the central questions it is useful to make some general observations about the development of "economics" itself. Insofar as one who is himself inside the discipline is able to discern movements in the whole, to me economics seems to be currently undergoing two apparently contradictory trend changes. The independence of "economics" in any broad disciplinary sense is rapidly breaking down, while, at the same time, specialization among the subdisciplines, within economics, is increasing apace.

Was "economics" ever so independent of its scientific neighbors as the bureaucracy of professional specialization makes it seem? Its subject matter emerged, scarcely a century ago, from "political economy," which, in its turn, sprang classical and full-blown from an earlier "moral philosophy." The scientific origins of economics lay hidden from their early expositors, and classical political economy was explicitly prejudiced toward reform. Its emphasis was on *improving* the institutions commanding its attention; *understanding* such institutions was always a secondary, even if necessary, purpose. Improvement did, as we know, materialize; the social transformation dictated by the classical precepts was, to an extent, realized.

The practical success of classical economics was responsible, in part, for its scientific undoing. The distinctions between scientific propositions and proposals for social reform were blurred from the outset. This led critics, who quite properly disputed classical prejudices toward social structure, to attack, and to appear to attack, the central propositions of the scientific analysis. This confusion has plagued economics and continues to plague it even now. The physical sciences have, by and large, escaped this confusion, and herein lies their prestige. Only in the recent discussions of the hydrogen bomb and radiation has there appeared anything akin to the elementary confusion between positive prediction and normative engineering that has pervaded economic discussion. Economists have, from the beginning of the discipline, been in the position faced by J. Robert Oppenheimer. And, they have, unfortunately for the science, chosen much as he seems to have done. As a result, the interests of economists have been rarely, if ever, wholly scientific, and, on occasion, have been explicitly ascientific. The personal inclination toward social involvement has proved too strong for most, even for those who shun the limelight and who remain, physically, within the ivoried towers. In this perspective, Pareto stands dominant over a narrowly confined group of lesser figures.

WHAT IS ECONOMICS?

The science advanced, nonetheless, despite the noise generated by inconsequential argument, and there has been, and remains, content in the words "economics" and "economist." Before the relationships among this science and its neighbors can be discussed, brief note of what this content is seems in order. What is the common language? What are the simple principles? How does one identify an economist?

By way of illustration, I propose to design here a simple conceptual experiment. One of the ancient Greek philosophers is credited with the statement: *Anything worth doing is worth doing well.* As our conceptual experiment, let us suppose that we select a randomly drawn sample from the general population. We give each person in the sample the adage cited above, and we ask him to comment upon it. We then observe their comments and attempt some sort of classification.

No single test could, of course, possibly be wholly conclusive, but it seems quite possible that the simple experiment proposed here would, in fact, provide us with a rough and ready manner of classifying economists and distinguishing them from the general public of which they form a part. There would be, in other words, a characteristic economist's response to the adage which would not be shared by large numbers of other persons. Additional, and more discriminating tests could, of course, be devised which would further delineate the economists from the remaining community of scientists. But these need not be elaborated here since the single experiment is sufficient to illustrate the elemental principles of the science.

The economist's stock-in-trade—his tools—lies in his ability to and his proclivity to think about all questions in terms of *alternatives.* The truth judgment of the moralist, which says that something is either wholly right or wholly wrong, is foreign to him. The win-lose, yes-no discussion of politics is not within his purview. He does not recognize the either-or, the all-or-nothing, situation as his own. His is not the world of the mutually exclusives. Instead, his is a world of adjustment, of coordinated conflict, of *mutual gains.* To the economist, there are, of course, many things worth doing that are not worth doing well since he is trained, professionally, to think in terms of a continuous scale of variation both in doing things and in criteria for judging them done well.

The theorems that are of relevance to the economist are all constructed from this simple base. These may be germane to the choices, the decisions, of individual persons, of organizations of persons, or of social groups. Care must be taken at this stage, however, to insure that too much is not claimed for the economist. His domain is limited to the behavior of individual persons in choosing among the alternatives open to them. This behavior provides the raw material for the economist, and his theory of economic aggregates is built on foundations of sand if the elemental units, behaving individuals, are overlooked. Individual persons choose among alternatives that they confront; their choices are not mutually exclusive; they do not choose on an either-or basis. Instead, they select the "goods" and reject the "bads" through choices of "more or less." There are few, if any, demonstrably universal "goods" which are desired independently of quantity variation; and, similarly, there are few, if any, demonstrably universal "bads." It is for this reason that the economist does not speak, indeed cannot, of "goods" and "bads" separately from the choices made by individual persons.

By examining such choices, the economist can, however, place some restrictions on human behavior patterns. He can develop testable hypotheses about behavior, which observations can refute. Once he has succeeded in identifying what individuals, on the average, consider to be "goods," the economist can predict that more of any "good" will be chosen the lower its "price" relative to other "goods." This is the central predictive proposition of economics, which can be all-encompassing provided only that the terms "goods" and "price" are defined in sufficiently broad and inclusive ways. This central principle amounts to saying that individuals, when confronted with effective choice, will choose more rather than less.

As such, this remains a very elementary, and, to the economist, self-evident, proposition. But the economist's task is that of extending the range of its application and usefulness. Individuals choose among the various opportunities that they confront, but, in so doing, they cannot treat other individuals as they can the physical environment. One means of choosing more rather than less is choosing to engage in trade; in fact, this is the pervasive means through which man has expanded his command of "goods." The institutions of exchange, of markets, are derived, therefore, from the mutual interactions of individuals who are continuously engaged in making ordinary choices for more rather than less. As a "social" scientist, the primary function of the economist is to explain the workings of these institutions and to predict the effects of changes in their structure. As the interaction process that he examines becomes more complex, it is but natural that the task of the economic scientist becomes more intricate. But his central principle remains the same; and he can, through its use, unravel the most tangled sets of structural relationships among human beings.

The economist is able to do this because he possesses this central principle—an underlying theory of human behavior. And because he does so, he qualifies as a scientist and his discipline as a science. What a science does, or should do, is simply to allow the average man, through professional specialization, to command the heights of genius. The basic tools are the simple principles, and these are chained forever to the properly disciplined professional. Without them, he is as a jibbering idiot, who makes only noise under an illusion of speech. The progress of a science is measured by the continuing generalization of its principles, by their extension into new applications. Economics is not different in this respect from any other science. Its progress is best measured by the extent to which its central propositions are pushed outward, are stretched, so to speak, to explain human behavior as yet unexplained, to provide new predictive understanding of institutions emerging from human behavior. Viewed in this light, John von Neumann's contribution lay in extending the principles to apply in a wholly new set of situations confronting the individual. Game theory takes its place within the expanded kit of tools that the economist carries with him.

Contrast this with the Keynesian and post-Keynesian attention on macro-economics and macro-economic models. Does this "theory" provide the economist with an additional set of tools? Does this extend the application of the central principles of the discipline? Unfortunately, the answer must be negative here. Precisely because it has divorced itself from the central proposition relating to human behavior, modern macro-economic theory is really no theory at all. It has evolved, and remains, a set of models for the workings of economic aggregates, models that have little predictive value. Lord Keynes, of course, recognized this, and it was for this reason that he tried to tie his theoretical structure to basic psychological propensities. These propensities, which were designed to replace the more simple neoclassical behavioral propositions, have never fulfilled the role that Keynes must have hoped for them, and the modern model builders seem largely to leave even these out of account.

Macro-economic theory may, of course, attain the status of science, when and if its propositions carry predictive implications. However, when it does so, it will be a wholly new science, not that of economics. And its practitioners will not be classified by the characteristic responses of economists to the simple conceptual experiment carried out above. It is the divergence of macro-economics from the central propositions that is tending, today, to create serious problems of communication within the confines of the same discipline that is professionally classified as "economics." Increasingly, it becomes difficult for those who have specialized in macro-economics to communicate with those who start from the traditional base.

SPILLOUTS TO AND SPILLINS FROM THE NEIGHBORHOOD SCIENCES—A SCHEMATIC PRESENTATION

The discussion to this point has been concerned with what "economics" is. This preliminary has been necessary before raising the main questions of this essay, those which concern the relations of this science to its disciplinary neighbors. Full-length, and useful, methodological essays could, of course, be written covering the relations between economics and each and every one of the neighborhood sciences. Obviously, selectivity and condensation are essential here. It will perhaps be helpful, nonetheless, to present, briefly and schematically, the totality or quasi-totality of relationships. It seems reasonable to think of these as falling broadly within two sets. First, the contributions that economics can make to the other sciences or disciplines can be presented. These external effects can be called "spillouts," following another usage of this term by Burton Weisbrod. Second, the essential contributions that neighborhood disciplines can make to economics may be arrayed. These are, similarly, called "spillins."

In this section I shall present an array of spillouts and spillins, with only limited explanatory discussion under each heading. For simplicity in presentation, I have organized the material such that a single term represents the spillout contribution of economics to each discipline and a single term represents the spillin contribution of each other discipline to economics. Those relationships which will be discussed in more detail in the following section are marked with an asterisk.

What Can Economics Contribute to Its Neighbors?

To Engineering——an Attitude *
To History——Constraints
To Humanities——dashes of Reality *
To Law——Limitations *
To Mathematics——Applications
To Physical Science——an Appreciation
To Political Science——a Theory *
To Psychology——a Challenge
To Statistics——Problems

The above is, of course, shorthand. And, as with much shorthand, the schema may raise more issues than it resolves. Some brief clarification may be attempted here for those items which cannot be elaborated on in more detail below.

Economics can impose on the study of history essentially a constraining influence. The reconstruction of past events is circumscribed by the predictions that can be made concerning man's responses to his economic environment, and the viability of institutional arrangements may, in a sense, be tested. In fact, one of the interesting developments in economics, which amounts to an extension of its simple principles, involves the work of economic historians in applying data from past years to test the central hypotheses.

Economics offers little to the pure mathematician, at least at first hand. However, to the applied mathematician, the problems posed by the economist can offer fascinating and fruitful challenges to his ingenuity. And, to the extent that the "twisting" of pure theory by the applied mathematician generates a secondary reaction from the purist, there may be ultimate influence on the development of pure mathematics itself.

The physical scientist can, I think, learn much from the economist. Essentially, he can learn humility as he appreciates the limitations of science and scientific method in application to the inordinately complex problems of human relationships. To the extent that he can learn that, by comparison, his own problems are indeed elementary; despite his great achievements, he becomes both a better scientist and a better citizen.

To the psychologist, the economists offer a standing challenge. Provide us with a better explanatory behavioral hypothesis! Economists know, of course, that ordinary utility maximization does not "explain" all behavior, or even a predominant part of it. Their success is, however, measured by the relevance of this hypothesis. Psychologists object to the economists' behavioral assumptions, but they have not provided sufficiently explanatory alternative hypotheses for the development of a general theory of human behavior in social structure. Perhaps they will do so; the challenge remains with them until they do.

The statistician is in much the same position as the applied mathematician, if, indeed, these two need be distinguished at all. The tests that the economists seek, the aid that they request from him in devising such tests, may open up areas of research that otherwise remain closed.

What Can Economics Learn from Its Neighbors?

From Engineering——a Warning *
From History——Hope
From Humanities——Inspiration
From Law——a Framework *
From Mathematics——a Language
From Physical Science——a Morality *
From Political Science——Data
From Psychology——a Damper
From Statistics——Design *

We may now examine, quite briefly, those spillins to economics, and to economists, from disciplinary neighbors not marked with asterisks on the above listing and thus not reserved for further elaboration.

The idea of progress that pervaded liberal scholarship in the two preceding centuries has, to an extent, disappeared. Nevertheless, history teaches economists, and all others whose subject matter is human civil order, that there is ultimate hope. Man may, and does, behave badly, by almost any standards, on many occasions. Yet learning more about how he does behave can mean only that, ultimately, he may choose to reform his institutions so as to bridle his impulses properly. History should teach the economist that the grievous mistakes of past epochs need not be repeated in future. History should provide him with hope.

The arts and the humanities have been too long neglected by the economists, through simple error and confusion. The "goods" that men pursue should in no manner of speaking be conceived as vulgarly materialistic, in the common-sense terminology. The economist takes man essentially as he is, and he observes man selecting his own "goods," while shunning his own "bads." But as affluence allows man to rise above the subsistence minima, his "goods" expand to include those things that only the arts and the humanities discuss. Man wants to want better things; he wants to change his own tastes, and he deliberately chooses to modify his own listing of the "goods" that matter to him. It is appropriate that competent research scholars are now devoting attention to the economics of the fine arts.

The language that mathematics provides to economists, supplementary to their own, is widely recognized and understood. Its contribution to the productivity of economists, at the margin, may be questioned, but the integral of the product function must be large indeed.

What can political science, in its traditional disciplinary organization, contribute to the economist? Basically, it provides him with a record, data, of socio-political structures that he may, if he chooses, utilize in conducting his conceptual and actual experiments. Governments tend to do many things, and many of them foolishly. Political scientists keep the institutional record.

Psychology always threatens to undermine altogether the economist's simple principles, to make his model as a house of cards. Human behavior is erratic, nonrational, and often wholly unpredictable. Nonlogical explanation often supersedes logical explanation. The psychologist, by emphasizing the nonlogical, the "deeper" motivations and urges that guide the human psyche, chips continuously at the economist's predictive models. To an extent, these models remain in a state analogous to Newtonian physics, while the psychologist hopes to achieve the relativity breakthrough. To date, he has not succeeded, but the economist who is wise always keeps out a weather eye.

The two listings, those for spillouts and spillins, are not complete, and the brevity with which the relative directional contributions have been discussed has surely served to confuse as much as to enlighten. And especially for noneconomists, the necessary sketchiness may have served to raise more red flags than intended.

THE IMPORTANT SPILLOUTS FROM ECONOMICS TO NEIGHBOR DISCIPLINES

I now propose to discuss the four important spillout relationships marked with asterisks in the above listing more thoroughly.

Engineering

In the simple schema on page 171, I suggested that economics contributes an attitude to the engineer and to the engineering sciences. With the latter term, I refer to all those studies that are instrumentally oriented toward the accomplishment of specific objectives. That is to say, the aim of the science is not understanding, but rather improving, making things work. Under this heading, therefore, I place not only physical engineering, as usually conceived, but also business engineering, most often labeled as business administration, and, likewise, social engineering.

As I have suggested, economists have often conceived themselves primarily as social engineers, and their interests have been more oriented to improvements in social structure than to predictions of a scientific character. This has led, and continues to lead, to much confusion. There is, of course, no reason why social engineering need not be a legitimate activity, in certain limits. But the activity of the social engineer is not that of the economic scientist.

Similarly, with the business engineer. It is one of the many American tragedies in education that has caused economics to be blanketed with business administration in professional association. Again, the business engineer serves a proper task, but a wholly different one from the economist. However, and this should be noted with some emphasis, the business engineer stands in precisely the same relation to the economist as the social engineer. The presumptive arrogance of those who call themselves economists and act as social engineers while scorning the role of the business engineer should be called promptly to account.

Having defined what I mean by "engineering" and "engineer," I can now elaborate what I mean by saying that the economist can contribute an "attitude" that is extremely helpful, as ample evidence reveals. The economist is trained to think in terms of alternatives; his attitude is one of searching among available alternatives for some optimal solution, and the study of the behavior of persons as they carry out such search. Engineers, far too frequently, fail to embody, as a "natural" thought pattern, sufficient concern for *alternatives*. They tend, by contrast, to think in terms of defined objectives and of specific means.

The best examples of the economist's contribution to engineering in this respect is provided by the whole field of operations research. Here the central idea is essentially that of searching out from among the available alternatives and examining the possibility of accomplishing the same objectives with other alternatives, arrayed finally in accordance with some acceptable criteria. A predominant share of the developments in this area of study belongs to those who are trained, professionally, as economists.

The *attitude* that is relevant here is the one which emerges quite naturally from a concentration on the allocation of scarce means among alternative ends—the traditional definition of an economic problem. To many of my professional colleagues, this attitude is the peculiar talent of the economist, and he works always essentially as an engineer. I do not, of course, deny his value to the engineer, be this technical, organizational, or social, but I prefer to divorce this spillout effect from the central principles of economic science. This is not, of course, to deny that the contribution made by economists here is highly productive. It is essential that some professionals specialize, explicitly, in measuring and analyzing the relative costs of alternatives. And, given the state of the scientific world as it is, economists are better equipped to do this than almost anyone else. In the process, however, I should emphasize only that they work as engineers, not as economists.

Humanities

Scholars in the humane studies should maintain at least a nodding acquaintance with economics and with economists. The spillout contribution here is that of imposing reality upon man's natural proclivity to dream. The economist, almost alone, takes man as he exists, and he does not spend his effort in dreaming of man's perfectibility. To the humanist, therefore, the economist's prospect is indeed a dismal one, and his concern with baser motives of man is held to scorn. This is as it should be; the humanist should not be expected to "love" the economist as fellow scholar. Indeed, his very purpose is to stretch the economist's model of ordinary man beyond its natural limits, and his success is measured by his ability to do so. The economist serves to provide the base from which the humanist begins. Essentially, the economist represents an ever-present Hobbesian realism standing counter to the innocent romanticism of all Rousseaus.

Utopianism is not the disease it once was, and to the extent that it has disappeared, the economist's constraints now have less value for the humanist than before. Even the last vestiges of utopianism, represented by the romantic conception of the ever-benevolent bureaucracy, the all-embracing despotism of the state, seems to have been dealt a crushing blow by the turn of events through history. Perhaps there is need now for a new utopianism rather than for its opposite, which seems reflected in the modern waves of disillusionment and despair. What is the future for humane studies in an absurd world? Perhaps the role of the economist has come full circle: Is it too much to claim that sober realism can, in fact, focus renewed attention on attainable human order? When it is finally recognized that man is neither the noble savage nor beset with original sin, the elemental rationality that is central to the economist's model may too become the stuff of dreams.

Law

The medium through which human beings impose constraints on their own interaction, one with another, is provided by the law. The simple principles of economics impose limitations on the operation of these constraints, much as the simple principles of physics impose limitations upon the engineer's working models of machines. Law can modify the conditions under which human beings choose among alternatives; it cannot directly affect the behavior in choosing. Economics seems to generate nonsensical statements by its critics, but none takes precedence over the discussion about the "repeal of the law of supply and demand." Intelligent and sophisticated men, who remain economic illiterates, talk as if human behavior in choice situations can be modified by legal restraints, as opposed to modifications in the conditions for choice. And on the basis of such discussion laws are enacted and enforced which have the effect of preventing the attainment of the very objectives that they are designed to promote.

Minimum-wage laws provide perhaps the best single example. Reasonable men support such legislation on the grounds that the poorer classes will be aided. The effect is, of course, the opposite, as the simplest of economic principles must state. By requiring the payment of a legal minimum wage, employers must choose fewer of the lowest paid workers rather than more. Low-productivity workers must be unemployed, or must shift into employments not covered by the legal restrictions. The laws harm the poorer and less-productive workers.

Such examples could be multiplied. The laws enacted in the ignorance of simple economic principles can do great damage, yet we observe little progress in the recognition of the limitations that economics should impose on legislation. This is the continuing despair of economists who want to see their science applied in practice.

Political science

To orthodox political scientists, it may seem the height of presumptive arrogance to say that economics can provide "a theory" for explanation and prediction of political decisions. Nonetheless, it is becoming increasingly evident that the important theoretical advances in the explanation of political phenomena have been made primarily by those who approach the subject matter as economists. The reason for this is not far to seek. The political scientist has not, traditionally, incorporated a theory of human behavior into his structure of political process. To him, "theory" has never implied prediction. Instead, political theory has suggested normative philosophical discourse on the objectives and aims of political order. Little, if any, positive science is to be found in this tradition.

The economist, shifting his attention to man's behavior in reaching collective decisions in concert with his fellows in some political arrangement, brings with him, ready-made so to speak, a basic behavioral postulate. He is able, through its use, to make predictions, to advance hypotheses that are conceptually refutable. He does so in the full knowledge that the predictive value of his propositions is much less than that for the corresponding propositions relating to man's behavior in the strictly defined market relationship. He is prepared to accept the fact that his "explanation" of politics falls far short of completeness. But he can claim that he has a "theory of politics," of the way men do behave in collective decision making.

It is essentially this "economic" approach to politics that has come into attention as an important interdisciplinary area of scholarship since the 1940's. Work here remains in its infancy, but scholarship will surely accelerate over the decades ahead.

IMPORTANT SPILLINS TO ECONOMICS FROM OTHER DISCIPLINES

Having discussed the four most important spillouts, the contributions that economics and economists can make to its scientific neighbors, I shall now discuss spillins. The "exchange" among disciplines is clearly multilateral, and the economist can learn much from the larger world of scholarship. Writing this paper as an economist, I find it more difficult to discuss spillins, which are more or less unconsciously allowed to affect our thinking, than I find it to discuss spillouts.

Engineering

In the schema above, I have suggested that the contribution of engineering to economics consists of a "warning." Stated in an obverse way, we can say that the engineering sciences offer a constant "temptation" to the economist, and he must ever be on his guard lest he forget his own special position in the scientific world. The argument here is much the same, in reverse, of that offered above concerning the economist's contribution to the engineer. The economist's task is not properly that of *improving*, or making things work, whether these things be technical equipment, a business organization, or the social system. These are engineering tasks, and the economist must warn himself not to assume the role of the engineer too readily. There are specific contributions that the economist can make to engineering, as discussed above. But engineering is engineering, not economics. And the engineer, be he business, social, or technical, can best contribute to the development of economic science if he acts jealously concerning the intrusion of economists in his field. Professionally, the engineer should refuse association with the economist, and he should shun all attempts of the latter to enter into the confines of his discipline. "Management science" should be isolated and should isolate itself from economic science. But so should "social engineering," or "the science of social management," which far too many economists claim as their own bailiwick.

Law

What can the study of law contribute to economics? The answer is clear, but its implications are too often overlooked. Economics seeks to explain human interactions within an emerging-evolving institutional setting, and this setting is best described in terms of the set of laws that condition human choices. The essential subject matter for the economist consists of human behavior in social institutions, not of human behavior in the abstract. The tendency of economic theorists to overlook this simple fact provoked the reaction of the American institutionalists, a reaction which surely was misguided in its emphasis, but which, nonetheless, pointed up a serious deficiency in the evolution of economic science. Imaginative and critical work in economics remains to be done in extending the applications of principles to the legal setting that is actually observable in a specific society.

To what extent are the rules, the laws, the institutions of social order assumed to be variable in the implied setting of theoretical welfare economics? The economist who has examined this literature will know that there is no answer suggested. Yet it is surely evident that the whole exercise has little significance until and unless such questions are answered. If, in fact, no laws are to be changed, Pareto optimality is automatically attained by each individual acting within the constraints imposed upon him. The whole discussion of Pareto optimality must, therefore, imply some change in the laws governing human conduct. But just which laws are to be subjected to change? Are overriding constitutional provisions to govern the changes that are allowed? These questions shall not be answered here, but merely raising them will suggest the need for some greater tie-in between the structure of economic theory on the one hand and the legal-institutional framework on the other.

How should such work begin? The logical starting place seems to be with the institutional structure that actually is observed. To this factual base can be applied the theoretical analysis. Fruitful results should emerge from such institutional theorizing. It is in such a context that productive work on the economics of property relationships has been done, and is being done, by such economists as Armen Alchian and Ronald Coase.

Physical science

Frank Knight has said that economists should learn *morals* not method from the physical sciences. There is a point in what Knight says, and it is worth discussing. The physical scientists are scientists in a fuller sense of this emotive term than are most economists. They have been able, with rare exceptions, to conduct reasoned argument critically and dispassionately without the ideological overtones that have plagued effective communication among economists. They have a higher respect for "truth"; at least this appears to be the case to one who stands outside their pavilions. Perhaps this is because their standards are more precise; this, in itself, breeds a scientific morality that social scientists seem to lack. Hobbes is widely credited to have made the statement that general agreement would never have been reached on the proposition that two and two add up to four if it had proved to anyone's interest to argue otherwise. To an extent, this is surely true. The physical sciences have advanced so rapidly because their own advances have been divorced from direct social implications. Economics, and economists, have been placed at a great disadvantage because they cannot, even if they try, divorce their theory from social implication.

Should economists try to be pure scientists? Should they seek truth independently of values? This continues to be a debated question, and the fact that it is debatable, or thought to be so, suggests the state of the science. Gunnar Myrdal, and others, argue that there are no independent propositions; that the "truths" in economics emerge from basic value postulates that had best be stated at the outset of discussion. Taken seriously, this position removes all scientific content from the discipline and reduces discussion to a babel of voices making noise. The economist, to maintain his self-respect, must hold fast to the faith that there does exist an independent body of truth in his discipline, truth that can be discerned independently of value judgments.

Theoretical statistics

Rutledge Vining has impressed upon me the contribution that theoretical statistics can make to the economist and to the study of economics. Practitioners in our discipline have been too prone to look directly at the instantaneously observable results of economic process and to infer from these implications that carry both theoretical and policy content. Statistical theory forces a recognition of the temporal sequences of results that are observable and the variations in distributions over time. The very presence of randomness in the economic universe seems to have been largely neglected in the formal development of the theory that we use. Once we begin to recognize that each and every event in time-space is not predetermined but contains some randomness in its generation, direct inferences from instantaneously observed results become much more difficult.

To what extent can the distribution of income among persons be explained by random variation? To what extent can the distribution of persons over space be explained by random selection? It is clear, once such questions as these are asked, that until and unless we can have some approximate idea as to the answers we cannot really evaluate the implications of any observable distribution. In designing his conceptual experiments, the economist cannot now fail to allow for the relevance of randomness, or chance, in determining outcomes. This makes the refutation of his hypotheses much more difficult, of course, but it is best that he proceed without false hopes of rigor that does not exist. Truth is not so easy to come by in a world of uncertainty, but, once having recognized this, we are better off as scientists.

Theoretical statistics can contribute to the design of experiments, and to the economist's thinking about design, in yet another way. The statistician recognizes that he does not choose directly among outcomes, allocations, or distributions. His choice is among *rules* that will restrict or confine the range of possible outcomes and among the criteria through which the operation of these rules shall be judged. This attitude is of major importance to the economist, and it can teach him a major lesson. The overemphasis on allocation problems has taught far too many economists to think in terms of directly choosing allocations of resources, distributions of income, etc. Reflection on this indicates at once that such variables are not within the range of social choice, even if social choice be accepted as appropriate for the economist's advice. The society chooses among the several possible rules which restrict or condition human behavior. These rules will generate outcomes, which may be examined in terms of allocations or distributions. Once the emphasis is shifted to the choices among rules, however, the whole structure of discussion of welfare criteria is shifted, and with obvious advantage.

SPECIALIZED INTERDEPENDENCE—A SPECIFIC EXAMPLE

In the introduction I suggested that two trends could be observed in the development of modern economics. First, the independence of the science from its neighbors seems rapidly to be disappearing, while, at the same time, professional specialization within the discipline is proceeding apace. These are, at first glance, contradictory trends, but upon closer examination the contradiction disappears. What seems to be happening in most instances is the emergence of a new orientation of professional specialization, and one that has not, as yet, found its place in the structure of professional organization and educational curricula. It becomes increasingly clear that the channels of effective communication do not extend throughout the discipline that we variously call "economics," and that some "economists" are able to communicate far more effectively with some scholars in the noneconomic disciplines than with those presumably within their own professional category.

I shall illustrate this development, which I think can be generalized for several areas, with reference to a single cross-disciplinary field, one with which I have personally been associated. I refer to the work that has been done by economists in extending the simple principles of their discipline to political decision making, to the making of decisions in a nonmarket context. As I have suggested earlier, much of the early work was done by economists, but more recently a few political scientists have been directly engaged in this field of scholarship. At the same time separate but closely related work has been done in other areas. Economists who have worked on the "theory of teams," on the "economics of information," on the "theory of organization" have all been concerned with similar constructions. Psychologists who have been concerned with small-group theory, all scholars who have worked in game theory, and especially with nonzero sum cooperative games, also fall into the cross-disciplinary field that is emerging. There are even a few philosophers who, in their concern with what is called "rule-utilitarianism," fall among the interdisciplinary communication network.

Through this development, it becomes far easier, and more interesting as well as more productive, for the economist who works with non-market decisions to communicate with the positive political scientist, the game theorist, or the organizational theory psychologist than it is for him to communicate with the growth-model macro-economist, with whom he scarcely finds any common ground. This specialized interdependence, if it is, in fact, general over several emerging specializations, can be expected to result, ultimately, in some movements toward professional institutionalization. To an extent, this has already happened in such areas as regional science. These movements should not be discouraged by the inherent conservatism of established disciplinary orthodoxy. Insofar as interdisciplinary specialization emerges genuinely from the changing channels of effective scholarly communication, steps taken to further such communication, while breaking down traditionally established disciplinary lines, represent added efficiency.

CONCLUSIONS

The starting point for this essay has been the empirical embodiment of "economics" as a scientific discipline. I have deliberately interpreted economics narrowly, as a science and as a positive set of conceptually refutable propositions about human behavior in a social organization. The normative content that is often alleged to be present in the discipline has been simply defined as outside the pale of discussion here. This is, I think, as it should be, although I recognize that many highly competent methodologists will sharply disagree with my position on this. There is, I submit, positive content to the science that is economics, and it is this positive content that is currently deserving of stress and emphasis, both on the part of its own practitioners and on that of its neighboring scholars. The role of the economist, at base, must be that of attempting to understand a certain type of human behavior and the prediction of the social structures that are emergent from that behavior. Ultimately, the economist must hope that his simple truths, as extended, can lead to "improvement" in the structure of these institutions, through the ability of institutions to modify the conditions of human choice. But improvement must remain his secondary and subsidiary purpose; he verges dangerously on irresponsible action when he allows his zeal for social progress, as he conceives this, to take precedence over his search for and respect of scientific truth, as determined by the consensus of his peers.

This does not imply that the economic scientist must remain in the realm of pure theory and shun all discussions of economic policy. There can be, and should be, a theory of economic policy. And the economist, by analyzing the results of alternative lines of action, can be of great assistance to the social decision maker. But, as such, the economist has no business at playing the social engineer. He can hope that his light will ultimately be used to generate some heat, but he should live with his hope and refuse to become an activist. He can point out to men the opportunities for reorganizing their social institutions in such a way as to achieve the goals that men desire. But the final choices in a free society rest with individuals who participate in that society. Men may choose to live primitively and to refuse to recognize the simple principles that economists continually repeat. If they so choose, they will so choose, and it is not the task of the economist, or anyone else, to say that they "should" necessarily choose differently. The task of the economist, and of economic science, is done when the simple propositions are presented.

If the economist can learn from his colleagues in the physical sciences, and learn in sufficient time, that the respect for truth takes precedence above all else and that it is the final value judgment that must pervade all science, he may, yet, rescue the discipline from its currently threatened rush into absurdity, oblivion, and disrepute. In the large, he does not seem to be learning, and, if anything, the physical scientist seems more in danger of accepting the perverted confusion that has plagued the economist through generations. But there are a few encouraging signs, and these are to be found in the genuinely exciting areas of specialized interdisciplinary interdependence that are blossoming in full flower. A second ray of hope lies in the attitude of the young scholars, in economics as well as its neighbors. Their attitude is properly critical of all ideologues. To the emotionally committed socialist or libertarian, who parades also as economist, these young scholars may appear as disinterested, lacking passion, as "cold fish." But to the extent that they are, economics is gaining stature as a science and is shedding off its burdensome overgrowth of social involvement. The economics that may gain full stature as a science will not excite the reformers who have occupied too many of its chairs in past decades, but to those who seek for truth the discipline will be worthy of their efforts.

The challenge remains with those who are and will become economists. The pessimist observes the prostitution and worries about scientific morality. The optimist seizes the rays of hope and projects the millennium. The final response will depend perhaps as much upon the unpredictable evolution of social institutions, guided only in part by rational choices, as on the deliberate decisions made by the professionals.

BIBLIOGRAPHY

Alchian, Armen and W. R. Allen, University Economics. San Francisco: Wadsworth, 1964.

Coats, A. W., The Role of Value Judgments in Economics. Monograph 7. Charlottesville, Va.: Thomas Jefferson Center for Studies in Political Economy, 1964.

Friedman, Milton, Essays in Positive Economics. Chicago: University of Chicago Press, 1953.

Hutchison, T. W., Positive Economics and Policy Objectives. London: G. Allen, 1964.

Kirzner, Israel M., The Economic Point of View. New York: Van Nostrand, 1960.

Knight, Frank H., Intelligence and Democratic Action. Cambridge, Mass.: Harvard, 1960.

————, On the History and Method of Economics. Chicago: University of Chicago Press, 1956.

Myrdal, Gunnar, The Political Element in the Development of Economic Theory, trans. P. Streeten. London: Routledge, 1953.

Vining, Rutledge, Economics in the United States of America. Paris: U.N. Educational, Scientific, and Cultural Organization, 1956.

BENJAMIN WARD

Benjamin Ward, Ph.D., University of California at Berkeley, is Associate Professor of Economics at the University of California. He has written on comparative economics and is the author of Greek Regional Development. *He is currently active in research in the fields of economic development, comparative systems, and the application of economic reasoning to the other social sciences.*

ESSAY

12

Institutions

and

Economic

Analysis[1]

NEARLY ALL ECONOMIC ACTIVITY IS STRONGLY permeated with habitual, organized, customary elements. This is as true of decisions made within corporations as it is of political decisions about taxes and expenditures of governments, as true of the market place as it is of the family. As a consequence, one might expect that economists would devote a good deal of their effort in theory building to the systematic incorporation of such factors into their explanations. Yet there is a widespread feeling that these factors are largely ignored by economists, a feeling which, though most commonly held by noneconomists, is by no means their exclusive property.

I suspect that within the mainstream of economic analysis this indictment was more nearly true thirty to fifty years ago than it was a century ago, and that it is

---

[1] This is a revised and expanded version of a paper presented at the Atlanta, 1962 meetings of the Southern Economic Association. I am indebted to Jack Wiseman, Bertram F. Levin, and Sherman Krupp for critical comments.

much less true today than in the period that straddles World War I. In this essay I will not attempt to test this assertion. Instead I will try to indicate the general strategies by which economic theorists have dealt with institutional aspects of their problems and offer a few examples of ways in which some political and sociological factors have been and may be introduced into current types of economic analysis. In doing this it will be useful to introduce one piece of jargon: a specialized definition of the word "rule." This will provide a unified framework within which to discuss these interdisciplinary matters.

RULES AND ECONOMICS

A rule is a device by which some people may influence the behavior of some (possibly the same) people. It has two key properties: a communication and a set of sanctions attached to obedience or disobedience. The effect of a rule is to change the relative valuation of alternatives by some of the participants and thus, at least potentially, to affect their behavior. We shall be thinking here only of rules which *are* effective, which *do* affect human behavior.

There are many forms for rules, but three types are perhaps most common and inclusive. First there is the *prescript*, which essentially, via implicit or explicit sanctions, points to the need for a revaluation of alternatives. The revaluation occurs because some of the alternatives now have—implicitly or explicitly, with certainty or without—additional rewards and penalties attached to them. The communication of a prescript may be imperative or even threatening in mood, but it need not be. The description of the sanctions is enough.

Then there is the *exhortation*. There are no threats or rewards attached to the environment in a pure exhortation. Rather the assumption is that utilities are either interdependent or manipulable. By exhorting we appeal to fellow feeling or to self-feeling, and presumably we often succeed if admen and propagandists are to be believed.

Finally, there is simply the *communication* of new information to an individual or group. Though it may seem somewhat removed from current usage, informing is rule making at least in its two general effects: it is a communication, and, when "useful," it influences behavior, primarily by leading to a revaluation of alternatives.

Rule making is obviously one of the most common forms of human behavior. In fact, one might well define social science as the study of rules and rule making, with behavioral science emphasizing their effects, while normative branches of the social sciences deal with the designing of optimal systems of rules. The definition does not exclude internal rule making by individuals: both New Year's resolutions and assumed roles fall under the rubric. It is safe to say that rules have some influence on all social behavior and that rule making constitutes a very large part of social behavior, though not all, as will be seen.

It is no surprise to find that rule making, given its scope, is a very complicated business. The student who aims at explanation and prediction in this area faces appalling difficulties. For example, exhortations lead us to study the properties of interdependent utility systems. Where are we to find either theoretical or empirical guidance through the vast maze of possibilities? Interdependence requires a tremendous complication of the assumed nature of the individual. It is only made worse by the possibility that new criteria of decision making may be created by suggestion or other forms of exhortation. The problem of the individual is still further complicated by his ability to make rules for himself, to alter his own behavior. In effect, a set of preferences is an internal behavior rule. The individual may seek to change his own rules by actions such as study or experiment. What regularities in this type of behavior can we cite with any confidence?

The formal content of the communication of a rule is, of course, not to be trusted. The sanctions may not be stated at all but merely be implicit. And if they are stated, it is typically not at all clear how effective they will be. Some system of control must be available for the inspection of possibly sanctioned acts, the evaluation of performance, and the levying of the sanctions. Sanctions are not always easy to observe nor easy for an outsider to understand. The study of control systems is an essential and difficult part of the study of rule making.

There are hierarchies of rules which may interact. Constitutional rules are rules which prescribe the scope for rule making in given environments. Much of the content of constitutions and bylaws consists of constitutional rules, though for fundamental political organizations explicit sanctions for violation of constitutional rules may be absent. It is hard enough to understand the effects of rules on behavior. Often the still more difficult task of assessing the impact of rules for rule making on behavior is faced by the social scientist, for example, whenever he is studying comparative government. In principle, at least, levels of rule making can be piled upon one another at will.

When rule making is ubiquitous, it is natural to assume that one way or another everything depends upon everything else. And when to this is added the methodological constraint that there be virtually no experimentation, one might well expect the Angst of the social scientist to transcend that of the existentialist by an order of magnitude. That this is not the case is perhaps more a tribute to the narrowness of his outlook than to any rational assessment by social scientists of their achievements. Nevertheless, this narrowing of perspective is the very essence of scientific procedure. For simplification of problems by isolating a few key variables and positing relatively limited and specific interactions has been the standard, and is indeed the only, expedient reaction to complexity. The very serious constraints faced by the social scientist inevitably restrict the confidence which can be placed in his results, but more productive alternative procedures do not seem to be available.

TYPES OF ECONOMIC ANALYSIS

The tradition of economic analysis carries four distinct types of reactions to the problem of understanding aspects of economic activity in such a complex environment. Each may serve partly as an example or inspiration for future work and partly as a warning of the dangers of inappropriate simplification. The elements of this fourfold classification, each of which will be described in a paragraph or two are: institutionalism, magnificent dynamics, general equilibrium analysis, and game theory.

More than any other school of economists the institutionalists were concerned with rules. John R. Commons called the customs and laws regulating human interaction "working rules," and most institutionalists devoted a major portion of their effort to the study of these working rules as they applied to developing capitalism. In one of the most interesting of these works, *Legal Foundations of Capitalism*,[2] Commons followed the changes in the idea of property rights from medieval times to the early twentieth century in the United States. For example, the slow and complex process by which promises acquired legal sanction provides some fascinating insights into the ways in which everyday life was being affected by economic change.[3]

Commons' purpose in writing this book, however, was not to provide a history of economically relevant legal concepts. "The aim of this volume is to work out an evolutionary and behavioristic, or rather volitional, theory of value." [4] In this he fails, and for the same reason that much of the other institutionalist work is unsatisfactory. The institutionalists seem to have suffered from a methodological confusion regarding the nature of theory. They thought a description was a theory: or alternatively, they thought that a good theory should explain everything. They were wrong, and nowhere is this more apparent than in *Legal Foundations of Capitalism*. Commons' theory of value is derived from what he takes to be the juristic concept. This he asserts is based on the judgment or classification of human actions as moral or immoral. In application this approach provides us with a series of dichotomies based on the properties of particular

---

2 (New York: Macmillan, 1924.)
3 *Ibid.*, see especially Chap. 7.
4 *Ibid.*, Preface.

actions. Often such an approach works well; however, it breaks down whenever the dichotomies lead to conflicting judgments—that is, when the action is moral in terms of one property and immoral in terms of another (killing to protect, for example). Without a criterion for the relative valuation of these individual criteria among one another there is no resolution provided in difficult cases. Because Commons was unwilling to compromise accuracy for simplicity, his theory of value has left us with concepts but without results.

At a more pragmatic level the institutionalist message was that the complexity of the behavioral effects of rule making was such that grand generalizations would not be forthcoming, at least not until a body of studies of relatively small-scale rule changes had been developed. Through the study of laws and cases the institutionalists made their contribution to economics in a series of insights and intuitive judgments of the impact of just such changes.

A second approach was more fruitful in the sense that it led at least to proposition-generating theory. Under this heading fall the magnificent dynamics, as William J. Baumol has called them.[5] They are the grand schemata, usually naturalistic in orientation, for which rule making is either purely epiphenomenal or strictly determined. Marx and the Social Darwinists shared at least this trait in common, that they considered the broad, long-run economic movements to be determined by forces built into the economy and over which man had very limited control. However, the Social Darwinists, like Adam Smith, believed that bad rules could distort natural development. William Graham Sumner at any rate does not seem to have had a clear notion as to what the consequences of bad or unnatural rules might be—beyond the slogan, "not-liberty, equality, survival of the unfittest." [6] In Book III of the *Wealth of Nations,* however, Smith develops at some length a theory to explain a reversal of the natural order of relative rates of development of town and country. This reversal he attributes to the relative power positions and propensities to form alliances among kings, barons, and towns. The result is the establishment of constitutional rules which are favorable to urban development, but these unnatural rules hinder greatly the development of the countryside. This must represent one of the earliest attempts at theorizing about the effects of rules on economic outcomes. However, one is never clear as to the extent to which naturalistic theories which admit unnatural outcomes are explanatory or normative in content. One might feel that this theory asserts no more than an irregular swerve in an essentially determined historical path from which rule-making behavior and its effects are derived rather than exerting any independent causal

---

[5] *Economic Dynamics* (New York: Macmillan, 1951).

[6] See the discussion in Richard Hofstadter, *Social Darwinism in American Thought* (Philadelphia: University of Pennsylvania Press, 1944).

impact. On the other hand one might feel that they assert that the "natural" way, though not strictly determined, is the best way, the one that ought to be followed. Only the first of these interpretations fits our methodological classification.

In the Marxian scheme, of course, rule making played an important role. The *bourgeoisie* made the rules of society in its own interest, thus bringing misery, then resentment, and finally revolution to the proletariat. But bourgeois behavior was determined by forces beyond the control of the individual, and at times Marx is even prepared to find their role as pawns of history pitiable.

For the most part the magnificent dynamists eliminated the process of rule making from their theories by assuming that rules, as the outcome of the rule-making process, can be considered to be determined by other factors in the environment. That is, since similar rules tend to be chosen in similar environments and to have similar consequences, the process of rule making can be skipped in the theory without having much effect on the accuracy of hypotheses generated by the theory. "In the long run differences in rules wash out."

A third approach—the general equilibrium analysis—has consisted in trying to find classes of situations in which it is not possible for individuals or groups to make rules. The competitive market environment was the great discovery in this area. The individual cannot make rules because all other participants in the market are indifferent to his behavior. Whether he enters or withdraws from the market, each buyer can buy what he wants from another seller and is indifferent as to the person of the seller. All participants have the information they need to make their decisions correctly, and utilities are independent so that informing and exhorting are excluded as effective or rational behavior. Buying above the market price or selling below it are possible instances of rule making, but they are excluded by the interests of the participants and the assumed unfeasibility of tied sales.

This is a powerful theory. It provides a very large number of mutually integrated results, describing aspects of the behavior of individual participants and the economy as a whole in terms of the amounts of goods and services produced and distributed among participants. It remains today the single most powerful and most important piece of analytical equipment available to the economist. This is true despite the many refutations that have appeared over the decades attacking as unrealistic the assumptions concerning tastes and technology. Even economists at times have seemed to accept the idea that the competitive model was at best of only normative significance. This is far from the truth, however, for much of the quantitative empirical work of economists is based on the assumption that prices are a reasonably accurate measure of relative scarcity and of the opportunity cost of alternative courses of economic action, an assumption whose only justification lies in the further assumption that the economy does indeed provide a rough approximation to the results of general equilibrium theory. However much one may rail at this theory, a preferable alternative *of comparable power* has yet to be developed.

Rules do play an important role in competitive equilibrium theory. The constitutional rules which define the organizational environment and set limits to the types of admissible actions are essential to the operation of a competitive economy. But these rules are assumed to be made by a political process which is exogenous to the economy. They are taken as given on the rather weak and often undefended ground that participants will see that it is in their own interest to make precisely these rules. This is an extension of the internal assumption that material self-interest governs the action of participants, a simplifying assumption whose prodigious power in an environment where individuals cannot make rules is the prime mover of the theoretical system. It is this assumption which constitutes the heart of the difficulties of communication often experienced between economists and other social scientists. The one side fails to appreciate the importance of rule making in many social contexts, while the other fails to appreciate the scope of the results obtainable when it can be assumed that rule making is a matter of secondary importance.

The last of the four great simplifying approaches of economics has been provided by game theory. It is difficult to characterize succinctly the nature of the contribution of game theory because a good part of its influence in social science has been indirect and intuitive. However, strictly speaking, games are events in which there are several participants (for our purposes all human), for which constitutional rules have been clearly prescribed and accepted by the participants (presumably because of attached sanctions), for which the possible outcomes are also clearly known, and for which the values of the outcomes to each participant are known to all. Within this context participants are allowed to make limited rules influencing the alternatives available to other participants. They may also make rules by simulating preferences (e.g., bluffing, a kind of *mis*informing) or possibly by making rules in small groups, i.e., forming coalitions. Even when the properties of games are thus drastically limited, there are few general statements that can be made about them; and, even for particular types of games, only a limited amount of information is available as to the nature of optimal behavior. Even less, often nothing, can be said about the *actual* behavior of participants so that the theory remains still almost entirely normative in content. Game theory provides even these limited results only for those situations in which the constitutional rules provide clear and unequivocal characterizations of the alternatives open to participants and precise information on the payoffs resulting from given choices.

Of these four approaches the two that appear to have been most successful—magnificent dynamics and competitive theory—in the sense that they generated a significant body of results, of conceivably falsifiable theorems, are the two that avoid dealing explicitly with rule making. Game theory, while admitting limited types of rule-making behavior, has produced propositions about games for the most part only in quite specific situations. To put it another way, the outcomes of most games are quite sensitive to a large number of environmental factors; consequently, only where the environment is specified in great detail can the outcomes be predicted with any confidence. It is rather ironic that this quite abstract theory should lead in the same direction that the institutionalists tried unsuccessfully to lead economists—toward study of the detail of the environment with little attempt at broad theorizing—though for different reasons.

Not all dynamics are magnificent. However, even at much lower levels of generalization the same methodological principle—that is, the assumption that rules are epiphenomenal—may be applied to model building. An example may be cited from the theory of the firm. Within traditional economic theory there has been no satisfactory analysis of the determinants of the relative sizes of firms in a given market environment. The problem which required explanation was generated by the empirical observation that in many industries firms of widely varying size and share of the market were able to persist for long periods of time while, on the other hand, the traditional theory of the firm at least suggest that in equilibrium surviving firms should have closely similar characteristics.

It cannot be said that this problem has been solved. However, two long steps toward explanation seem to have been taken. The first was the discovery that if firms are ranked in order of size—size being measured for example by value of assets—then there is a linear logarithmic relationship between rank number and size. The second was to point to the fact that this relationship is the steady state distribution of a stochastic process whose basic assumption is that at any point in time the probability of a given percentage increase in the size of a firm be independent both of its size at that moment and its past size.[7] The fit of the data to this relationship is far from perfect, but the data themselves are not of very satisfactory quality. The main point for our purposes, however, is to point to an explanatory theory which seems to have some power and yet makes no explicit assumptions about rules. There is only the implicit

---

[7] Apparently first formulated by R. Gibrat, Les inégalités économiques (Paris: Librairie du Recueil Sirey, 1931). Current interest seems to stem largely from Irma Adelman, "A Stochastic Analysis of the Size Distribution of Firms," Journal of the American Statistical Association, 53 (1958), 893-904, and Herbert Simon and C. Bonini, "The Size Distribution of Business Firms," American Economic Review, 48 (1958), 607-617.

requirement that, whatever the rules governing human interaction in this type of environment may be, they act in a manner which is consistent with the above mentioned independence. The assumption that size conveys no relative advantage in further size increases is surprising, and it may well be that the ultimate test of the theory will come from an empirical analysis of firm decision (rule) making with a view to evaluating this assumption. However, if further tests were to demonstrate that the theory has real power in explaining size distributions, then the shoe may well be on the other foot; that is, the assumption of the theory will be used to explain decision (rule) making in firms of varying size.[8]

This type of theory has other applications as well.[9] In all of them it seems that at best only a partial explanation of the observed phenomena can be offered in this way. When one considers the complexity of social life, it is after all a highly simplistic sort of theory. Though the results may be useful as they stand, further refinement would certainly be desirable; the question then arises: What procedure for refinement seems most promising? I suspect that methodological considerations do not give much insight here. It may well be that a few complications within the framework of magnificent dynamics will improve the theory a great deal; it may be that only by introducing rule making explicitly can further improvement be obtained. The obvious insight that at *some* point rule making becomes important is really of no help, even at this relatively low level of generalization.

THE CONCEPT OF ROLE AND ECONOMIC ANALYSIS

In the environment of theoretical competitive capitalism the behavior of the individual is not hard to understand. For example, the pressures on the firm are such that economic survival is achieved in the long run only by a maximum exertion of effort. A firm which does not achieve the best available technology will not survive in the long run. Nor can a family whose members' productivity does not provide a survival income survive in the long run within the economic system. In competitive capitalism the high pressure under which participants are forced to operate provides a strong justification for the emphasis on material interest as the dominant incentive.

---

[8] At present this would be a very shaky procedure indeed since the fact that this assumption generates the distribution does not imply that the observed relationship can only result from this assumption.

[9] It first became of interest to economists as "Pareto's law" of income distributions which was an inductive generalization to the linear logarithmic relationship. A stochastic process interpretation seems first to have been provided by D. G. Champernowne, "A Model of Income Distribution," *Economic Journal*, 58 (1953), 318-351. For a similar interpretation of city size distributions see Herbert Simon, "On a Class of Skew Distribution Functions," *Biometrika*, 52 (1952), 425-440.

However, it must be admitted that further refinements of the theory of competition have been in the direction of reintroducing rule making into the operation of the market system itself. To take a single example, George Stigler has investigated the effects of introducing into the competitive market ignorance by participants of sellers' prices.[10] Since acquiring information is costly, the participants will not generally try to discover the asking prices of all sellers. They will take into consideration several factors, including their own attitudes toward risk, in determining the amount of search they will undertake, and the range of asking prices that will persist in equilibrium. Under these assumptions price setting again becomes rule making since it significantly alters the environment of other participants.

Many of the results of the competitive model have also been derived for economies with quite different institutional environments. For such models the question arises as to whether under the new institutions it is reasonable to assume that rule-making behavior is excluded. In market socialism,[11] for example, the manager of a factory is a bureaucrat responding to instructions from the government in making decisions for the firm. Though his firm too may be eliminated by the market criteria, as applied by the authorities, he is presumably no longer fighting for economic survival in the sense of the competitive capitalist entrepreneur. But if this is the case, one may wonder whether the environment really compels or even encourages the hypothesized behavior by the managers. Obviously, someone is making rules for them, and we are back in that difficult and complex world of human interaction. The difficulty is that in shifting from competitive capitalism to market socialism there occurs some substitution of rules for impersonal market pressures.

At this point we may consider the way in which the concept of *role* may be applied in economic explanations. Problems of role arise when certain habitual forms of behavior occur which are not simply related to the personality of an individual viewed as a distinct and independent unit. Perhaps the most striking instance of role behavior is that of the actor, whose sudden assumption of manners and activities appropriate say only to a sixteenth-century king might otherwise seem most peculiar. More important, this behavior could not be predicted easily by reference to material interest. Not only do actors very frequently not have professional ambitions, but many important aspects of their behavior in their role seem inconsistent with interest: for example, displays of temperament. There does not seem to be any satisfactory theory of actors' be-

---

[10] "The Economics of Information," *Journal of Political Economy*, 69 (1961), 213-225.
[11] Reference, of course, is to the models presented by Abba Lerner and Oskar Lange during the 1930's, and not to later discussions of the problem by the latter author.

havior available, but should one develop, it would surely have to deal
effectively with the interaction of conflicting roles and of roles with
"basic" personality.

Though overt role contrasts are generally not so striking in other walks
of life, it seems clear that they are important in many situations, and
particularly in those in which behavior is strongly conditioned by frequent
human interaction, as is typically the case in the management hierarchies
of large organizations. It may be useful to suggest a way in which role
and role conflict may be used to describe such behavior and then to
interpret the behavioral assumptions of one or two recent economic
theories in terms of this description.[12]

From the point of view of the individual assuming it, there are essentially two elements in a role. The first is an environment, a set of
situations within which the role is deemed appropriate. The second is a
criterion which provides a decision as to which among the possible and
acceptable courses of action is best. To follow the simple example of the
actor, the environments in which it is appropriate to assume the role of
Henry VIII are easily discerned. The criterion is that assumed in determining which modes of behavior are best in this role, in making decisions relating to bearing, phrasing, extent of acceptance of director's
instructions, and the like. Though it would be very difficult to work this
characterization of the role out in detail, the nature of the approach
seems clear enough.

So it is with a bureaucrat. On accepting employment within a large
organization he is expected to make decisions in a special way within the
range of environments of interest to the organization. He assumes a role
criterion for these situations. If he assumes the role prescribed by his
superiors and if the role is feasible, in that it does lead unequivocally to
behavior which can be executed, the actions of the bureaucrat in his role
environment may be predicted with some accuracy. On the other hand,
the new member of the organization has been making decisions all his
life by some criteria. When faced with comparable situations as an em-
ployee, he may be aware of a conflict between the old and new criteria.
Or he may misunderstand the role expected of him. Or the role may not
be well defined. To the extent that these anomalies arise, the bureaucrat's
behavior becomes much less certain.

There is, however, a feature of economic organizations which may

---

[12] A highly simplified version of the role concept is presented here, as seems fitting,
since the aim is really to simplify things still further. However, it does not conflict
with some sociological definitions, for example, Talcott Parsons': "A role is the organized system of participation of an individual in a social system, with special
reference to the organization of that social system as a collectivity." *Social Structure
and Personality* (New York: Free Press, 1964), p. 261. An exception to the rule that
economists make little explicit use of the concept is Harvey Leibenstein, *Economic
Theory and Organizational Analysis* (New York: Harper, 1960), Part III.

provide a basis for substantial simplification of this problem. Economic organizations are typically rather worldly in their atmosphere and oriented toward the serving of rather well-defined material interests. To the extent that this ambience is absorbed by participants in economic organizations, a basis exists for evaluating and predicting behavior within the framework of defined roles.

Take the example of market socialism: the bureaucratic manager is instructed to adjust the rate of output of the product of his firm to the point at which price, which he takes as given, is equal to the marginal cost of producing the last unit of output. This role criterion is easy to state but not so easy to apply. If he is appropriately trained, the manager may understand its significance and in fact be able to apply it successfully. But he will frequently face situations in which because of uncertainties in his information the appropriate decision is not clear. To some extent his uncertainties may be reduced by including a rule for dealing with risk in his role criterion, but by the nature of things the uncertainties can never be eliminated. What is more, his superiors will often be unable to give good advice on these decisions because the decisions must be based on detailed information which either is not available to them or would be rather costly to assimilate. In such cases the role does not determine the decision, and the manager must fall back on some other criterion.

At this point the worldliness of most economic organizations may be called to the rescue. The manager may be assumed to act in these ambiguous cases in ways which tend to be of most benefit to him personally. And once his superiors recognize this behavior tendency, they may well find it expedient to cater to it. By providing material rewards for performing effectively in his assigned role the authorities not only provide themselves with a basis for controlling outcomes in ambiguous situations, but also provide the bureaucrat with a new role; for the authorities will rarely have direct evidence as to the extent to which a bureaucrat has actually assumed the assigned role criterion in his decision making. What they observe, and what they must reward if they are to provide rewards, is the manifestations of decision making—the results achieved. But if the bureaucrat comes to recognize this action on the part of his superiors, he may well assume yet another role: that of simulating as high a level of performance as possible. His superiors too are then faced with a new task: they must determine a set of rewards and sanctions which will tend to make actual performance, from the manager's point of view, at least equivalent in value to the simulation of maximum performance.

The trend of the argument should now be clear. It is suggested that in environments in which worldliness is important roles may be characterized in terms of the self-interest of the participants. To the extent that this is true, it will be possible to anticipate role behavior by studying the environment within which participants function, with a view to understanding their interests. This cuts through much of the bewildering maze of interactions that constitutes the daily life of most bureaucrats. Of course, it is an oversimplification. Cultural traits, personality types, ignorance [13] and many other factors either distort the operation of self-interest or make it difficult for the participant to apply his criterion. But it does appear to be a suggestive device for at least sketching in the probable actions of members of a bureaucracy.

This assumption that role criteria are dominated by interest appears to be the standard interpretation of economic analysis. It motivates both game theory and the earlier analyses of market conflict. It makes possible a separation of the role of an actor in economic organizations and the role of family member, a dichotomy which permeates economic analysis though it is not generally made explicit. It has been used in hypothesizing alternative objectives for decision makers in various types of organizations, such as large oligopolistic firms and socialist firms controlled by worker managers. It is in applications such as these that the power of the approach becomes apparent. In such situations the environments are fairly well specified, so that if a means can be found for determining the criterion for a participant, outcomes can be determined with some precision. And interest provides the basis for determining the effective role criterion.

By no means is all economics based on this assumption about behavior. Already mentioned is the special case of competitive capitalist theory; though in refining the theory, interest-dominated roles are being introduced. Implicit in the competitive model (as in some other more recent applications, such as team theory) is the assumption that a great many participants do as they are told. Each organization in competitive capitalism is a successful dictatorship ruled by an omniscient dictator, whose power is limited only by the existence of comparable alternatives for each successful participant. In team theory cooperation under uncertainty is analyzed with a view to determining optimal rules of behavior for participants, on the assumption that they will in fact assume the assigned roles.[14] The danger in this approach lies in what might be called the assumption of institutional stability. Participants, especially

---

[13] For an analysis of attitudes and background on role criteria see the pioneering work of R. A. Gordon, *Business Leadership in the Large Corporation* (Washington: Brookings, 1945), especially Chap. 11. Anthony Downs of the Rand Corporation has developed a theory of bureaucratic behavior in which personality types are distinguished in terms of their adjustments to formalized roles. For an assessment of research on the effects of ignorance and uncertainty on the decision process see James March and H. Simon, *Organizations* (New York: Wiley, 1958), Chap. 6. It should be noted that none of these approaches has as yet resulted in a broad substantive theory of the results of decision making of a scope and power remotely comparable to that of the competitive model of capitalism.

[14] J. Marschak, "Elements for a Theory of Teams," *Management Science*, 1 (1955), 127-137.

those under considerable pressure, may seek other forms of behavior whose results are preferable when all factors, including the likely re-actions within the environment, are taken into account. Thus, competi-tive capitalist entrepreneurs have an incentive to merge in order to reduce the risk of ruin in the short run, an incentive which can easily destroy the properties of long-run equilibrium derived from the theory. Similar possibilities emerge from team-theoretic solutions to organiza-tional problems, just as bluffing changes the outcomes in a poker game. This danger can be avoided only by examining carefully the options available to participants in the hypothesized environment from the point of view of some estimate of the roles they will actually assume, that is, taking account of the ways in which the assigned roles will be modified by the interest of the participants.

POLITICAL DECISION PROCESSES AND ECONOMIC ANALYSIS

A somewhat different problem arises in highly structured decisions such as those of the formalized political process. In this type of situation the constitutional rules for the organization have been fully legitimated —that is, the participants are willing to seek their various goals subject to the constraint that the constitutional rules not be broken.[15] A case of some interest within this framework is that in which the preferences of participants, whatever they may be, are to be converted into decisions. Majority-rule voting is perhaps the most common procedure of this kind.

It would seem that the study of these processes stands clearly outside the realm of economics. However, there has recently been a good deal of interest in such processes among economic theorists, an interest which was aroused by some problems in welfare economics. As the study of the properties of competitive capitalism continued, it became clear that a number of deviations from conditions consistent with the optimality of competitive equilibrium were essential features of modern capitalism. Since they could not be eliminated from consideration, it became a matter of interest to economists to find ways of generating optimum results in these areas. Examples are technology, for which average costs cease falling only after a firm has produced a substantial fraction of total out-put, so that technology itself imposes monopoly elements on the market if production is to be efficient; and external effects, in which the action of one decision unit affects the environment of others—the case of inter-dependent utilities or technology.

---

[15] The legitimation may be thought of as arising because of a valuation of the gains and losses in terms of security and stability of expectations which result from general acceptance of these rules; that is, these are the—positive and negative—sanc-tions attaching to the constitutional rules.

In the case of external effects it appears that there are no market-like decentralized processes which will lead participants to an optimum.[16] However, there may be an optimal equilibrium point if the state levies appropriate taxes and subsidies on participants. Having thus reached the conclusion that political decision making would necessarily play a role in optimal economic decision making, some economists have gone one step further and asked what sort of political decision-making apparatus would yield the desired results. Since majority rule is a very common decision-making process and can be idealized into a relatively simple formal characterization,[17] the properties of majority rule and majority rule-like processes came under study first.

The first result of this study was rather surprising. It was found that majority rule is in general an inconsistent decision process.[18] That is, if the preferences of participants among alternatives are not limited, except to assume that each participant acts consistently, then the ranking of alternatives which results from majority-rule voting will at times be inconsistent in the sense that, though say alternative A is preferred by a majority to B and B to C, alternative C is preferred to A by a majority.

As yet no optimal political decision process has been discovered which will serve to eliminate cases of nonoptimality in the economic results of the freely competitive market system.[19] Indeed one may question the meaning of the term "optimum" where group decisions are made in an environment of conflicting wishes.[20] However, there is one possible approach which integrates role analysis with political decision processes to analyze decision making within an economic environment, thus providing a highly interdisciplinary, formal analytical framework. Suppose that majority rule, or some other specified group decision process, is to be used to make group decisions in an economic context, such as that of the

---

[16] Kenneth Arrow and L. Hurwicz, "Decentralization and Computation in Resource Allocation," in *Essays in Economics and Econometrics*, ed. R. Pfouts (Chapel Hill, N.C.: University of North Carolina Press, 1960).

[17] Kenneth May, "A Set of Independent Necessary and Sufficient Conditions for Simple Majority Decision," *Econometrica*, 20 (1952), 680-684.

[18] Kenneth Arrow, *Social Choice and Individual Values* (New York: Wiley, 1951).

[19] Arrow, in the work referred to in note 18 above, actually studied a class of such decision processes which is more general than simple majority rule. There has been a good deal of controversy over one of his assumptions about the properties of a "good" social decision process. This is the assumption that the introduction or elimination of alternatives to be considered will not affect the ranking of alternatives which occur in both situations. Not much effort has been devoted as yet to the study of social decision processes in which this assumption is relaxed, partly because majority rule is in such common use, but partly too because bargaining and the simulation of preferences seem to play a more central role in this more general case, and these phenomena are notoriously intractable to analysis.

[20] James Buchanan, "Social Choice, Democracy and Free Markets" and "Individual Choice in Voting and the Market," both in *Journal of Political Economy*, 42 (1954), 114-123, 334-343.

board of directors of a nationalized firm or the members of a regulatory commission. Each member of the board represents certain interests which define his role as a board member. The environment in which the board functions determines the range of decisions to be made and may be sufficiently specific to provide a good basis for estimating the interests of represented groups. Armed with a knowledge of preferences determined by role analysis and a knowledge of the decision process, the analyst may be able to predict the range of likely choices by boards of varying composition.

Of course, the usefulness of such a procedure depends entirely upon the extent to which the results are influenced by the particular simplifications built into the model. When viewed as a general description of political decision making, the idea that roles and rules interact to generate some decisions smacks of the descriptive vacuity typical of much institutionalist programmatics. The two key assumptions which give the approach some specific content, namely that role is dominated by the interests of represented groups and that decisions are the direct result of aggregating the resulting preferences in accordance with the constitutional rules, will be most likely to work for economic decisions, but even here the assumptions may at times involve excessive oversimplification from the point of view of generating *useful* results.

INTERDISCIPLINARY ECONOMIC ANALYSIS

The isolation from other disciplines which has marked economics in the past has not yet disappeared, but it is certainly on the wane. Probably the major forces tending to break down this separation have come from the press of practical problems and the revolutionary increase in information available about society. As we come to know more about society, the details of human interaction in all their complexity become more obvious and the rigidity of current disciplinary partitions tends to be revealed. And for the problem-oriented, this is all the more true. In research on such problems as war and peace, education and city planning, interdisciplinary communication has become a commonplace. Such contacts naturally generate an interest in integrated analytical approaches.[21]

To some extent theory has lagged behind the practitioners in looking to other fields for insights. This is a reflection partly of the more extensive formal development of economic theory than of other social sciences, partly of the greater amenability of much economic activity to quantitative description, and partly of the growing importance of activities burdened with externalities. Even that bastion of isolationism, the study of

---

[21] An example of such an attempt is Kenneth Boulding, *Conflict and Defense* (New York: Harper, 1962).

the competitive model and welfare economics, appears to be crumbling before the need for a more inclusive theoretical treatment.

Interest in expanding the scope of theory is not necessarily a harbinger of results. There is no theory of rules at present, and it may be that there never will be. At present economists and others will have to work up bits and pieces of rule analysis on their own, tailoring their work to suit the particular organizational environment in which they find their research problems. The institutionalists have shown us that premature generalization leads to programs but not results; the magnificent dynamists and competitive theorists have shown us that excessive simplification leads to error. But the former have also shown us that rules play a vital role as external effects in much social action and the latter that *appropriate* simplification can yield a rich harvest.

KELVIN LANCASTER

Kelvin Lancaster, Ph.D., University of London, is Professor of Political Economy at Johns Hopkins University. He has been engaged in research in the fields of economic theory and mathematical economics. He is currently carrying on research in the problems of utilizing qualitative data in economic and other systems, and in the development of a new approach to the theory of the consumer.

ESSAY

13

PROBLEMS OF THE RELATIONSHIP BETWEEN the behavior of individual elements and the behavior of aggregates are not peculiar to economics, but these problems appear in economics in a context which is often crucial and in a form which is relatively intractable.

In comparison with the aggregation problems of physics, those of economics differ most in that the level of direct awareness in economics is at the individual (micro-) level, while the aggregates (macro-variables) are abstractions. The reverse is typically true of physics, where, for example, the pressure of a gas (aggregate behavior of molecules) is observable about as directly as any physical phenomenon, while the behavior of a single molecule in that aggregate is observable only in an indirect fashion. Furthermore, since the population of molecules in a cubic centimeter of gas (a volume small for an ordinary laboratory experiment) is something like 100 million times the whole human population, the reliance on large-number

Economic

Aggregation

and

Additivity

statistical generalizations in physics is more valid than in economics even if human populations were composed of individuals much less diversified than is the case.

Among the behavioral sciences, economics occupies a special place in its willingness to attempt to treat micro- and macro-relationships on an equal footing within the same discipline. Compare, for example, the division of labor, technique, and theory formulation between psychology and sociology. Economists working primarily with macro-relationships may often wish they were freed from the burden of continuous comparison with the results of micro-economics.

The aggregation problem in economics is concerned with the relationship between four kinds of things. These are micro-variables (the variables which impinge directly on the individual decision maker), micro-relationships (the results of individuals' actions with respect to the micro-variables), macro-variables (variables which have lost some of the labeling, e.g., with respect to individual decision makers, individual commodities, or individual time periods that characterize micro-variables), and macro-relationships (relationships holding between variables, at least one of which is a macro-variable). The aggregation problem arises because the macro-variables are functionally related to the micro-variables, the micro-variables to each other, and the macro-variables to each other. There are more relationships than can be chosen independently and the problem is that of consistency between them.

A classic aggregation problem is that of the aggregate demand function for, say, bread. Consumer theory leads to the statement of a micro-demand relationship between each individual's demand for bread, the price of bread, prices of other goods, and the individual's income. By analogy, the most fertile breeder of macro-hypotheses, we might investigate whether we can find a satisfactory relationship between the total demand for bread (a macro-variable), the price of bread and of other goods (note that prices, in perfect markets, may be both micro- and macro-variables), and the level of some macro-variable which we can regard as aggregate income. The same model may be more highly aggregated by replacing the individual prices of commodities other than bread by some macro-variable representing the "general level" of prices.

Although the above formulation of the classic problem conveys the spirit of the quest, it is too imprecise to set up the problem for solution. Taking the micro-relations and the micro-variables as given, we have alternative approaches to the macro-problem. We can define the macro-variables and search for the form of the macro-relationship that is compatible, or we can posit the existence of a macro-relationship of a certain form and then search for compatible relationships between the micro-variables and the macro-variables.

Aggregation is not a single problem, but a set of related problems since macro-variables are constructs rather than "natural" variables (although some constructs, by virtue of usage and data processed in some standard way, may come almost to be accepted as "natural" variables—e.g., Gross National Product). Therefore, freedom in the construction of macro-variables and freedom in the construction of macro-relationships are substitutes for each other. Although a macro-variable may be thought of as representing some general concept, such as the price level or national income, from an operational point of view it is simply a functional relationship between a set of micro-variables, typically linear, and frequently a simple sum of micro-variables.

Given the freedom of construction of both macro-variables and macro-theory, aggregation theory is primarily concerned with consistency between variables and relationships. Two main approaches have already been suggested.

(1) Given micro-theory and micro-variables, posit a macro-theory; then search for relationships between macro- and micro-variables consistent with the relationship between the micro- and macro-theories. Since we choose the MICro-theory, MAcro-theory and macro-Variables in that order, we shall refer to this approach as MICMAV.

(2) Given micro-theory and micro-variables, define the macro-variables and then search for the consistent macro-theory. We shall refer to this as MIVMAC, since we choose MIcro-theory, macro-Variables, MACro-theory.

The MICMAV approach has been championed by Lawrence R. Klein and used extensively by Henri Theil, the MIVMAC by Kenneth O. May. As we shall see, one approach or the other may be useful in given circumstances. On the whole, the MICMAV approach has been more popular in empirical work; the MIVMAC approach is perhaps more appealing at the theoretical level.

A third approach—which does not exhaust the possibilities—is to come in from the other direction. It may be that the macro-theory presents itself directly, perhaps based on some observed empirical regularity at the macro-level. It is implicit in this approach that the relationships between macro- and micro-variables must be part of the data, and the problem is to discover the implicit restrictions on the micro-theory. In conformity with the terms already introduced, we shall refer to this third approach as MAVMIC.

We can examine the simpler aspects of the aggregation problem in terms of a simple model of the Keynesian savings function. This model was, historically, the seed from which grew modern macro-economics, although some of the important aspects of the aggregation problem had arisen in earlier discussions of the Index Number Problem.

We assume the existence of a simple micro-theory which states that, for each individual, saving is a function of both his income and the rate of interest. We shall further simplify the relationship by supposing it to be linear (this linearity assumption is crucial to most aggregation) with constant coefficients. In a complex economy, it should be noted, the relationship under discussion may not truly be at the micro-level since the consumer's decision to save in each of the ways open to him (cash, bonds, capital goods, etc.) will have its own functional relationship and the total savings of the individual (in money terms) will involve aggregation over these different commodities. Furthermore, the relationship will often involve aggregation over time since we may be concerned with total savings over a period longer than that for which the individual actually makes his decisions. In our assumptions we shall overcome these problems by supposing that savings can only be made in one commodity, and we shall also set aside a set of difficulties that may be critical in an operational model by supposing that all prices (other than the rate of interest) are constant. Given all the above, we can write the savings relationship for the ith individual as

$$s_i = a_i + b_i y_i + c_i r \tag{1}$$

where

$$s_i, y_i = \text{savings and income}$$
$$r = \text{rate of interest}$$
$$a_i, b_i, c_i = \text{constant coefficients.}$$

All individuals will be assumed to possess savings functions of the same form, but with their own personal values of a_i, b_i, c_i.

By analogy with the micro-relationships, we shall examine the possibility of a macro-relation of the form

$$S = A + BY + Cr \tag{2}$$

where S, Y are macro-variables analogous, in a manner yet to be determined, to the micro-variables s_i, y_i and A, B, C are coefficients. The rate of interest, being an information variable rather than an operational quantity, is the same in both macro- and micro-relations.

As pointed out above, we may take approach MICMAV, provisionally accepting (2) and seeking definitions of S, Y (in terms of s_i, y_i) which are consistent with both (1) and (2), or we may take approach MIVMAC in which we accept definitions of S, Y (chosen, perhaps, to conform with empirically available macro-quantities) and examine whether (1) and (2) can be consistent.

Let us first simply sum the relationships (1) over all individuals (n in number), obtaining

$$s_i = \Sigma a_i + \Sigma b_i y_i + r \Sigma c_i \tag{3}$$

If we define the macro-variable S as the sum of individual savings, the direct summation immediately gives the relationships

$$S = \Sigma \; s_i$$

$$A = \Sigma \; a_i$$

$$C = \Sigma \; c_i$$

between (2) and (3).

It is the macro-variable Y and its corresponding coefficient B which present the aggregation problems. These problems would disappear if all individuals had identical marginal propensities to save (i.e., $b_i = b$, all i). In this case, which involves one of the simplest forms of an *aggregating postulate*, we would have $BY = b \; \Sigma \; y_i$, so that on the MICMAV approach, defining Y as the simple sum of individual incomes would solve the problem. Since this definition would be the most likely to be chosen in the MIVMAC approach, there would be a simple solution here also.

It should be noted that the above aggregating postulate requires identity only for the coefficients in the term with aggregation problems. The coefficients a_i and c_i may differ between individuals to any extent, provided the b_i coefficients do not. In spite of the simplicity of this aggregating postulate, we do not expect that individuals will have identical parameters; in fact, it is already assuming a great deal to suppose that the functional form of the savings relationship is the same for all. Nevertheless, the identity postulate, which gives consistency between the micro- and macro-theories under all circumstances, is implicit if not always explicit in many economic models. Most models in which aggregation has been carried out, but no explicit discussion of the aggregation process is given, are operated upon in a way which implicitly requires the identity postulate.

We shall assume henceforth that the identity postulate, which solves linear aggregation problems, but not necessarily others, is not applicable.

If we take the MICMAV approach, consistency between the micro- and macro-relationships can only be obtained by defining either S or Y to be a *weighted* sum of the corresponding micro-variables. If we take S as the direct sum of the s_i's, then we have

$$BY = \Sigma \; b_i y_i$$

Since we have assumed, on this approach, that the macro-coefficients are constants and independent of the micro-variables (but not, of course, the micro-parameters), let us try the relationship

$$B = \frac{1}{n} \; \Sigma \; b_i$$

with the macro-coefficient a simple average of the micro-coefficients. Substitution in the macro-relationship gives immediately the consistency condition, that

$$Y = \sum (b_i/B) y_i \tag{4}$$

that is, Y must be defined as the weighted sum of the individual incomes, the weight for each individual being the ratio of his marginal propensity to save to the community average. This definition of Y is not a "natural" definition; it does not conform to any standard statistical series; it is a solution only to the problem in hand and has no special use for any other aggregate income problem; it depends upon the exact distribution of income at each period; but it makes the micro- and macro-relationships always consistent. In spite of these apparent drawbacks, the above type of solution has been called by Theil *perfect aggregation* because of its consistency properties when the micro-quantities are not known a priori but must be estimated from a mixture of micro- and macro-data. Because of the inherent disadvantages of the method, however, Theil's designation is not a happy one. Indeed, there is no such thing as perfect aggregation; so no aggregating technique should bear the name.

If one takes the MIVMAC approach, and chooses the definition of Y as the standard one of the direct sum of individual incomes, then it is clear that B must be a weighted sum. Substitution gives, as the relationship between the macro- and micro-coefficients,

$$B = \frac{1}{n} \sum \frac{y_i}{(Y/n)} b_i \tag{5}$$

where B is the weighted average of the b_i's, the weights being the ratio of the individual's income to the community average. This solution has the same consistency properties as the previous one. We now have the macro-variable in the form in which it is generally used in economics and in which empirical data will generally be obtainable, but at the expense of having the coefficient B sensitive to changes in the distribution of income.

It is obvious at this point that the choice between the MIVMAC and MICMAV approaches is not between an approach which solves the problem and one that does not, but simply between having a fixed coefficient and recomputing the variable with changes in the income distribution, or using standard statistical macro-variables and recomputing the coefficient when income changes.

In this case, but not necessarily in other models, income distribution between individuals is not a macro-effect. A satisfactory macro-theory should surely have both coefficients and variables which are independent of phenomena that are regarded as essentially micro-effects. Such a theory can only be founded on an *aggregating assumption* of some kind, additional to the asumptions of the micro-theory, macro-equations, and macro-variable definitions. The nature of this assumption is more crucial than the choice between MIVMAC and MICMAV approaches. The aggregating postulate will depend upon the model in question, but we can distinguish between postulates that are essentially deterministic and those that are essentially statistical in character.

A deterministic postulate in the example with which we are concerned would be the "identical individuals" postulate. Another, weaker, would be the assumption that the income distribution is constant, i.e., all incomes change in the same proportion. Then, if $Y = \Sigma\ y_i$, we have $y_i = k_iY$, with k_i constant, and

$$BY = Y\ (\ \Sigma\ k_ib_i) \tag{6}$$

where the expression in parentheses is constant, so that the problem is easily solved. The constant distribution postulate is superior to the identical individuals postulate since it provides both for an heterogeneous population and a course of action if the income distribution does change.

At the level of simplification of some macro-theories, a deterministic aggregating postulate of this kind may be a relatively small addition to the list of other abstractions from a complete description of the economy.

A statistical aggregating postulate may be more rewarding and more acceptable. Continuing with our example, let us denote the simple means of the individual incomes and the marginal propensities to save by y, b. We then have

$$b_iy_i\ =\ nby\ +\ \Sigma\ (b_i{-}b)\,(y_i{-}y)\ +\ \Sigma\ b(y_i{-}y)\ +\ \Sigma\ y(b_i{-}b)$$

$$=\ nby\ +\ \Sigma\ (b_i{-}b)\,(y_i{-}y) \tag{7}$$

$$=\ bY\ +\ nCov(b_iy_i)$$

if Y is defined as the simple sum of individual incomes.

If the marginal propensities to save are uncorrelated with the incomes, the expected value of the covariance term is zero. We can then write the macro-equation

$$S\ =\ na\ +\ bY\ +\ ncr \tag{8}$$

where all the coefficients are simple averages of the individual coefficients in the micro-equations and the macro-variables are simple sums of the micro-variables. Although we have referred to this postulate as a statistical postulate, all we have done in fact is use arithmetic and terms from statistics. The extent to which the macro-theory is truly statistical depends upon whether we assume, deterministically, that the covariance term is always zero, or, statistically, that the actual set of individuals being aggregated is a sample from a population with a bivariate distribution having zero covariance over the whole population.

A statistical assumption of the above kind is in the true spirit of the aggregation method. Whether a particular statistical aggregating postulate is acceptable must be decided separately, either on a priori grounds or by a test of macro-predictions. In the example given, some would argue that there are a priori grounds for expecting the covariance term to be positive since the marginal propensity to save would rise with income. If this were true, however, it would be a denial of the linearity of the micro-equations (1), and we cannot expect inappropriate micro-theory to lead to satisfactory aggregation.

So far, we have been concerned with a completely linear aggregation problem, in which the micro-equations, macro-equations, and macro-variable definitions were all linear functions.

A good example of a nonlinear aggregation problem, and at the same time an illustration of the so far neglected MAVMIC approach (proceeding from the macro to the micro) is provided by the Cobb-Douglas production function. This function was originally advanced as the form that fitted empirical relationships discovered between certain macro-variables. In one of its simpler versions, the Cobb-Douglas function is of the form

$$X = aK^b L^c \tag{9}$$

where the macro-variables X, K, L represent the aggregate output of manufacturing industry and the total capital stock and labor used in manufacturing. X and K, and possibly L, involve problems of commodity aggregation, but for the present purpose of illustration we shall assume that output and capital are single commodities.

We face a straightforward problem of the MAVMIC kind, namely what production functions for individual firms are consistent with (9) and with the definitions of X, K, L as simple sums?

The obvious approach is to try the hypothesis that individual firms are miniature versions of the whole manufacturing sector, with coefficients a, b, c the same for all firms and for the sector. In the straightforward linear case this identity postulate reduced the aggregation problem to a triviality. This is no longer true since we know from classical inequality theory that, in general,

$$(\Sigma_i k_i)^b (\Sigma_i l_i)^c \neq \Sigma_i k_i^b l_i^c$$

We can make the aggregating postulate that the capital to labor ratio, r, is the same for all firms, a condition that is known to be satisfied if firms behave in accord with the micro-theory of perfect competition and have identical production functions. With this postulate we have

$$(\Sigma_i k_i)^b (\Sigma_i l_i)^c = r^b (\Sigma_i l_i)^{b+c}$$

and

$$\Sigma_i k_i^b l_i^c = r^b \Sigma_i l_i^{b+c}$$

If, and only if, $b+c = 1$ (the production functions exhibit constant returns to scale), is the aggregating postulate sufficient to solve the problem. In general, if $b+c = l$ there is no solution to the aggregation problem except that, if all firms have identical sizes (measured by l_i) as well as identical capital to labor ratios, then the sum of the micro-relations differs from the macro-relation only by the constant multiple n^{b+c-l}, where n is the number of firms.

The above examples have all involved but a single aggregation, over individuals or over firms. Typically, macro-theory may require aggregation over commodities as well as, or in place of, aggregation over individuals, and may also require aggregation over time. Aggregation over time is frequently implicit in macro-models, and, although it presents problems, no different in principle (though usually less difficult in practice) from those of other types of aggregation, it is infrequently discussed explicitly. A general macro-theory may contain, therefore, a double or triple aggregation, compounding all the problems of a single aggregation.

Suppose we have a micro-theory giving a simple linear relationship, for the ith individual, between his demand for the jth commodity, the price of that commodity and of other commodities, and his income, of the form

$$x_{ij} = a_{ij}p_j + b_{ij}y_i \qquad (10)$$

where there are m commodities and n individuals. Relations of the same form, but with different coefficients, are supposed to hold for all commodities and all individuals. This is an extremely simplified relationship since no price other than its own is assumed to affect the demand for the commodity.

We seek to determine whether, and under what conditions, an analogous macro-relationship

$$X = AP + BY \qquad (11)$$

is consistent with the micro-relationships. The variables X, P, Y represent, in a yet undefined way, the aggregate demand for commodities in general, the general level of commodity prices, and aggregate income.

Since we are faced with a double aggregation, over commodities as well as individuals, there is a choice as to which aggregation should be carried out first. If we aggregate over individuals first, then we have a problem, in this phase, exactly analogous to that of the savings function discussed earlier. Now, however, the success of the first phase of the aggregation must be judged in the light of its suitability for the second phase. In particular, the MICMAV approach with macro-variables chosen as weighted sums (so called perfect aggregation) presents great difficulties here if it is applied to a first phase which consists of aggregation over individuals. For, as we have seen, the macro-variable representing income will be a weighted average with different weights for each commodity so that the second phase of the aggregation (over commodities) will involve aggregating these commodity-specific income variables as well as the commodity and price variables. If, on the other hand, the first aggregation is in terms of the MIVMAC approach, with Y defined as the simple sum of individual incomes, then this variable requires no further aggregation over commodities.

We shall adopt the MIVMAC approach, choosing the macro-variables before the macro-theory. The variable X involves a double aggregation over individuals and over commodities, and we shall assume that it is the direct sum over individuals, to obtain a total demand X_j for each commodity, and that the aggregate demand is defined as the weighted sum of the X_j's, with weights assumed to be given. These weights can be supposed to be those of some published series of indices of total demand, subject to a scale factor. In the same way we shall assume that some published series for the general level of prices is to be used and that the macro-price variable P is the weighted sum of the prices of individual commodities with given weights, there being no aggregation problem over individuals. Finally, we shall assume that the income variable, which has no problem of aggregation over commodities, is the simple sum of individual incomes. The macro-variables are then specified:

$$X = \sum_j \; (w_j \sum_i \; x_{ij})$$

$$P = \sum_j \; k_j p_j \tag{12}$$

$$Y = \sum_i \; y_i$$

where the w's and k's are the weights of the commodity index and the price index, respectively.

First, aggregate the micro-relationships (10) over individuals, obtaining the total demand for each commodity in the form

$$X_j = p_j \sum_i a_{ij} + \sum_i b_{ij} y_i \tag{13}$$

The price term presents no problems and the income term can be treated as in the earlier example. In a form amenable for the introduction of a statistical aggregating postulate, we can rewrite (13) as

$$X_j = n a_j p_j + b_j Y + n Cov(b_{ij} y_i) \tag{14}$$

where a_j, b_j are the simple averages, over all individuals, of the coefficients relevant to the jth commodity.

The second aggregation involves weighting the relationships (14) in accord with the weights used in the definition of X. Carrying out this aggregation, we obtain

$$X = \sum_j w_j x_j = n \sum_j a_j w_j p_j + (\sum_j b_j w_j)Y + n \sum_j w_j Cov(b_{ij} y_i) \tag{15}$$

Consider the price term. Our macro-price variable is a weighted sum of the p_j's, but with weights k_j. Manipulation of the term, however, immediately gives

$$n \sum_j a_j w_j p_j = n \sum_j a_j (w_j/k_j) k_j p_j = na'P + mCov(w_j a_j/k_j, k_j p_j) \quad (16)$$

where a' is the weighted sum of the a_j's, using the ratios w_j/k_j as weights.

From (11), (15), and (16), we can identify the coefficients of the macro-equations as follows

$$A = \sum_j (w_j/k_j) \left(\sum_i a_{ij} \right)$$

$$B = \sum_j w_j \left(\frac{1}{n} \sum_i b_{ij} \right)$$

and write the results of the double aggregation as

$$X = AP + BY + c_1 + c_2 \quad (17)$$

where c_1, c_2 are the covariance terms

$$c_1 = n \sum_j w_j Cov(b_{ij}, y_i)$$

$$c_2 = mCov(w_j a_j/k_j, k_j p_j)$$

We can consider the aggregation solved if we can make statistical aggregating postulates which reduce the covariance terms to zero. The first covariance term presents no great problems. It is certainly zero if, for each commodity, income effects vary between individuals independently of incomes. This is a restriction that is not unacceptable in principle, although its acceptability in a particular model must be judged *ad hoc*. In fact, we can make do with a weaker assumption that the weighted sum of the covariances vanishes, an assumption that will be satisfied if the mean covariance is zero and the distribution of the covariances is independent of the distribution of the commodity weights.

The second covariance term presents more considerable problems. The variables whose joint variation is under scrutiny are composite, with k_i appearing as an element of both. It is well known that, in general, the covariance of these composite variables will not be zero even if the components w_j, a_j, k_j, p_j are all unrelated. The existence of a variable on both sides will give rise to "spurious" correlation which gives rise, in spite of the name, to a real problem. The only simple assumption that will remove this spurious correlation is one that removes k_j from one of the composite variables. If we are free to choose the weights for the macro-variables X or P—which runs contrary to our MIVMAC approach—then we can choose either the w's proportional to the k's or the k's proportional to the a_j's so that the k_j's cancel out of the composite variable $w_j a_j/k_j$. In fact, choosing the k's proportional to the a_j's makes economic sense since we are weighting our commodity price index in accordance with the average effects, over all individuals, of price on quantity demanded. This, however, is equivalent to adopting a MIVMAC approach to the aggregation over individuals and a MICMAV approach to the aggregation over commodities. There is probably no harm in this, but if the aim of our macro-theory is to utilize some existing price index, it is not useful.

Another possible approach to the problem of the covariance terms, especially c_2, is to find an aggregating postulate that makes them constant and independent of the macro-variables, even if not zero. In the case of c_2, for example, if the parameters a_j, w_j, k_j are uncorrelated, the value of the spurious correlation between the composite variables in c_2 can be computed easily in terms of the variances of the components. Since all these variances except that of p_j are constant for all values of the macro-variables, if it is possible to postulate that p_j has a constant variance (a postulate that might be acceptable in some circumstances), then we can obtain a macro-equation of the form

$$X = AP + BY + C \qquad (18)$$

where C is constant. This amounts to incorporation of the "aggregation bias" (i.e., the covariance terms) into the macro-system itself, always possible if this bias is constant.

So far we have proceeded on the assumption that the micro-theory is established and that the coefficients of the micro-equations are known at the outset. This is the situation usually assumed in theoretical problems of aggregation or in theoretical model building. In a typical situation of an empirical kind this may not be so, and the coefficients of the micro-equations may have to be estimated from a mixture of macro- and micro-data. It is not proposed to deal with such estimating problems here, or with the allied problems of using the results for prediction, since they are technical in character and have been extensively discussed by Theil. Broadly speaking, Theil's technique is to regress each micro-variable on the macro-variables, then to derive the coefficients of the equations from the resulting coefficients of the regression equations.

As already mentioned, aggregation over time may occur instead of, or together with, other forms of aggregation. Either of the micro-relationships (1) or (10) may be considered to refer to some time period, say a month. The behavior over a full year then involves aggregation. For an individual, time aggregation may be quite simple. The aggregation is likely to involve simple summation, and the simplest aggregating postulate—that the coefficients are invariant between one period and another (equivalent to the postulate of identical individuals in the case of aggregation over individuals)—is usually quite acceptable. Not all time aggregation involves simple sums, however, since some macro-variables may be "seasonally adjusted" or involve some other form of weighting. In any case, if time aggregation occurs as part of a multiple aggregation problem so that, for example, income varies over individuals and over time, while prices vary over time as well as between commodities, the resulting problems are anything but trivial.

In this rather pragmatic study we have made of typical problems of aggregation and additivity in economics, two aspects of the problems have emerged as of special importance. These are the linearity of the relationships and the nature of the aggregating postulates. We shall now turn briefly to examine the light thrown on these by the ordinary structure of economic theory.

Although nonlinear aggregation problems may sometimes be solved on an *ad hoc* basis, the apparatus of ordinary aggregation techniques is based on the linearity of the micro-equations, macro-equations, and macro-variable definitions. To what extent does economic theory support the use of linear relations in these contexts?

It is useful to distinguish between three types of linearity here. If the fundamental relationships are themselves of a strictly linear form, we have strict linearity. If the fundamental relationships are nonlinear, but can be represented by a linear relationship to a sufficient degree of approximation (which ought to be, but never seems to be, specified) for variations over the relevant range (again, this is usually left unspecified), then we have approximate linearity. Except in the definitions of the macro-variables, strict linearity is rarely characteristic of micro-theories. Approximate linearity is very widely used and the basic arithmetic of aggregation is the same for strict and approximate linearity but, as we shall see, the acceptability of an aggregating postulate may depend crucially upon whether the linearity is strict or only approximate.

Another form of linearity also emerges from the structure of economic theory. This, which we may call quasi-linearity, exists when the fundamental relationships are nonlinear, but the actual behavior is linear because it is confined to a linear path on the behavior functions. Quasi-linearity occurs over a wide area of economic theory. Among the best-known examples are the long-run behavior of a firm when factor prices are fixed, the productive characteristics of an economy with fixed factor proportions, the validation of the Leontiev system by the Samuelson substitution theorem. If the conditions for quasi-linearity exist—typically fundamental relationships which are homogeneous of degree one and the continuous attainment of equilibrium—the system is amenable to the same treatment as a strictly linear system. Quasi-linearity occurs mainly in production relationships.

Let us turn now to aggregating postulates. The simplest deterministic postulate, that of identical individuals, is rarely appropriate (although widely used implicitly) for consumers, but it may be appropriate for firms, especially in circumstances in which quasi-linearity is also appropriate.

The simplest statistical aggregating postulate—that variation between individuals in the coefficient of some micro-variable is independent of the variation between individuals in the micro-variable itself—is not unattractive. For a strictly linear micro-system, in which neither the variations of the coefficients nor the variations in the variables are causally linked into the system, it is a very attractive and very powerful postulate.

For an approximately linear system, however, a severe problem arises. Consider the earlier example of the savings function. Suppose that saving is a nonlinear function of income, well represented by a linear function over the range of variation expected for the typical individual during the time period under consideration. We shall think of this range of variation as the *time-series range*. But the aggregation at each point in time involves aggregation over different individuals, with different incomes. The range of incomes over which we aggregate is the *cross-section range*. Obviously the range between the poorest and richest United States citizen in 1965 is many times greater than the range over which a typical citizen's income may be expected to vary over the next ten years, so that it may well be, in a particular case, that the cross-section range may be very much greater than the time-series range. The cross-section relation between marginal propensity to save and income may then exhibit noticeable nonlinearity even though the time-series relationship is well represented by a linear equation. If, for example, the marginal propensity to save rises slowly with income, the above effect will appear. There will then be a positive correlation between the income coefficient and the income variable over the cross section, and the aggregating postulate that the correlation is zero cannot be used.

The only conclusion to a study of the problem of aggregation in economics is that there is no single conclusion to be drawn. Each aggregation problem must be solved in its own way, choosing the most useful approach in the light of the use that is to be made of the macro-model and of the nature of the information on which empirical estimates must be based. The consistency of the aggregation chosen depends upon the acceptability of the aggregating postulate that is made implicitly or explicitly, and that, too, must be judged for each model individually. If any conclusion is to be drawn at all, it is that problems of aggregation in economics are usually swept under the rug.

BIBLIOGRAPHY

Allen, R. G. D., *Mathematical Economics*. New York: Macmillan, 1956.

Green, H. A. J., *Aggregation in Economic Analysis: An Introductory Survey*. Princeton, N.J.: Princeton University Press, 1964.

Klein, Lawrence R., "Macroeconomics and the Theory of Rational Behaviour," *Econometrica*, 14 (1946), 93-108.

———, "The Aggregation Problem for a One-Industry Model," *Econometrica*, 14 (1946), 303-312.

May, Kenneth O., "The Aggregation Problem for a One-Industry Model," *Econometrica*, 14 (1946), 285-298.

Theil, Henri, *Linear Aggregation of Economic Relations*. Amsterdam: North-Holland, 1954.

PART 4

VALUES

IN

ECONOMIC

THINKING

ROTHENBERG
Values and Value Theory in Economics

CHURCHMAN
On the Intercomparison of Utilities

BRANDT
The Concept of Welfare

INTRODUCTION

THE RELATIONS BETWEEN HUMAN VALUES AND THE PROCEDURES OF SCIENCE have been actively explored during the last ten years. In part, this was in reaction to the spread of logical positivism which had called for a value-free science and had banished values to the limbo of the a priori and the prescriptive. In the social sciences, the continued exploration of utility theory and decision-making gave explicit impetus to the formal integration of values into scientific inquiry. As a consequence, the sharp hiatus between values and science that the positivist had advocated underwent substantial modifications.

Values, according to Viennese positivism, expressed subjective states of mind that eluded measurement and comparability. Though it was always possible to observe the behavior of individuals, one could never be sure of the mental states that gave rise to their actions. Moreover, these mental states were internal and individual; they could not be compared. This purist position had important policy implications for economics. If subjective states cannot be compared, then utilities cannot be added. Thus, it is impossible to formulate general welfare criteria by compounding individual choice. Under any collective policy, some people were sure to lose. What was gained by the winners could not be measured against losses by the losers. Consequently, the scope of collective policy was a narrow one. Nonetheless, common group values and successful public policy are an accepted part of our daily lives. It seems reasonable to find some paradox in the logic of purely individual choice.

The theory of values and choice is fundamental to reasoning in economics. Jerome Rothenberg surveys some of the main uses of value in economic theory. He distinguishes between values as phenomena of choice and the objective, measurable values of the market mechanism. In order to show just how values are being used in the thinking of economists, Rothenberg explores the problem of decision making. Values enable the decision maker to order alternatives, to rationalize choice. Rothenberg examines both economic and noneconomic choice, choice under conditions of uncertainty or where information is incomplete. The values of the decision maker also help explain the values of the market mechanism; they help define rationality, utility, wants, and demand. Observation of demand, utility, or revealed preference are various attempts to measure value. Normative economic theory, in particular, depends on the value problem. Collective human welfare and public policy imply some degree of value measurement and aggregation. The concepts and logical implications of value, in short, enter almost all facets of economic thought and action.

C. West Churchman and Richard Brandt turn to the question of individual choice and the problem of collective valuation. Churchman points out that knowing the minds of other people is crucial to collective valuation. If other minds can be perceived, they can be compared. He argues that the subjective mind—the other mind—can be comprehended by the perceiving mind. A special case of this is the understanding of one's own mental processes; the perceiver may be the individual himself. Statements about one's self, it follows, are not basically different from other people's observations of us. Both may be reliable to some degree. This enables individuals, their minds and values, to be compared. Because a perceiver can order statements about similar phenomena along a common dimension, utilities can be compared. When utilities are compared, social valuations may be achieved. Consequently, a consistent public policy is possible based on rational, nonautocratic collective valuations.

Brandt, like Churchman, addresses himself to the question of individual and social goals. He draws upon the thinking of philosophical psychology and moral philosophy to argue the possibility of a collective welfare function. Using the methods of philosophical analysis, he demonstrates how other people's minds are taken into account in our everyday thought and action. This analytic method is applied to the common terms of economic understanding, the value concepts of "welfare," "happiness," "preference," "pleasure," "satisfaction," or "utility." Brandt shows that welfare and utility can be, and in fact are, formulated in an empirically meaningful manner. That is, it is reasonable to identify, discuss, and compare different levels of welfare. Since individual welfare can be identified and summed, a collective welfare policy is logically consistent and empirically meaningful. Like Churchman, Brandt essentially rejects the extreme atomism that underlies much of modern economic theory and welfare formulations.

JEROME ROTHENBERG

Jerome Rothenberg, Ph.D., Columbia University, is Professor of Economics at Northwestern University. He was a Ford Foundation Faculty Research Fellow, Nuffield College, Oxford University, and a Fellow of the Institute for Advanced Study in the Behavioral Sciences. He is the author of The Measurement of Social Welfare *(1963) and* The Economic Evaluation of Urban Renewal *(1966), as well as of many papers for professional journals. His research covers welfare economics, resource allocations, and decision-making theory, as well as the economic role of government and economic and strategic analysis of national security.*

E S S A Y

14

Values and Value Theory in Economics

"VALUE THEORY" IS ONE OF THE TWIN PILLARS supporting the edifice of economic analysis. (The other is income theory.) Contrary to what its name might suggest, it is not a branch of normative economics, but of positive economics. It is that branch of pure theory which deals with the determination of market prices on all commodities and productive services (including intermediate goods—capital) and with the influence which these prices have on the allocation of the economy's limited productive resources. The latter concerns which commodities will be produced and in what quantities, what methods will be used to produce them, and how they will be distributed among resource owners.

The "values" in "value theory" refer to market values—the market values of productive services or what embodies them and of commodities. These market values are anonymous, impersonal entities. But they are not abstract; they are concrete. They have their representation as market prices. Market prices are precise signals for action, and nothing else. They stipulate the terms on which a commodity can be exchanged on a market. At least in value theory (also known as "price theory"), they do not point into themselves in terms of any notion of intrinsic worthwhileness of the commodity. The market price is what a commodity is "worth" only in the sense that someone here and now who owns a unit of the commodity is willing to exchange it at this price.[1] It testifies neither to what terms the commodity can "rightfully" command, nor what it has commanded yesterday nor will command tomorrow.

The market values that economists are most interested in are equilibrium prices. Not only do these not reflect anything like a "just price" or intrinsic worthwhileness, they do not even represent a "use value" or a value of socially necessary labor involved in producing it or, indeed, a total cost of producing it. Value theory emphasizes that decision making rarely involves an all-or-nothing issue. It usually involves issues that can be broken down into relatively homogeneous parts—like *how much* to spend on spinach or diamonds or night-club entertainment. Choices are influenced by calculating the consequences of hypothetical shifts at the margins of alternative options. Market prices reflect the marginal, not total (or average), calculations of usefulness (to buyers) and opportunity cost (to sellers).

Finally, though market values are public, interpersonal phenomena, they do not refer to any social or group or corporative consensus: they are simply the public resultants of an interplay of the valuations of individual decision makers.[2]

So the values which form the central subject matter of value theory are objective, interpersonally comparable, impersonally arrived at, measurable resultants of individual valuations, which bear no direct relation to intrinsic worthwhileness or usefulness or social significance or total cost or persistent status of the corresponding commodities to which they refer.

THE NATURE OF VALUE THEORY

Value theory is a positive theory of behavior concerning resource allocation. Under a system of division of labor and decentralized decision making, there are three types of elements which must be coordinated:

---

[1] The market prices most importantly dealt with in value theory are "equilibrium prices," which means prices which achieve a balance of the amount of the commodity that sellers are willing to sell at each such price and the amount that buyers are willing to buy. Any such price shows the terms on which the economist predicts that a commodity *will tend to be exchanged*, not simply those on which some *one* owner will be satisfied to trade.

[2] Some of which may, of course, be themselves organizations like business firms.

resources, technological knowledge, and wants. These are coordinated by means of market values. Prices on the market perform as signals indicating to resource owners where they may most advantageously employ their resources, since prices serve to announce the returns available to such owners in alternative uses. Prices also perform as signals to ultimate purchasers of commodities, the so-called "consumers," announcing to them what they must sacrifice in order to achieve specific kinds of gratification, thereby making it possible for them to decide where to obtain the best compromise between liveliness of wants and budget constraints. Finally, market prices are perceived by entrepreneurs as signals as to where and how it would pay them to bring together and productively transform resources in order to meet the expressed wants of consumers. The result of these simultaneous forms of signaling is an exhaustive set of decisions determining what kinds of commodities will be produced, of what qualities and in which quantities, what kinds of resources will be used to produce these commodities, in what combinations and by what methods, and, since these decisions determine the whole set of resulting factor incomes, the distribution of produced commodities among resource owners. Changes in resources, wants, or technology will affect these decisions through their effect on the market signals.

At the level of specific markets, the character of the supply side of the market depends upon the opportunity costs affecting resources and the nature of the technology; the character of the demand side of the market depends upon the nature of wants and the distribution of purchasing power. These forces act on one another through the mediating communication performed by prices. But the prices are themselves determined simultaneously with the interplay of these forces. Price in any market will fluctuate whenever purchase decisions do not balance sales decisions at that prevailing price. Price comes to rest, for a given set of forces, when the two balance, i.e., when the market clears. In general, these forces change in any one market whenever changes occur in markets for related commodities. While a single market is seldom closely related to many markets, so that changes in the former will have substantial effect on the latter, any two markets, however unrelated directly, will have patterns of relatedness with other markets such that intermediate linkages of influence can ultimately be traced. In short, all markets are ultimately coordinated together in a network of relatedness. All market prices together, therefore, play the role of information carrier to coordinate resource use, production, and consumption decisions.

It is important to note that value theory is a theory of action, not simply of valuation. The valuation is at one and the same time the resultant of action (bids for exchange or actual exchanges) and the signal for further action (actual exchanges, resource use, and consumption choices). Indeed, the market values of value theory *are* a form of action.

There is a respect in which market values perform a referential, target function akin to, but not in fact equivalent to, the normative function of "philosophic values."[3] The economist's interest in *equilibrium* prices enables him to use them as targets of real-world behavior, even when actual behavior diverges from these targets. The use of the concept of the "long-run" time period unit of analysis facilitates this. "In the long run, prices in the butter market will be at level X, the long-run equilibrium price." Now, and tomorrow, and the day after, price will not actually be at X; but so long as the basic parameters which determine the supply and demand response remain unchanged, price will keep tending toward X. Theoretical values serve then both as predicted resting places and predicted goals toward which tendencies tend. This is again a positive role, not a normative one.

A final, related role should be mentioned. Some markets are observed not to be free: they are subject to certain restrictions, or interferences— e.g., legal price ceilings, monopoly restraints. The economist often explicitly compares the actual performance in such a market with what it would have been in the absence of restriction. He compares actual price with the free market equilibrium price and gauges the difference this makes in resource allocation. The pattern of resource allocation under free market pricing becomes a point of reference for the actual pattern both for purely descriptive (predictive) and for normative purposes.

NONMARKET VALUES IN VALUE THEORY: INDIVIDUALISM

The public, measurable, action-determined market values discussed are not the only values involved in value theory. At the base of value theory, and therefore at the base of the whole corpus of economic theory, are "economic values" held by the ultimate economic decision makers. These "values" refer to the basic incentives of these decision makers for economic activities. It is fundamental to all of economic theory that the goal of economic activity is to meet the wants of the ultimate consuming public and that these wants are the aggregated wants of individual decision-making units.[4] The majority of economists go further. They argue that it is only these "individual" wants that have reality; they contend that the wants which are aimed at by the action of representative government—the so-called "public wants" or "social wants"—are in reality only individual wants whose gratification can most efficiently be accomplished by collective action. Value theory is thus strongly individualistic.

---

[3] The use of market values for normative purposes will be discussed below.

[4] These units are spoken of as "individuals," but they are used to describe the behavior of households; and no analysis is given as to how truly individual wants are reflected in household behavior. See the next section on Wants and Individual Values.

This is true of the logical structure of value theory both as a positive science and as a springboard for normative economics.

Since they hold such a central position, individual values must be examined in some detail. It is the treatment of these that gives economic theory its distinctive flavor as a theory of human behavior.

WANTS AND INDIVIDUAL VALUES

The terms individual "wants," "incentives," and "values" have been used in speaking of the targets of economic activity. These are interrelated. Their interrelationship is best revealed by examining the economist's conception of the directionality of human behavior.

The individual is seen as possessing a set of drives. These are organic states which dispose him to activity aimed at reducing or transforming these same states in a way that leads to gratification.[5] Thus, they impose directionality on behavior. For one thing, they point to instrumentalities by which these gratifying transformations can take place. They become object-oriented—i.e., wants. The economist calls these instrumentalities "commodities." The wants which reflect such a selective attention to commodities may be innate, unchanged, and unchangeable or socially acquired and subject to various changes over time with changed internal and environmental circumstances. But the key features to which the economist points are that within a period of time considered appropriate as a decision-making unit (1) the individual experiences numerous wants, (2) there exists more than one commodity which can satisfy any want, (3) specific wants do not have totally independent effects on the individual, and (4) the combinations in which commodities are consumed possess enhancing or curtailing influences on their want-gratifying power.

In the presence of these characteristics the fundamental assumption made is that of scarcity, i.e., that the individual is faced with limitations on the total amount of commodities he can acquire, thereby preventing him from being able to satisfy all his wants. His budget constraint keeps him in a nonsatiated state. The presence of this budget constraint means that the individual is faced with a nontrivial problem of choice.

It is at this point that the most distinctively economic assumptions about behavior are made. The individual is assumed to be able to evaluate all the alternative total options of trading his available purchasing power for commodities so that he can order them in terms of preference. The ordering is assumed to be a complete (transitive) ordering. Now, the individual is assumed actually to choose to acquire commodities in conformity with his preferences. He is assumed to choose that attainable

---

[5] We allow, in this loose formulation, for gratifications other than from "drive-reduction," in the terminology of learning theory.

combination which is preferred to all other attainable combinations (or at least he will not select a combination with respect to which he has another attainable combination which is preferred). The last two assumptions essentially comprise the economist's definition of rational behavior (under certainty). The individual has commodity preferences which enable him to order all alternative commodity bundles completely, and he chooses his most preferred attainable bundle in conformity with this ordering.

The substantial assumption is that the individual possesses preferences which enable him to order completely the alternative commodity bundles. The stringency of this assumption will be examined later in the chapter. For immediate purposes we may reformulate this assumption. When faced with alternative patterns of consumption, the individual is able to make relative evaluations of these alternatives. It is these relative evaluations which permit the making of a complete ordering. We may call these evaluations the individual's values.

Standing just behind the individual's preferences, these values enable one to formulate another, more hallowed concept, in the economic theory of choice—the concept of utility. Utility is the indicator of the level of want-gratification. The main issue is the degree of measurability achievable. The information contained in the preference ordering just mentioned permits measurement on an ordinal scale. Given this preference ordering, an individual possesses a utility function at least in the sense that different alternatives can be assigned numbers which predict choice in terms of the relation "greater than." This suffices to predict the individual's choices in many types of market situations. In situations involving risky outcomes, and in certain nonmarket-type situations, the individual's choices cannot be predicted unless additional information is extractable from his values, namely, indications about the relative intensity of different preferences. If these are obtainable, the utility numbers assigned to different alternatives have the further significance that differences between them bear predictive power for choice, i.e., measurement is possible on an ordered metric scale. These considerations will be examined further below.

The individual's internal evaluation system provides a system of incentives for him when facing actual choice alternatives. It determines his choice. We assume that he is subject to two kinds of constraint: one, a given total limitation of general purchasing power; the other, the terms on which different commodities can be acquired (or the terms on which one commodity can be exchanged for another [6]). Together, the constraints determine a set of commodity bundles which are obtainable by the in-

---

[6] In this alternative formulation the limitation on general purchasing power gives way instead to a specification of the resources owned by the individual which are available for exchange into other commodities.

dividual. His preferences (values, utility functions) then determine his choice. Each such choice is identified as a demand response (or, if a choice among alternative sales of resources are involved, as a supply response). It represents an observable market action.

Thus, the internal dispositions, evaluations, tastes, eventuate in overt action—choice. Their function in value theory is, most importantly, to *rationalize* choice. Only secondarily is this internal and essentially unobserved (but not necessarily unobservable as will be noted) system used for predictive purpose. Predictions are largely based on the level of the pattern of observed overt choices.

It is important to note that though tastes eventuate in overt choice, overt choice fails in a crucial respect to reflect tastes. Actual choices result from tastes acting upon specific constraints, not tastes alone. In particular, it depends upon the distribution of income (or more anteriorly, on the distribution of the initial endowment of resources). Therefore, actual choices cannot be aggregated to produce a semblance of average or aggregate or normal or consensual tastes. The concept of public tastes, or the consensus of tastes, rests not upon the structure of aggregate market actions, but upon the structure of the set of individual tastes.

THE UTILITY FUNCTION AND "ECONOMIC MAN"

The concept of the utility function has been central to the economic theory of choice. Despite the sufficiency of ordinal measurement of preferences for rationalizing many choices, it has been mathematically convenient, and in certain respects philosophically advantageous, to speak of utility and utility functions. The reason hinges on the key function played in all of economic theory by the concept of maximization. In most of traditional theory economic behavior is conceptualized as an attempt to maximize something. In the traditional theory of the firm, for example, it is the attempt to maximize profits (expected profits, or the present value of expected profits, or some such variant). For consumers—and this means ultimately all decision-making units when disaggregated down to their final consumption role—it is the attempt to maximize utility. The concept of utility here has been a useful buffer between the action of choice and the supposed psychological ground of this action. By being able to speak of maximizing utility, the economist has not had to say that individuals try to maximize gratification, or satisfaction, or pleasure, or happiness, or virtue, etc., each one of which would seem to be making an empirical commitment in the field of psychology. Utility seems philosophically neutral, while the others seem to assert something about the substantive quality of the ultimate inner goad—if indeed, it is unitary.

The issue has been of some importance in the history of economic science. For considerable periods economists have been charged by non-economists with asserting that all men are hedonists. They seek only to maximize in terms of a "pleasure principle," neglecting every other ground of choice. This charge is, of course, incorrect. Utility maximization takes into account all grounds of choice. Indeed, it is logically incapable of excluding any substantive ground of choice because it possesses no content dealing with the substantive grounds of choice. It asserts that if an individual has preferences so structured that he can give a complete (transitive) preference ordering of all the alternatives, then his choices can be described as if he were assigning different levels of preference (utility) to these alternatives and selecting that available alternative (or alternatives) which has the highest level of preference of any which are available. It refers almost entirely to the *structural* characteristics of preferences—namely, the presence or absence of complete preference orderings of alternatives. The additional postulate, that an individual chooses his most preferred alternative, is nearly analytic, "nearly" because some slight synthetic content might be explicable.

Thus, rationalization of human choice in terms of utility maximization does not assert that individuals are motivated by pleasure or avoidance of pain. Utility may not even bear on pleasure or pain in a particular choice situation; other goals may be more important than either, where they do appear. Furthermore, it does not assert that individuals are selfish as opposed to altruistic. One's concern for others is as much a part of one's utility function as one's concern for oneself.

In addition to selfish hedonism, utility maximization has also been compacted into other characterizations. It has been closely associated by economists and noneconomists alike with constructs like "rationality" and "economic man." Both associations involve some deep issues.

"Economic man" is an "ideal type." It has two characteristics: extreme "calculatingness," and a preponderant (in some formulations, an exclusive) concern with so-called "economic goals" as opposed to other goals. The concept of "economic" as opposed to "noneconomic" has a long history of misinterpretation. It has often been used to denote a particular form of want-gratification, like an aesthetic or religious gratification. In reality, "economic" refers not to the type of want-gratification but to a characteristic of the instrumentalities for attaining any type of gratification.

In a market economy we call an instrumentality "economic" if it partakes of market transactions—if it has been *used as* a commodity. Being a commodity is not intrinsic to a good or service. Physically the same object or process may or may not be a commodity depending upon whether its use is part of a market transaction. The household services of a wife are not a commodity; the same services performed by a hired maidservant are.

In this sense the "economic man" pays preponderant attention to the commodity aspect of things—their market transactability. This characterization is more specialized than formal utility maximization. It is in fact a mis-characterization. We repeat that utility maximization is concerned only with the ordering of alternatives, not with what aspects of these alternatives are especially salient to choice. A preponderant concern for the commodity aspect of things is neither a necessary nor sufficient condition for utility maximization.

However, this emphasis should not be dismissed too soon. Economists have typically specialized the nature of the utility function they work with in a way that bears at least superficial resemblance to commodity-consciousness. It is worth examining this specialization.

The restriction involves using only what is called nonlexicographic utility functions, functions for which all of the arguments of the function are substitutable for one another in producing any particular over-all evaluation. There are no dimensions of choice which are so overwhelmingly important relative to the others that their effect on the over-all evaluation cannot be compensated for by *any* appropriate values of the other dimensions.[7] The relevance of this to the present point is that in nonlexicographic utility the change in a noncommodity dimension of want-gratification can be duplicated or offset in over-all evaluative impact by a corresponding change in a commodity dimension. Since the latter change is associated with a market transaction, and such a transaction can be expressed in monetary terms, this is tantamount to saying that "each man has his price"—and knows what it is. One might speculate that it was for this type of behavior that Oscar Wilde excoriated what he called the "cynic" as a man "who knows the price of all things, and the value of none."

But the Wilde quotation is, in fact, inappropriate, for the sense in which "everyone has his price" must not be misunderstood. It does not mean that money is all that is ultimately wanted, nor even that the goods and services purchasable with money—commodities—are more important than noncommodity means of gratification so that noncommodities can be "bought off cheaply" with commodities. It means only that there is a general substitutability of ingredients within the package alternatives of choice. Just as a commodity can offset a noncommodity in over-all evaluation, so too a noncommodity can offset a commodity: substitutability is twoway. The formulation of nonlexicographic utility does not really possess an ethical or pejorative content, but it does have descriptive empirical content. It is amenable to falsification (refutation). And the role of money

---

[7] Similarly, there are no dimensions so overwhelmingly trivial that their over-all effect can never be large enough to compensate for certain values of the other dimensions. Under lexicographic utility such overwhelmingly important and unimportant dimensions exist.

is not as a dominant focus of attention, but simply as a means of calculating the availability of different alternatives. Thus, the assumption of nonlexicographic utility touches on a component of the construct of "economic man," but the latter involves more restriction than the former. It is, in effect, a caricature of traditional utility theory in this respect.

The assumption of nonlexicographic utility does, however, make a difference. It has been argued that observable choice behavior can be better rationalized by introducing lexicographic utility, and treatments have been given of utility analysis under this approach.[8]

The other component of "economic man" raises even more fundamental questions. The decision maker must calculate in order to maximize utility. He is seen as a calculating chooser. This has two ramifications. On the one hand, his actions are considered to be the result of deliberate choices. They are not habitual, or random, or spontaneous. On the other hand, the choices are calculated. They are based on adequate information and full evaluation. Both of these are refutable, empirical assertions. Both go beyond utility maximization, but it is not clear how far beyond. The crux of the problem is that it is not clear how far utility maximization itself goes in terms of these issues.

Utility maximization implies that the individual (1) knows the available alternatives, (2) orders them completely in terms of preference, and (3) chooses the most preferred. The key assumptions are the knowledge of all available alternatives and their exhaustive relative evaluation. Two kinds of information are necessary for this, one external and the other internal. There must be information about which alternatives exist and which are available, and there must be information about the actual evaluation of the several alternatives. Neither kind is trivial or easily obtained information. Logically speaking, the search for all the available alternatives is open-ended. It is never known with certainty how much search is necessary to discover all—or even nearly all. This is partly due to the fact that the alternatives of choice are not single-dimensioned entities. They represent multidimensional commodity bundles, where even a knowledge of all the extant relevant *dimensions* is far from trivial. In the modern market context, an individual decision maker would have to learn about innumerable different types of commodity to be truly informed.

But knowledge of one's own consistent relative evaluations is extremely difficult to obtain as well. This also is due in large measure to the extravagantly multidimensional character of the alternatives of choice. Alternatives that differ from one another heterogeneously in many dimensions may be immensely difficult to compare. It begs the question simply to assert that somehow they *are* compared.

---

[8] See John S. Chipman, "The Foundations of Utility," *Econometrica*, 28 (1960), 193-224, for a systematic treatment and bibliography.

Both of these considerations together mean that decision making is itself a costly process. To assert the old adage, "I'm going to maximize my utility no matter what the cost," is humorous because it is inconsistent. Utility maximization requires taking the costliness of decision making into account when making choices. It is easier to state that it should do so, however, than to indicate how it should be done. How much information about alternatives *should* an individual amass in order to make a rational choice? There is no substantive answer. At most, one can give a formal answer consistent with the spirit of utility maximization. Additional information should be accumulated so long as the expected gain from such marginal accumulation exceeds its expected cost. But to indicate how the cost and benefit functions for relevant information are to be ascertained by the decision maker is something quite different, and has nowhere been definitively settled in the literature.

A qualitative implication can be given, however. Decision making is like a process of production. It feeds upon a flow of inputs to produce decisions as its output, and this entails using up scarce resources owned by the decision maker: time, energy, and general purchasing power. Thus, it must be operated efficiently to be consistent with the decision maker's over-all utility maximization. The use of inputs must be economized: their expenditure must be justified by expected results. This means that it will scarcely ever be rational to seek to exhaust all relevant information before making a decision. Short cuts will be called for; "rules of thumb" will be used.[9] Utility maximizing will call for decision making under incomplete information about alternatives and without an explicit exhaustive ordering of even the alternatives known to the decision maker.

One type of relevant rule of thumb may well be that the same action will be taken each time that approximately the same choice situation prevails. No elaborate new attempt will be made to marshal the alternatives, or deeply to re-evaluate them. In effect, habitual "choice" will be resorted to. Only substantial changes in the choosing situation will warrant wheeling out the elaborate paraphernalia of explicitly deliberate decision making.

That habitual choice may be consistent with, indeed entailed by, utility maximization, has important consequences. First, it means that the second ingredient of the concept of "economic man," his unrestrained calculatingness, is a caricature of the utility-maximizing decision maker

---

[9] Some recent work on the economic use of information has been done by Shubik, Stigler, Downs, Marschak and others. See, e.g., Martin Shubik, "Information, Risk, Ignorance and Indeterminacy," *Quarterly Journal of Economics*, 68 (November, 1954), 629-640; George Stigler, "The Economics of Information," *Journal of Political Economy*, 69 (June, 1961), 213-225; Anthony Downs, *An Economic Theory of Democracy* (New York: Harper, 1957); Jacob Marschak, "Towards an Economic Theory of Organization and Information," *Decision Processes*, eds. R. M. Thrall, C. H. Coombs, and R. L. Davis (New York: Wiley, 1954), Chap. 14.

just as is his supposed extreme economistic goal orientation. Second, it means that the notion that deliberate choice is a necessary condition for utility maximization may be suspect. It is true that *random, spontaneous* choice is still likely to be inferior to some deliberation and planning. But a strategy consisting of a combination of deliberate and *habitual* choice may well prove optimal.[10] It is often argued that habitual response does not involve a true choice at all. The present argument then appears to assert that utility can be maximized without choice being made at every choice point. But it is clear that the no-choice characterization is figurative. We must see choice as occurring on the broader integrative level: the level at which the over-all strategy about how information shall be processed is decided; how the decision-making process as a whole shall be employed vis-à-vis the choice problem on the one hand and the materials for meeting it on the other. Decision making involves two stages: first, the stage of structuring the decision-making apparatus and determining how it is to be employed; second, the stage of actually using the apparatus to make a specific decision. Utility maximization requires a true choice at the first stage. That choice may well, however, require much lower intensity use of the apparatus for some situations than for others. Such differentiation of use is not only consistent with utility maximization, it is very likely essential to it.

This emphasis on two-stage decision making—the emphasis on the importance of decisions about the decision-making process itself—has not been dealt with much in traditional decision-making theory of the individual. But it has been receiving increasing attention in the theory of decision making of organizations and in statistical decision theory. It is one of the central foci of organization theory and operations research. This is not surprising. The decision-making apparatus of organizations is overt in a way that is not true for the individual: explicit, complex institutions concretize it. Indeed, this overtness makes possible a paradigm for individual decision making. Just as external electronic systems have been used by Ashby and others to analogize the human central nervous system, so organization theoretic decision making can help to analogize the individual's (and household's) internal process.

We now summarize our discussion of utility maximization. What is essential is the marshaling and complete preference ordering of alterna-

---

[10] Herbert A. Simon has advanced the notion that, at least with respect to organizations, the objective is not to maximize some function, but to "satisfice"—that is, to obtain a *satisfactory* outcome (payoff). It is difficult to find specific content in this notion other than that of maximization subject to certain (suppressed) constraints—constraints like the cost of information or evaluation or (in the organizational context) interpersonal disharmonies. Thus, in our usage, the optimality of some combination that includes habitual choice represents utility maximization subject to constraints concerning the costs of decision making. See Simon, *Models of Man: Social and Rational* (New York: Wiley, 1957).

tives and the choosing in accordance with preference. Such choice does not characterize an ultimate psychological ground of motivation. It makes no reference to egotism versus altruism, or to an exclusive preoccupation with commodities or money. It does presuppose the absence of extreme hierarchies in want gratification. It implies that if the process of decision making itself be recognized as bearing costs, then decision making itself should be economized (i.e., efficiently organized) in making decisions. This implies that specific choosing situations may not be treated with unlimited calculatingness. Utility maximization is compatible with imperfect knowledge of alternatives and of the decider's own evaluations. It is compatible with habit. All in all, the construct of "economic man" diverges substantially from the character of utility maximization.

RATIONALITY

The concept of "rationality" may be dealt with more briefly since we already have introduced most of the relevant materials. As generally employed by the economist, "rationality" can be taken to mean "action in accordance with preferences" or "choices consistent with preferences." Where alternatives can be given a complete transitive preference ordering, it simply means utility maximization.[11] This use is descriptive. The concept has also been used by some economists in a normative way, typically in speaking of decision making under risk. Leonard J. Savage and others have presented axioms of decision making based on the Von Neumann-Morgenstern utility concept which they claim characterizes rational choice in the context of risky alternatives.[12] This normative characterization is controversial.

In the descriptive use, only those cases have been cited where the decision maker can give a complete, transitive ordering of alternatives. Empirical observations substantiate that individuals sometimes express

---

[11] This formulation is bypassing the distinction between choice under certainty, risk, and uncertainty situations. "Alternative," as used here, can refer to a certain outcome, a risky prospect, or an uncertain prospect. Whatever its character, the key to the present argument is that if such alternatives (and each combination of alternatives—as for example, a probability mixture—is itself an alternative) can be completely ordered, then the individual is rational if he selects in accordance with this ordering.

[12] Leonard J. Savage, *The Foundations of Statistics* (New York: Wiley, 1954); John C. Harsanyi, "Cardinal Welfare, Individualistic Ethics, and Interpersonal Comparisons of Utility," *The Journal of Political Economy*, 43 (August, 1955), 309-321; Jacob Marschak, "Rational Behavior, Uncertain Prospects and Measurable Utility," *Econometrica*, 18 (April, 1950), 111-141. In the language of the preceding footnote, the axiom systems indicate how preferences for one set of alternatives impose constraints—i.e., help determine—preferences for other sets of alternatives.

preferences which are not transitive, but cyclic.[13] In such circumstances, the individual cannot give a complete preference ordering. There is no consistent hierarchy.[14] The individual then does not have a utility function. Is the individual rational if he does not possess a utility function?

Economists have frankly not given this problem much attention. Some have held that rationality is so intimately associated with utility maximization that they cannot conceive of the latter without the former. It is not rational not to have transitive preferences and all alternatives ranked. Yet the basic usage of rationality in economics, like the utility function itself, concerns means and not ends, since ends are typically beyond question in economic theory. Rationality then would seem to concern the implementation of ends, not the ends themselves. In order to be rational despite possessing intransitive choices, the individual must choose in accordance with his ends.

But there is an ambiguity here. When preferences are transitive, no matter in what combinations and sequence the alternatives are presented for choice, selection according to preferences is always possible, and the choices are unchanged and consistent. When preferences contain some intransitivities, however, the combinations and sequence of presentation make a difference in outcome: selection is sometimes impossible, results of elimination contests depend on sequence, and sometimes choices are inconsistent. It is only where choice always relates to *pairs* of alternatives, with no elimination of alternatives occurring between different pairs, that intransitive preferences will generate unchanged, dependable, and consistent choices. Only then can an individual be said to be able to choose in accordance with his ends. But market choices almost never appear as paired comparisons without elimination. Therefore, rationality applies in very limited scope to intransitivity, a scope that does not include market situations.

This argument can be extended further. If rationality is a property of the adaptation of means to ends, can there be rationality when *the ends themselves are inconsistent* (even in pairwise comparisons)? The answer partly depends upon the meaning of inconsistent ends. We have implicitly been treating ends in this section as the system of preferences. On this level, inconsistency of ends simply signifies that the individual cannot give a consistent set of orderings. Thus, he cannot possibly choose "in harmony" with his preferences. He can neither feel that his choices

---

13 E.g., see Andreas Papandreou, "Experimental Testing of a Postulate on the Theory of Choice," paper read at the December, 1952, meeting of the Econometric Society in Chicago.

14 The diagnosis of inconsistent choices is by no means unproblematic. Such choices are often "explained" in terms of desire for variety, change in tastes, etc. The present discussion assumes a time unit long enough to accommodate desire for variety within it, and assumes also no changes in tastes. We are examining properties of a given set of tastes.

have or have not been true to what he wants. Indeed, at this level the distinction between means and ends breaks down and with it this conception of rationality.

Yet it is not farfetched to argue that the essential quality of irrationality is that the individual *acts* as if he did not know what he wanted. This usage is consistent with the case of transitive preferences. Where preferences are inconsistent, the individual will act as if he did not know what he wanted: since if he chooses inconsistently, this characterization holds *a fortiori*, and if he chooses consistently, this will not be in accordance with his preferences. In a deep sense, therefore, inconsistency of ends characterizes irrationality just as does nonmaximization of gratification where maximization is possible; for in the former the distinction between ends and their implementation becomes blurred.[15]

THE STRUCTURE AND SUBSTANCE OF INDIVIDUAL VALUES

This section will attempt to characterize the economist's view of the decision maker and the decision-making situation. First, the period for which the decision maker is deemed to make his decisions is long enough so that he must plan for satisfaction of the total organism. It must be possible for his chosen behavior over this period to be repeated over consecutive similar periods without his viability as a living inhabitant of his community being destroyed. This means that different modes of want gratification are not necessarily competitive; on the contrary, they are likely to be basically complementary. But within the basic indispensable needs there are substitute ways of attaining gratification. More-

---

[15] "Inconsistency of ends" can be used in a sense that does not automatically blur ends and "means." In psychological and psychiatric formulations ends may be thought of as particular organismic need directions—hunger, thirst, sex, power, etc. In psychological theory the engagement of any one of these at high intensity at some particular time is likely to preclude the actualization of the others at that time, since it tends to monopolize the individual's perceptual and evaluative capacities for its own fulfillment. Need gratification is characterized by this "pre-potency": different gratifications come sequentially, if at all. Inconsistency of ends in this kind of formulation may be a matter of extremity in preclusion—where the dominance of any one is so protracted as to leave too much of the organism unsatisfied. Or, in contrast, there may be not enough pre-potency, so that the enjoyment of any one mode of gratification is constantly interfered with by the presence of the other drives.

These formulations retain the distinction between means and ends somewhat better than the earlier "economic" one. They are not equivalent to the economist's formulation because the economist takes as the temporal unit of decision making a period long enough to bypass the pre-potency of single want gratifications: the individual is asked to choose commodities for a period during which he will have to meet "all" his wants in some degree. But inconsistency in these psychological formulations can be a source of inconsistent preferences too, in that the attempted satisfaction of certain wants is expected to result in actions, attitudes, and/or experiences which will make the individual less capable of satisfying other wants.

over, the specific objective means of securing gratifications—the commodities—typically affect more than a single mode of gratification. Automobiles, for example, in addition to transportation serve power and
self-esteem and many other socially acquired and socially significant
wants. So it is with food, clothing, shelter, and recreation. Thus, while
basic needs may or may not be competitive, the commodities that serve
them, being composite gratifiers, often represent competitive complexes
of want gratification. Commodities are related both as completing (complementary) elements in over-all styles of consumption and as competing,
more or less interchangeable, elements in such styles. Besides, over-all
styles are themselves competitive, viable patterns of total organismic
gratifications.

For this reason, the basic alternatives of choice are considered not as
different quantities of individual commodities, but as different market
baskets of commodities—different over-all consumption patterns. These
commodity combinations incorporate within them the various complementary and substitutive relationships among clusters of commodities. Thus, the significance to an individual of consuming one more unit
of a certain good depends heavily upon the consumption context—on the
presence and absence of specific other commodities in the bundle to
which this marginal unit is being added.

Incorporation of commodity relatedness patterns into the units of
choice has substantial conceptual advantages. It also has costs, as has
been hinted previously. The alternatives are radically multidimensional.
This multidimensionality prevents the predicting of the preferences of
decision makers easily. The basic predictor is the assumption that for
any individual the quantities of each commodity involved in attainable
alternatives, and the size of the commodity bundles as a whole, fall in the
individual's nonsatiation range. He prefers more of any one commodity
to less, and he prefers a larger total bundle (income) to a smaller one.[16]
This assumption does not permit prediction of preferences or choice when
the alternatives are multidimensional because heterogeneous differences
in different dimensions cannot be evaluated without reference to the individual's particular (idiosyncratic) preference system.

An additional difficulty is, as we noted earlier, that the economist cannot even guarantee that individuals will possess transitive preferences or
a complete ordering of all the (even relevant) alternatives. Individuals
may well have difficulties in comparing such composite bundles. Their
actual market choices—which the economist ascribes to the interaction
of a budget constraint with transitive preferences relating to this type
of alternative—may not be such at all. Utility theory may in fact be a

---

[16] The satiation range in both senses has been dealt with in the formal exposition
of the theory, but it is usually disregarded in actual analysis.

poor theory. It has not been employed demandingly enough in terms of specific predictions to be tested. But such a test would bear on whether the units of choice selected by the economist—these complete commodity combinations—are indeed the most appropriate ones for "explaining" consumer choice.

The economist believes in a hierarchy of preferences for commodity bundles, but neither a precise hierarchy of wants nor one of individual commodities. Some wants are more basic, less dispensable than others; but the truly indispensable ones are several. Moreover, any one of them, and certainly the whole family of indispensable ones, can be fulfilled by a huge number of combinations of commodities. No one commodity is indispensable, nor even any one combination of commodities. This is the reason economists do not employ a lexicographic utility function. There is general substitutability across all classes of commodities (while not necessarily across all types of want gratification).

Most of what economists have to say about utility, rationality, values, etc., concerns only these structural characteristics, like transitivity, general substitutability, and maximization. Economists have deliberately refrained from paying close attention to the specific arguments of the utility function—the substantive nature of the things that motivate people. There has been no real attempt to evaluate the strength of different types of motives (or rewards)—e.g., of the relative strength of prestige vs. convenience vs. value of time in the attractiveness of different modes of transportation. An important comparison in many problems (for example, occupational choice and brand selection) concerns how important a money payoff is relative to nonmonetary aspects of reward. By not committing themselves on substance, economists have kept their neutrality about the ultimate nature of gratification, but at the cost of being unable to predict even relatively uncomplicated choices.

ULTIMATE AND NONULTIMATE CONSUMPTION

Want-satisfaction is usually treated as the specialized business of the ultimate consumer. It is the consuming unit which consumes, and the producing unit which produces. Production is treated as entirely instrumental, an intermediate process devoid of want-satisfying power in itself. Consumption is treated as entirely an ultimate want-satisfying activity in itself, with no instrumental facet (except, of course, in the broader sense that all commodities are simply means to want-gratification).

In fact, both of these are incorrect. The business of the consumer in his use of commodities is partly the productive, instrumental activity of supporting and maintaining himself over time as a viable consumer. Food, clothing, shelter—almost every other consumption category—possess such intermediate, nonfinal, consumption facets. Similarly, the activities involved in production possess important elements which are prized for themselves: social intercourse, sense of achievement, power.[17] A production unit like the business firm is far from being purely an instrumental shell with no rewards other than the money incomes generated. The traditional assumption of complete producer-consumer specialization makes it especially difficult to predict a variety of choices where money rewards are explicitly associated with the several alternatives but where nonmonetary rewards are only implicitly associated with them and are often neglected entirely.

Thus, our characterization of individual values should apply not solely to a role called "consumption," played only by an actor called (definitionally) the "consumer," but to all ultimate consumption elements—and only those which are ultimate—whether they occur during a process called "consumption" or "production." This has in fact been formalized in economic theory. The household is deemed to perform both production and consumption actions in the course of buying commodities and selling productive services. No attempt is made to separate out the two types.

THE MEASUREMENT OF VALUES

The economist treats the values we have been speaking of as measurable in principle. This is not the place where the technical problems of value measurement can be discussed, but the issue can be be broadly characterized. The place of measurement in value theory has been influenced by economists' views on the place of utility theory in value theory. Earlier in the century, practitioners like Alfred Marshall, A. C. Pigou, Henry Schultz, and Ragner Frisch believed that utility was necessary to rationalize consumer market-demand behavior, that the latter truly depended on the former for integrity. The task was seen as that of postulating the strongest assumptions that seemed to be true and seeing what overt choosing behavior could be inferred from them. Measurement of utility was, therefore, part of the task of setting a justification for, and prediction of, market behavior, and therefore had to be done independently of market behavior. Techniques were developed to measure utility scales under approximately experimental (laboratory) conditions. The psychologist Thurstone delved heavily into experimental methods for explicitly deriving individuals' preference scales. Utility functions and indifference curves (a graphical formulation of preference orderings) being deemed in principle observable, such techniques may have been

---

[17] And some elements disliked in themselves: poor working conditions. These also are consumption elements.

imperfect, but they were not epistemologically suspect. John Von Neumann and Oskar Morgenstern's axiomatization of utility theory in the context of risk (1947) [18] gave additional impetus to the search for experimental techniques to measure utility functions. These efforts were largely attempts to provide a quantitative basis for predicting market choice, to offset the substantive vagueness noted earlier.

Another tradition began around 1938 with Samuelson's revealed preference theory. This essentially argued that individual market behavior was the ultimate observable. Preferences, the utility function, were only logical entities useful for achieving logical closure of the system. The chief task of analysis was seen to be to postulate what was logically the *weakest* assumptions about preference that could deductively generate the properties of observable market choices. This tradition has since become very important. There has been some linkage between the two traditions in measurement technique in connection with the quantification of Von Neumann-Morgenstern utility. An increasingly behavioristic interpretation of this utility concept has led essentially to the notion that Von Neumann-Morgenstern, utility is simply a construct revealed by the pattern of observed risk choices. One important feature of this construct is that it is used for predictive purposes, not solely to achieve logical closure of the system.

INDIVIDUAL AND HOUSEHOLD VALUES

In our section on individualism we noted that the values which we have been referring to as "individual values" really refer to the values of the individual consumer decision-making units, which are households. These values are employed to rationalize the market behavior of households. Yet we noted also the critical emphasis given to individualism, to asserting the absence of "social values" or "social wants." Economists have not explicitly traced household values down to the true individual constituent values, being generally content to assume informally that the family operated as a "team," that is, that all members had identical tastes and identical values for the group as a whole. Problems of internal distribution could be dismissed as being sociological, just as the mainsprings of motivation (the substance of utility "payoffs") could be dismissed as being psychological.

But the household is in reality much more like a coalition, where only some tastes (or none) are alike, and only some values concerning the group as a whole are shared. Internal differences about the group's use of resources are too well known to require elaboration. Thus, the house-

---

[18] *The Theory of Games and Economic Behavior* (Princeton, N.J.: Princeton University Press).

hold is like a small society, and the united face which the economist assumes it shows to the external world must, therefore, represent some group-resolved values—compromise or consensual values: a form of social value. The economist has not generally been willing to analyze the nature of this group resolution or its projection onto the larger society.[19] In effect then, there rests an important, largely unexamined element of social valuation at the very foundation of a system of individualistic values.

VALUES IN NORMATIVE ECONOMIC THEORY (WELFARE ECONOMICS)

If individual values are important for positive economic theory, they are absolutely crucial for normative economic theory—welfare economics. In the former they perform the function of rationalizing the micro-observations which provide the foundations of actual analysis. In the latter, however, they constitute the essential criterion of welfare, without which there is no analysis at all.

The economist's basic connection between individual values and the welfare criterion is a proposition in philosophic psychology (or psychological philosophy). The well-being of an individual involves the satisfaction of his needs. But these needs are not innate. They are largely modified, extended, or acquired within a social context. They become wants. Wants are capable of explication within a system of attitudes and values. They are projected in the tastes or preferences of the individual. Thus, somewhat crudely, individual preferences bear upon the welfare of the individual. Abstracting from unconscious preferences (stemming from unconscious motivation),[20] the individual knows what is good for him. There is sometimes a discrepancy between the individual's preferences and his own welfare (as for example, when unconscious motivation is serious). His own valuations are likely to be only an imperfect projection of what is good for him. But it is likely to be a closer approximation than an outsider can give (except *possibly* a psychiatrist or spouse or parent in intimate and prolonged attendance on him). On the level of any particular individual, there can sometimes be found a more perspicacious outsider. But on the level of the population as a whole, no concentrated group of outside evaluators can be found which come anywhere near as close to expressing what is good for them as the individual members of the population themselves. Thus, the set of individual preferences becomes accepted as the arbiter of their own

---

[19] An exception is the present author's, *The Measurement of Social Welfare* (Englewood Cliffs, N.J.: Prentice-Hall, Inc., 1961), especially Chap. 13.

[20] Unconscious preferences raise problems with our earlier close association between preferences and choice since the essence of the unconscious process is that it is not overtly recognized.

welfare. Descriptive individualism in positive economics becomes transformed into normative individualism in welfare economics.

The set of individual values comprises the criterion of social welfare. But this is a *set* of preference scales (utility functions), not a unitary scale. Such a set is extremely awkward to employ in practical evaluations. The question arises whether the separate scales of the set can be aggregated together. Can individual values be aggregated?

Earlier economists like Marshall and Pigou were willing to do so, to add together the utilities of different individuals and obtain a grand sum. But the influence of Max Weber and Lionel Robbins introduced a normative purism into welfare economics. Interpersonal comparisons of utility had no scientific validity. They could be employed only by making explicit value judgments, and such value judgments could not gain general assent. Thus, individual values had validity, and no outside authority could conclusively either challenge *or* second their substance. Moreover, since the individual was the ultimate decision-making authority, there could be no such thing as social values or social judgments without unanimous individual agreement.

On this basis, Paretian welfare economics was established, and it has formed the mainstream of welfare economics since about 1935. The key is the Pareto welfare criterion—that alternative situations can be compared only where the totality of individuals give unconflicting individual evaluations. Situation *A* is judged to be Pareto superior to (better than) situation *B* only if everyone is at least as well off in *A* as in *B* while at least one person is better off, and vice versa. If *everyone* is equally well off in both, *A* is judged to be as good as *B*, and vice versa. If individuals give opposing preferences, then no judgment can be given.[21] A Pareto optimal situation is one for which there is no other *attainable* situation which is judged to be Pareto superior to it. No improvement is possible to a Pareto optimal situation in Paretian welfare economics. It can be proved that under circumstances abbreviated as individualistic perfect competition, the general (static) equilibrium of markets, with their corresponding, mutually consistent set of equilibrium market prices, achieves Pareto optimality.

As might be expected, a welfare economics based on the Pareto criterion will be strongly restricted in scope. This has provoked much dissatisfaction. There have been many attempts to formulate alternative frameworks. They focus especially on: (1) the limitation of attention only to preference ordering, attempting in addition to introduce information about preference intensities; (2) the injunction against interpersonal comparisons of utility, indicating how and when such comparisons may be properly considered; (3) the absence of a framework for introducing

---

21 These properties can be summarized as vectoral dominance.

value judgments into the analysis, formulating an explicit apparatus for incorporating a variety of value judgments (the social welfare function); (4) the existential rejection of social values or social evaluation, attempting instead to establish the reality and importance of group value consensus in going social processes.[22] These various approaches have not been definitely developed as yet, and no one approach now commands either much satisfaction or general acceptance. The optimal direction for the development of a welfare criterion is not at this time clear. Consequently, the employment of individual and social values in this branch of economic theory is uncertain as well.

---

[22] See the author's *The Measurement of Social Welfare* for an extended discussion of these approaches and a bibliography.

C. W. CHURCHMAN

C. W. Churchman, Ph.D., University of Pennsylvania, is Professor of Business Administration, and Associate Director of Space Sciences Laboratory, University of California at Berkeley. He was Editor-in-Chief of Philosophy of Science (1949–59) and of Management of Science (1956–61). He was President of The Institute of Management Sciences (1962) and Chairman of TIMS Council (1963) as well as member of the Council of the ORSA. He has published many articles and books in operations research, management science, and philosophy of science. He currently heads a large project at the University of California which is studying the management of research in industry and government.

ESSAY

15

MAN CAN BE CONSIDERED TO BE A DECISION maker whose values in part determine the behavior he exhibits. The intellectual problem of this manner of viewing man and his behavior is to determine these values, explain why and how they occur, and in what manner they "determine" behavior. The problem is still a very open one, in that no aspects of it are clearly settled. In the past, for example, it has been proposed that man's values are completely determined by his environment and his physical structure so that a knowledge of these is sufficient to predict behavior, according to this mechanistic viewpoint, "values" are merely a convenient way of describing the process and have no inherent reality. On the other hand, there is the philosophical "vitalist" position that man is possessed of a completely free component which can decide solely in terms of its own will and the behavior of which cannot be predicted from any knowledge of environment or internal physical structure; according to this position, values are inherent in the decision maker.

On

the

Intercomparison

of

Utilities

Although the mechanist-vitalist dispute about values was a central topic of discussion several decades ago, today the attention of the academic community has turned to another problem of values that seems more critical in our times. This is the problem of designing a society that is in accord with man's basic values. The attack on this problem requires an understanding of the basic value structure of each man and the way in which individual valuations can be combined to form a rational society.

In this essay we consider one proposed model of man's basic value structure, a model that certainly is reminiscent of mechanism and a model that makes the problem of passing from individual to social values especially difficult. The aim is to criticize certain underlying assumptions of this model. These underlying assumptions are frequently taken to be obvious in academic discussions, and indeed they seem to be a part of what T. S. Kuhn calls a "paradigm" of a scientific community:

> [By "paradigm"] I mean to suggest that some accepted examples of actual scientific practice—examples which include law, theory-application and instrumentation together—provide models from which spring particular coherent traditions of scientific research. . . . The study of paradigms . . . is what mainly prepares the student for membership in the particular scientific community with which he will later practice. Because he there joins men who learned the basis of their field from the same concrete models, his subsequent practice will seldom evoke overt disagreement over fundamentals.[1]

In the language of model builders, the paradigm forms the set of axioms of the model that the research community is most reluctant to change, either because the axioms are taken to be "obvious," or are agreed to by all, or even assumed without any awareness.

MAN AS AN INFORMATION PROCESSOR

The model of man's value system which we wish to examine is one in which each man is taken to be an information processor: he has a sensor, a way of coding information, storing it, and retrieving it; the stored information may become lost or distorted over time; at any moment of time, the mind may attempt to retrieve information from its memory bank and if the information corresponds with reality, the mind has an accurate picture of its world. Information is processed by the usual computational methods, which permit aggregation, condensation, abstraction, etc. Furthermore, each mind is endowed with a "preference processor," which operates over a set of alternative actions. This processor, in effect, scans a set of alternative "choices" which can be formed out of

---

[1] *The Structure of Scientific Revolutions* (Chicago: University of Chicago Press, 1962), pp. 10-11.

the information memory of the mind. These choices may be real, which means that the individual can realize them in action, or imaginary, or distorted. The preference processor is assumed to operate on pairs of choices so that it generates as output one of three possibilities: A is preferred to B, B is preferred to A, or the choice is indifferent. As soon as the preference occurs, it becomes a part of the memory of the mind by an act of "reflection." Finally, if the choices are real, and if A is preferred to B, then the individual will actually choose A instead of B according to the reports of an unbiased observer.

The first question for empirical research is how we learn about such a mind. Since the "we" in this question designates minds, the question is how one informative, evaluating mind of the type just described learns about another informative, evaluating mind. In order to keep the cast of characters clearly in mind, we shall think of two minds—the one that is to be investigated and the one that is to do the investigating. The first we call the "subjective" mind, the second the "inquiring" mind. We are specifically interested in the strategies available to the inquiring mind in its attempt to learn about the subjective mind, under the assumption that both minds are information processors and preferences processors. In other words, how can one design an inquiring mind to learn about the processes of another mind?

It should be emphasized that the model we are to explore is not the only one possible. Indeed, many people are appalled that any intelligent mature person could think of describing the human mind in this manner; the schism between points of view of psychology is too well known to elaborate. But this essay is written much more in the spirit of a sympathetic criticism of the "paradigm," than of a direct attack upon it.

The paradigm we are examining is reminiscent of the first part of John Locke's *Essay Concerning Human Understanding* (1689); indeed, this treatise could be considered as an early attempt to describe the fundamentals of information processing. Interestingly enough, the same puzzles, paradoxes, and difficulties that George Berkeley and David Hume later pointed out in connection with Locke's work reoccur in the modern discussions of the information processor. Of chief interest is the ability of the mind that observes its own state to communicate this information to other minds.

INFORMATION ABOUT OTHER MINDS

Perhaps more fundamental still is the subjective mind's ability to comprehend anything but its own processes. In this connection Berkeley [2]

---

[2] *A Treatise Concerning the Principles of Human Knowledge.*

showed that any input-output information processor must rely solely on internally generated criteria to distinguish between reality and non-reality. This rather obvious point, which may indeed be a tautology, came as something of a shock to many extroverted minds of his day. It was merely the beginning of the whole trend toward solipsism in British empiricism, in which evidence for the existence of other minds is quite different from evidence of the processes of one's own mind. For example, what can an inquiring mind infer about the preference structure of the subjective mind? If one assumes that the information stored in the other mind is accurate, so that the other mind perceives the alternatives clearly and realistically, then the inquiring mind can infer that a given expressed choice is indeed a true preference. Since there is no information about the preference processor other than these expressed choices, the inquiring mind cannot seemingly go much beyond this simple information without assuming too much. Thus it cannot safely infer stability over time in preference orderings of other minds; it cannot safely infer choices that have not yet been made, or the same choices in risky situations. Worst of all, it cannot "compare" its own preferences with those of the subjective mind except to say that they are alike or different. All of this sounds very much like Hume's skeptical arguments in his *Treatise of Human Nature* (1739) and his *Enquiry Concerning Human Understanding* (1748).

As in Hume and later writers like John Stuart Mill,[3] the delicate problem is to decide, on more or less practical grounds, how far the inquiring mind is justified in going beyond the mere data—in this case the mere expression of preference as exhibited by the spoken word or other appropriate action. Most writers of today seem to believe that there are a few "rational" rules that every well-adjusted preference processor must follow. By "well-adjusted" they mean that the mind is mature, normal, and can be persuaded by argument to follow the rule if it deviates from it for some reason. A great many such rules have been proposed, e.g., the asymmetry, transitivity, and connectedness of preference. J. von Neumann and O. Morgenstern's *Theory of Games*,[4] K. Arrow's *Social Choice*[5] and volumes of subsequent literature explore the extension of these rules to the "fair" choices of social individuals. In all this literature there is an attempt to be very cautious about making inferences that cannot be supported by the raw data of preference choices; concerning the subjective mind, the inquiring mind knows only the exhibited preferences and perhaps the simplest rational rules.

---

[3] *Logic* (1843).
[4] J. von Neumann and O. Morgenstern, *Theory of Games and Economic Behavior* (Princeton, N.J.: Princeton University Press, 1947).
[5] *Social Choice and Individual Values* (1951).

The suggestion of F. P. Ramsey,[6] J. von Neumann,[7] and others alleviated this very stark isolation of minds somewhat; if the preference processor of the subjective mind can process "gambles," then one may feel justified in some cases in inferring something more than preference orderings. (A gamble is simply a "risky choice" in which one receives outcome A with probability $\propto$ or outcome B with probability $1 - \propto$). If the inquiring mind assumes that the preference processor can process gambles according to a fairly simple set of "rational" rules, then it can infer a sort of theory about the processor. According to this theory, the processor behaves as though it locates all choices on a continuous scale, to which it arbitrarily assigns a zero point and a unit. In any risky situation the processor will most prefer that choice which maximizes the "expected utility," which is obtained by multiplying the scale values of each specific outcome by the probability that the outcome will occur. Whether or not there is ever sufficient evidence for the inquiring mind to infer such a theory of the preference processor is a debatable issue even among those who work within the information-processing paradigm. But there is almost unanimous agreement that there is no way for one mind to communicate to another anything about how its scale is constructed; the choice of a unit and zero point must always be taken as arbitrary. Thus, there is no way that the subjective mind can ever tell the inquiring mind how much he prefers A to B, no matter how hard he tries. "I love you far better than any one else I've ever known" can at best simply mean "I prefer you to anyone else"; the "far better" is a meaningless emotive term for the believer in this metaphysic.

The consequence is that there is no way in which the inquiring mind can "compare" its preferences with those of another mind in any rich manner. For example, if one man prefers golf to fishing, and the second fishing to golf, we cannot generate a group decision from the individual preferences that in any reasonable sense constitutes a consensus of the two. D. Luce and H. Raiffa explain the matter as follows:

> The non-uniqueness of the zero point is of no real concern in any of the applications of utility theory, but the arbitrary unit of measurement gives trouble. The trouble may be illustrated most easily by a fictitious example in the measurement of distances. Suppose two people are isolated from each other and each is given a measuring stick marked off in certain and possibly different arbitrary units. With such limited communication it is clearly possible for the second man to construct a scale model of the object, but it will only be of the correct size if it happens that both measuring rods are marked in the same units. Clearly, once the barriers on communication are dropped, the two men can determine with fair accuracy the relationship between

---

[6] *The Foundations of Mathematics and Other Logical Essays* (New York: Harcourt, Brace & World, Inc., 1931).

[7] J. von Neumann and O. Morgenstern, *Theory of Games and Economic Behavior*.

their two units. . . . The big difference between utility and length measurement is that we do not seem to have any "outside thing" which can be measured by both persons to ascertain the relation between the two units.[8]

Thus what is paradigmatic in the model of human values is the axiom that there can be no direct intercomparison of individual preferences. This axiom produces great difficulties in constructing fair, rational bases for the criteria of design of social systems.

SOLIPSISM

The paradigm creates the image of a lonely subjective mind, cut off from the rest of the world as far as its feelings are concerned. It alone can understand the intensity of its desires. Indeed, if we wished to go the whole way, one mind could never be sure that another mind even exists. This is solipsism in its strongest but probably least interesting form. In the form that interests us, one mind can only receive information about the choices another mind makes.

What is strange about this paradigm to the world outside is that its adherents do not regard this result as a *reductio ad absurdum* of their own position: that is, they apparently fail to realize that any position leading to solipsism must *ipso facto* be wrong and in need of reconstruction. If any rationalization of this rather strange attitude exists, it lies in the conviction that the study of human decision making must begin with the "simplest" kind of model and proceed thence to the more complicated. This aspect of the paradigm is well depicted in Von Neumann and Morgenstern's *Theory of Games*. Whatever one may feel about the historical accuracy of this account, its strategic implications for the inquiring mind are questionable. The implied strategy is one of starting with simple, well-defined problems and working up to complicated ones; but how can one know which simple problems provide the correct starting points without having some idea of the nature of complicated problems and their solution?

This question suggests another, more basic one: What is it that an inquiring mind must assume in order to know anything, even the most simple things?

KANTIAN CRITICISM

Such was the question that Immanuel Kant posed in his first *Critique*.[9] In view of the fact that the paradigm we are examining is a reliving of

---

[8] *Games and Decisions* (New York: Wiley, 1957), pp. 33-34.
[9] *Kritik der Reinen Vernunft* (1781).

eighteenth-century empiricism, it is certainly worthwhile asking what later philosophy had to say of the weaknesses of empiricism. Kant's critical question about any information processor can also be stated as follows: What must it presuppose in order to collect information, or, in modern terms, what aspect of the data is simply a result of the internal structure of the processor? For example, a digital computer has its information stored in bits; such a computer, were it reflective, might believe that all reality is digital in nature, not realizing that this aspect of its stored information was of its own making. Kant's criticism restricted itself to finding a minimal internal structure, in his case an elementary logic and an "address system" (space and time). Since the information processor, for example, must have some sort of an internal clock, it necessarily views its world of information as subject to certain minimal regularities; but these regularities are produced out of its own processing. Hence, Kant's well-known statement: "The understanding does not derive its a priori laws from nature, but prescribes them to nature." [10]

The relevant question here is whether the inquiring mind can choose the design of its own internal structure. If so, and there is a choice between alternative designs, then the preference processor has some control over the information. These speculative questions are usually phrased in terms of the debate about the role of "values" relative to "facts." Those who believe that the information processor cannot design its own internal structure view the two processes—the one of data collection, the other of choice between alternatives—as two separate functions. This position is very difficult to defend, however, in view of the fact that minds seem perfectly capable of looking at the world with many different kinds of spectacles, and of designing machines with built-in designs of quite different kinds.

Nevertheless, even if the preference processor of the inquiring mind does have something to say about the form of the data, does this change the basic problem of the communication between minds in any way? If anything, it seems to make it worse since there is no way in which one mind can judge the importance to another mind of a given information-processing strategy. On the other hand, the simplicity of the image of the information processor is shattered because one now requires a model in which the preference processor in part shapes the basic information.

THE REFLECTIVE MIND

A far more serious defect in the paradigm is its concept of the reflective part of the subjective mind. According to the paradigm, this part of the subjective mind can "directly" record the results of the preference

---

[10] *Prolegomena* (1783).

processor's scanning of alternatives. Locke in his *Essay* states that the mind has two sources of information, sensation and reflection. The latter is the information about the mind's own operations. He is not at all clear how the subjective mind is capable of observing itself,[11] and indeed no obvious representation of this process was at hand. One can readily represent how sensation takes place, just by imagining a black box receiving inputs, or, as Karl Pearson put it, a telephone operator receiving calls.[12] But there seems to be no comparable way of representing the manner in which the subjective mind knows its own processes. How *does* it know that it prefers A to B?

One rather bad answer to this question is to take preference as a "primitive," i.e., as an indefinable, idea so that there is no analysis which can possibly explicate its meaning. The concept of a "primitive idea," seems to have originated in symbolic logic. There it refers to the end point of the process of formal definition: primitives are the set of symbols in terms of which everything else is defined. If the primitives are "independent," then in this formal way of defining there is no further defining of the primitives themselves. There has been some considerable effort to adapt this concept of a primitive idea to empirical methodology in such a way that in the world of observables there are primitive properties that can only be understood if they are observed. Locke called these "simple sensations," and others have called them the sense data, the directly observed, etc. A large literature has pointed out that there is no possible basis for any useful application of the concept of an empirical primitive in science. The main gist of this criticism is that a scientific result must be communicated. If one tries to explain a primitive idea like color to another mind, one must point or otherwise narrow the attention of the other mind. But any such process of "pointing out" becomes *ipso facto* a part of the idea being explained; the process is indeed the "operational definition" of the idea. Hence the idea itself is not a primitive. Since the argument applies in general, there cannot be any primitive ideas in operational defining, and consequently no primitives in empirical science.[13] Furthermore, the introduction of an unanalyzable primitive is quite contrary to the spirit of empirical objectivity on which the paradigm we are examining is based. It is most inappropriate simply to say that the subjective mind apprehends its own states directly, but we cannot observe or represent this directness.

---

[11] A few sentences give the flavor of Locke's idea of reflection: "The other fountain from which experience furnishes the understanding with ideas is the perception of our own mind within us . . . which could not be had from things without. . . . This source of ideas every man has wholly in himself, and though it be not sense . . . yet it is very like it, and might properly be called internal sense. . . ." *Essays Concerning Human Understanding* (1689), Book I, Chap. 1, Sec. 4.

[12] *A Grammar of Science* (1892).

[13] C. W. Churchman, "Concepts Without Primitives," *Philosophy of Science,* 20 (1953).

Actually, there is at hand a rather obvious way to explain the reflective component of the subjective mind. This consists of representing the reflective mind as another mind that receives inputs from the preference processor. A computer representation of this reflective mind would be very easy to conceive: the "reflective" computer simply receives as inputs a certain type of output of another computer. Indeed, this reflective mind could be taken as a part of the information processor. The question is how this reflective part does in fact process the preference information it receives.

OBJECTIVE VS. SUBJECTIVE: HEGELIAN CRITICISM

Now if the "reflective mind" processes information about how the subjective mind makes its preferences, then the reflective mind is an inquiring mind. In this regard, should we think of the reflective mind like any other inquiring mind? If so, then we see that its problems are exactly the same as the problems of any inquiring mind: it cannot be sure that the inputs express true preference; it cannot know the intensity of a preference; etc. But also the inquiring mind is on an equal basis with any other inquiring mind, and it can communicate as readily as any other one. Hence, if the reflective mind is like any inquiring mind, one's own reflections on one's own preferences are a priori no better nor worse than any other sources of information.

In order to maintain the idea of the "pure" subjectivity of the subjective mind, one might argue for a very privileged relationship between a processor and its "own" reflective mind. Specifically, one might imagine that the link between the two is so excellent that the personal reflective mind has a far greater accuracy in determining preferences than any outer mind; furthermore, this internal reflective mind settles on a unit for the preference scale, but because of its close linkage to the preference processor it is unable to communicate the unit to any other mind. Such an account of subjectivity does seem to correspond to the inner feelings of at least some people: they truly believe that they are directly and accurately in touch with their own desires.[14]

However, there is the almost overwhelming weight of evidence to

---

[14] Luce and Raiffa's concentration on the distinction between "inside" and "outside" is not only apparent in the quote given on page 247, but also in the following discussion: "We imagine that most people feel it is easier to make operational sense of interattribute comparisons within an individual's mind than to make sense of interpersonal comparisons. Anyhow, we do. Why? Primarily because the individual himself can compare his psychological reaction to one (alternative attribute) pair versus another pair. *Games and Decisions*, p. 353.

One can see here the unquestioned attitude that what is "inside" can be known better by the insider than the outsider. In the quote given above they fail to realize that the "outside thing" they seek as a standard might will be the preferences of a third party, as each perceives him.

support the opposite point of view, namely, that people are often confused about their own feelings, do not know what they want, etc. There seems to be no a-priori nor common-sense reason why the inquiring mind should assume higher accuracy on the part of its own reflective part, unless it simply wants to maintain the mystery of subjectivity.

The effort to maintain the mysterious, internal reflective mind recalls the equally fantastic story which Luce and Raiffa created in the quote on page 247. One could address a number of embarrassing questions to anyone attempting to pass their story off as the truth. Obviously, if someone has "given" each man a measuring rod, then why did he not give the standard unit along with his other gifts? Furthermore, the two men must have transmitted a great deal more than mere numbers; they must have been able to tell each other that they were measuring lengths. To do so, they must have been able to transmit their respective techniques of calibrating and controlling their measurements, else neither one would feel that the other was really measuring lengths at all. Yet, they were able to transmit this enormous amount of information without once "leaking" the secret of the unit! It would require some ingenuity to reveal the calibration method without saying a good deal about the units of various scales used in the calibration. Any scientific group so bent on keeping secrets is better ignored by the rest of the scientific community.

In short, either the story teller is telling us about two isolated men who can pass no information to each other except for some meaningless bleeps, or else he is telling us about two men who can tell each other that they are measuring lengths and how they are measuring them. In the latter case, the men know a great deal about each other and are in a sound position to infer a great deal more.

The same point can be made in another way. If any mind is capable of learning the truth but not of transmitting it, has such a mind attained any degree of scientific validity? The answer must be in the negative: wherever communication fails to occur, science is absent. In other words, if there is a mind that is incapable of transmitting its calibration techniques and unit of measurements, then it should be ignored. We must conclude that the reflective part of the subjective mind is an inquiring mind and is not itself subjective. It has the same status as any other inquiring mind, except perhaps for a heightened degree of curiosity in some cases. This is not an argument against introspection, for one may come to believe that the internal reflective mind can be a reliable inquirer.

To conclude these remarks on subjectivity, we can point out that there is one sense in which it is true that no one can feel my toothache, but this sense is the trivial, tautological sense in which one mind and its state is necessarily different from another mind and its state. But there is a far more significant sense in which someone else can feel my toothache and judge how much alike it is to his aching foot; the judgments of his reflective mind and mine are two pieces of evidence about the true state of affairs of our respective preference structures, and the evidence in each case is to be used according to acceptable calibration and control processes of measurement.

We have reached a representation of minds in which "subjective mind" refers only to a mind that is being observed by other minds; it gains its subjectivity only by being an object of inquiry. The problem of inquiring minds is to learn about the states of this subjective mind, that is, to be objective about it. We have also reached that point in the history of thought when it was realized that the concept of mind necessarily involves both a subjective mind and a reflective mind; neither can exist without the other. It was Hegel [15] who developed the philosophy that something becomes real, i.e., objective, only by virtue of its being observed from all possible points of view. A simple analogy is to be found in the set of descriptions of a chair provided by a carpenter, artist, homeowner, and cat. Each will tell us in his own way what the chair is for him; what it is objectively is the meaningful composite of these descriptions. To create such a composite is that aim of objective science called "measurement." In the same vein, a person's preferences at a stage of his life are objectively ascertained only by being observed from many points of view—his wife's, his children's, his friends' and enemies'. What he "really" prefers is the ideal composite of all these points of view. To create such a composite is the goal of the measurement of utilities.

We note one other significant contribution of Hegelian thought: A mind is conscious only to the extent that it can be observed, and a fully conscious mind is an ideal of a mind observed from all points of view. In other words, a conscious mind is fully objective, not subjective. E. A. Singer [16] has described the point very well, and has shown how British empiricism converted the original meaning of consciousness, "knowing-with," into a knowing-alone.

SUBJECTIVE VS. OBJECTIVE EMPIRICISM

Indeed, it seems that Locke and his school, by paying too much attention to the immediacy of sensation and reflection, turned empiricism into a basically subjective philosophy. The strength of empiricism lies in its demand that knowledge be based on observation; the weakness of the British form of empiricism lay in its peculiar insistence that observation is ultimately grounded in an unanalyzable, subjective reaction. Yet this quirk of thinking persisted down to the present time, especially in

---

[15] *Phenomenology of Mind* (1807).
[16] "On Conscious Mind," *Journal of Philosophy,* 26 (1929).

the philosophies of the social sciences. Apparently many spokesmen for the social sciences feel that the security of their discipline lies in the elementary fact of subjectivity so that every issue is supposed to be "put to the test" of "direct" observation.[17] Here there is a confusion between the idea of grounding the theory of evidence in observation, which is needed, and the idea of a subjective, direct observation, which is not needed. In all these instances, there seems to be the underlying fear that if one doubts the validity of what is directly observed, one must give up the whole enterprise. But this is clearly not the case, as physical science and indeed the practice of social science show; it takes a very subtle process to elevate a set of observations to the status of accepted fact in the scientific community. Whenever one analyzes this process and attempts to justify it, one sees how "fact" is the product of many tentative judgments. By far the best analysis of the process is to be found in E. A. Singer's *Experience and Reflection*.[18]

Excessive attention to the observational "elements" of inquiry has also led to a peculiar attitude in the social sciences with respect to measurement; here the whole theory of measurement is taken to be embedded in a classification of scales.[19] Useful as this exercise has been in many respects, it has led to a faulty and superficial concept of the measurement system. Measurement is not merely the assignment of numbers to phenomena according to a rule; such a description ignores the empirical methodology completely. Measurement also includes all the operations required to calibrate and control. Measurement is essentially teleological, not merely structural. Its purpose is to provide a wide use of important information; the structure of this information is important, of course, but so are all of the control operations required to transmit the data so that it can meaningfully be applied in other places at other times.[20] Furthermore, one cannot decide whether a given measurement process provides information of a certain structural kind without knowing the calibration and control method.

ON THE COMPARISON OF UTILITIES

The conclusion is that preferences and utilities of different people can be compared *if* preferences and utilities can be measured at all. In other words, *if* one can obtain some knowledge of the preferences of an individual, then one can compare the preferences of two or more in-

---

17 For example, see M. Friedman, *Essays in Positive Economics* (Chicago: University of Chicago Press, 1959).

18 *Experience and Reflection* (Philadelphia: University of Pennsylvania Press, 1957).

19 S. S. Stevens, "Psychophysics and Utility," in *Measurement, Definitions and Theories*, eds. C. W. Churchman and P. Ratoosh (New York: Wiley, 1959).

20 C. W. Churchman, "Why Measure," in *Measurement*, eds. C. W. Churchman and P. Ratoosh.

dividuals. *If* the preferences of two persons can be predicted each by means of a scale, then the units of the two scales can be compared.

All the conditionals of the above statements are important, for if we grant that the true preference of an individual is the result of many ways of looking at his behavior, then we may want to question whether any preferences can ever be ascertained.

Once we accept the principle that knowledge of another does not proceed from simple, subjective reflection, but rather is the result of co-ordinating observations of many reflective minds, then the whole methodology of individual and group preferences must change. Welfare economics is sometimes described as trying to create a social utility function in terms of individual utilities; this again is reminiscent of a one-directional empiricism. The problem of a democratic society is not only the problem of creating social choice from individual preferences; it is also the problem of ascribing preferences by means of the most objective means available. We all know how a public can be made to believe that it prefers certain states of affairs; the social problem is to create valid sets of preferences.

In a society thus devoted to creating knowledge about human wants as well as policy based on these wants, the society is both the investigator and the decision maker. It must create the criteria of objective evidence of wants, and in a democratic society these criteria must be communicable and understood. Utilities can be compared, of course, but this is only a part of the picture. The rest is an enormous intellectual effort to create a coordinated picture of human wants in which conflict of desire is not destructive of the society nor does it bias the society's estimates of the wishes of certain segments.

We are certainly far from any such ideal of the democratic society. While appreciative of the gains that have been made in understanding conflict by means of game theory, I cannot help feeling that game theoretic methods have often reinforced the old notion that fairness in social life can be built up from given individual utilities and self-evident rational rules. Since no mention is made of the social choices that determined the given individual utilities, the whole question of the rational resolution of conflict is begged. At the very least, game theory should be given the license to assume an intercomparison of utilities because this freedom must have been granted in determining the individual utilities in the first place. Whether then game theory could be a fruitful ground for defining rational social choice remains to be seen.

CONCLUSION

We have reached the conclusion that one cannot measure an individual's preferences without creating a system of "reflective minds." This system is capable of generating evidence about the preferences, calibrating (adjusting) the evidence, and transmitting it to any mind of the system. The "true" preference of an individual is a limiting concept of this whole system; it is not a property of nor is it known by any of the reflecting minds.

The conclusion implies that utilities of different persons can be "compared"; alternatively, the unit of measurement of utility, if one exists, can be transmitted; alternatively, utilities are not merely unique up to a linear transformation except in the obvious sense that the scale unit can be picked arbitrarily for all persons by the measuring system. The implication is based on the notion that measurement consists in a set of strategies of a sufficiently large group of reflective minds. The philosophy of subjective preferences is based on the notion that one is fundamentally constrained from "peeking into" another's mind and that there is no way to design an inquiring system so that the constraint is removed. If one is so wedded to a paradigm that for him the world must of necessity be viewed in one particular way, then the paradigm has become a metaphysics in the worst sense of the term. The problem is not how to generate models of preference orderings under the constraint that scalar comparisons cannot be made. The problem is: Are such scalar comparisons desirable and what kind of an inquiring system design, or world, would permit such comparisons?

In the end, however, I cannot avoid the looks of those whom we glided by earlier who are appalled by the whole notion of a "preference processor." So am I, if it is intended to stand for all that a man wishes, hates, and loves. There is no doubt that much has been accomplished in economics, operations research, and management science by imagining a "decision maker" who makes choices by means of a preference processor of the sort discussed in this paper. The imagery seems to prove most successful when the decision does not touch the issues of social conflict too deeply or when the decision maker clearly operates in his bounded freedom to maximize some quantity. In politics and love, however, the imagery is of dubious value. At best it is merely one way to look at the subtleties of the human psyche.

RICHARD B. BRANDT

*Richard B. Brandt, Ph.D., Yale University, is Professor of
Philosophy and Chairman of the Department of Philosophy
at the University of Michigan. He was a Guggenheim
Fellow in the year 1944–45. He has contributed to
learned journals in the fields of moral philosophy and
epistemology.* He is the author of Hopi Ethics: A
Theoretical Analysis *(1954),* Ethical Theory *(1959), and is
the editor of* Value and Obligation *(1961), and, with
Professor Ernest Nagel, of* Meaning and Knowledge *(1965).
He has been Vice President of the Eastern Division of
the American Philosophical Association, and is President of
the American Society for Political and Legal Philosophy.*

ESSAY

16

ONE AREA IN WHICH THE MORAL PHILOSO-
pher might say something useful for the
thinking of economists is that of welfare
economics—not by improving formaliza-
tions or criticizing proofs as to conditions
necessary or sufficient for an optimum
situation, much less by suggesting what
particular state of society would be optimal. Rather, he can do this by pointing
out some distinctions (e.g., explaining why
assigning "social welfare" a certain meaning obscures important points), by suggesting how some terms used by economists
can profitably be defined, and by question-
ing some assumptions which seem to lie
behind the thinking of some economists.

The following discussion is aimed along
these lines. The main goal of the argument
will be to produce helpful definitions of
"increase the welfare of an individual" and
"increase social welfare." But the logical
points and distinctions introduced in the
course of the discourse may be of more
interest to the economist and can be accepted on their merits irrespective of one's

The

Concept

of

Welfare

appraisal of the main definitions. My discussion will draw upon recent work in "philosophical psychology" and moral philosophy, but it would be misleading, in view of controversies among philosophers, to suggest that it represents any "agreed results" of philosophical inquiries.

THE WELFARE OF INDIVIDUALS

The term "welfare" seems to carry a meaning, in ordinary talk about the welfare of individuals, different from what it carries in many recent discussions in which it appears in the expression "social welfare." Hence, it will be useful to begin by examining the meaning of "welfare" in our more familiar discourse about the welfare of individuals. Since I shall argue later that a useful concept of social welfare *involves* the concept of individual welfare, it behooves us to be clear about the latter notion before we try to define the former.

The *Shorter Oxford Dictionary*, among others, equates the meaning of "welfare" with that of "good fortune, happiness, or well-being; prosperity." This proposal is hardly helpful for our purposes. For if clarification of "welfare" is needed, it is equally needed for the terms "well-being" and "good fortune." The other two terms are at least somewhat more explicit, although for "prosperity" one may wonder whether money income, real income, or something else is meant. But in the case of these two terms it is mistaken to assert an equivalence of meaning with "welfare." It is untrue that a person's welfare increases if and only if his prosperity increases, for, to cite an example, we should say that a person's welfare was enhanced by a happy marriage, although such a marriage need not contribute to one's prosperity. "Happiness" is rather closer; but we should not want to say that a person's welfare is increased *only* if, and *to the extent that,* his happiness is increased. There is room for reasonable doubt about this last point, partly because "welfare" is a somewhat vague term; the reader will be in a better position to judge at a later stage.

A different reason for objecting to the Oxford proposal is that it undiscriminatingly mixes terms of entirely different kinds. "Well-being" and "good fortune" appear to be value-words and probably do not designate anything observable (probably are not parts of an "empiricist language"); whereas "happiness" and "prosperity" are not value-words and, with reservations about vagueness, are parts of an "empiricist language." Since it is helpful to place these distinctions in clear focus, in view of their importance for the confirmation of judgments containing these terms, let us pause to formulate the concepts of "empirical language" and "value-judgment" (or "value-word").

Let us consider the notion of an "empiricist language." [1] Such a language may be explained or defined in terms of its vocabulary. First, it includes words for the concepts of logic—those essential for discourse and argument about any subject matter—and in particular words like "all," "some," "the," "if . . . then . . ." (and including "if it *were* the case that . . . then it *would be* the case that . . ."), "not," and "or." Second, it includes terms for *observable* properties and relations, such as "red," "between," "painful," and "joy." There are debates about which terms should be classified as observation terms, but for the present this rather technical epistemological point may be ignored. Third, it includes all terms synonymous with any complex of terms formed from the vocabulary already admitted. Fourth—and here we get into deeper water —it includes other terms (like "electron") which are tied to terms of the second and third classes by virtue of appearing in laws or rules in which terms of the other classes also appear. Such laws or rules are often said to accomplish a "partial definition" of terms of this fourth type. Rudolf Carnap has argued that this fourth class is very large indeed, in science, but we need not pursue this question.

Whether a statement belongs to an empiricist language in this sense is an important matter. For any statement in an empiricist language is open to assessment by the methods of empirical science, whereas this is not possible for any statement which does not belong to an empiricist language.

If we overlook some points of vagueness, it is clear that "happiness" and "prosperity" belong to an empiricist language; the same is true for "welfare" *if* its meaning were equated with that of these terms. (I. D. M. Little has doubted this claim about "happiness" in contexts of talk of "increasing the happiness of the community"; explanations are needed if we are to use the term in such a context.)

Let us turn now to the concepts of "value-judgment" and "value-word." Some writers classify a judgment as a value-judgment if and only if it *cannot be formulated in an empiricist language.* If this proposal were acceptable, we could drop "value-judgment" as a *second* conceptual tool, and get along with the first one alone. But the proposal is too broad. Statements in books on theology, or on metaphysics, or even inductive logic (statements containing "probable" or "well-warranted") appear not to be formulable in an empiricist language, but it would be odd to say that they necessarily express value-judgments. Moreover, some philosophers ("naturalists" in value theory) hold that value statements *do* belong to an empiricist language, and we do not wish to prejudge this

---

[1] For a discussion of the concept of an empiricist language, and some of its difficulties, see C. G. Hempel, "Problems and Changes in the Empiricist Criterion of Meaning," reprinted, with afterthoughts, in A. J. Ayer ed., *Logical Positivism* (New York: Free Press, 1959). This paper includes a useful bibliography.

issue by linguistic legislation. (Even if we did, we should not succeed in settling any important issue, for the question could still arise whether judgments to the effect that "It is a good thing that . . ." were value-judgments in that sense.) I believe, then, that we should adopt a neutral definition of "value-judgment" which at least begs no important questions. I propose the following, while conceding that it needs to be spelled out more elaborately than is possible here. Let us say that a judgment is a value-judgment if, and only if, it entails or contradicts some judgment which could be formulated so as to involve any one of the following terms, in its ordinary sense, in an essential way: (1) "is a good thing that" (or "is a better thing that"), (2) "is morally obligatory," (3) "is reprehensible," and (4) "is morally praiseworthy." If one wishes to use "value-judgment" more narrowly, so as to distinguish it from specifically ethical or moral judgments, one could define it by reference to just the *first* of the foregoing phrases. Now a "value-word" or "value-phrase" is one the occurrence of which in a statement marks the statement as a value-statement expressing a value-judgment. "Is a good thing that" is a clear case of a value-phrase.

If we ask whether, by this criterion, judgments about the welfare of individuals are value-judgments, the correct answer appears to be affirmative. For take the phrase, which is the important one for the economist, "is on a *higher level of welfare.*" The statement, "X is on a higher level of welfare if he is in situation S rather than S'" appears to imply or even mean the same as "X is *better off* in S than in S', if we abstract from all questions of moral obligation and the rights of others"; and the same for, "If we abstract from all questions of moral obligation and the rights of others, it is a *better thing* for X to be in S than in S'." If this is correct, then such judgments are value-judgments in our sense, and "welfare" appears to be a value-word. The same is not, however, true of "happiness." From "X is happier in S than in S'" it does not appear to *follow* that he is necessarily better off. This is shown by the fact that it is not inconsistent to think that knowledge is better than ignorance, and therefore, that, whereas a person might be happier in S than in S', he is worse off because he is more ignorant in S (perhaps he is happily half-witted in situation S). "Happiness," then, is not a value-word—which is an additional reason for denying that it is synonymous with "welfare."

So far, then, our tentative conclusion about "welfare" is (1) that it is a value-word and (2) that it does not mean the same as either "prosperity" or "happiness." Since we have defined "value-word" (and "value-judgment") in a neutral way, so as not to commit us on the question whether value-words belong to an empiricist language, we are not yet committed to any conclusion about whether welfare-judgments can be confirmed by the methods of science.

It might seem that the next order of business, then, must be to state the outcome of the enormous philosophical literature on the meaning and function of value-words in general and then to attempt to map the place of "welfare" among value-words (viz., map the logical relations to other value-words) as all of these are used in ordinary speech.

This undertaking would be all very well for the authors of a dictionary, but I do not believe it would be very profitable for economists or philosophers.[2] The fundamental reason for this is that value-words, in their ordinary use, are very vague, and the authors of value-statements do not have any definite meaning in mind when they make them. Moreover, there is some reason to think that what meaning they have varies a good deal from one person to another, the extent depending largely upon the cultural history of the individual. What is called for, in contrast to laboring with ordinary usage, is that we *assign* some definite meaning to these terms, doubtless within the rough and vague limits prescribed by present usage, and that we do so for definite, statable, and relevant reasons. This holds, I believe, for the term "welfare."

It may seem that the job of picking a useful and relevant meaning for "welfare" is a wholly amorphous one, too indefinite to qualify as a job at which one could either succeed or fail. But let us see. In fact, it will be possible to be quite brief, although at the outset we must consider some facts which may seem extraneous to our concern about "welfare."

Let me begin by pointing out that there are a great many choices or decisions which an individual has to make when we think he is free to attend only to his own welfare—when no moral obligations to others are involved and no considerations of the rights of others arise. An example of such a choice, in normal circumstances, is which profession to prepare for, whether law, or teaching philosophy, and so on. Another and humbler example is whether to enter this drugstore for a breakfast egg or to seek the same in the cafeteria across the street. Let us consider only choices of this sort.

Suppose there is such a choice to be made. The agent may be in doubt what to do. Or, having made the choice, he may be in doubt whether he did not "make a mistake." If there is this element of doubt or puzzlement, the question arises whether one possible choice may be defended, supported, or justified, as compared with others. It is obvious that people *do* engage in some sort of reflection which they think sometimes results in a justification of a choice, to their own satisfaction.

About this process of reflection, we can sensibly raise two questions: Is there any particular kind of consideration or reflection which in prac-

---

[2] I have argued this at some length in *Moral Philosophy and the Analysis of Language*, The Lindley Lecture for 1963, published by the Department of Philosophy, University of Kansas, 1963. I have discussed the varieties, and difficulties, of various theories about the meaning of value-words in ordinary language in *Ethical Theory* (Englewood Cliffs, N.J.: Prentice-Hall, 1959), Chaps. 7 to 9.

tice thoughtful people in general find weighty or conclusive support or justification of this sort? And, if so, is it possible to give an account, universally persuasive to thoughtful people, of *why* attention should be given this kind of consideration, in guiding one's conduct? [3]

I believe there is a particular kind of reflection which thoughtful persons do find weighty, and for good reasons. Something close to it was indicated by John Stuart Mill, when he said that the only way to find whether something is desirable is, in the end, to find whether people do desire it. A more adequate account is, roughly, to say that a choice is considered justified, and with good reason, if it is shown that it is one which the agent, if he were "rational," would prefer to any alternative open to him. Or, to spell out the term "rational" just a bit, a choice is considered justified, and with good reason, if it is shown that the agent would prefer it to any other open to him at the time, if he were in a normal frame of mind and believed correctly all the facts relevant to the choice and had them vividly before his mind. To say this is still so brief as to be cryptic: I shall, therefore, proceed now to spell out what I mean by "prefer," and by "rational"; and I shall sketch the reasons which may be given for saying that one should pay attention to one's rational preferences in making one's decisions.

But first let me acknowledge that other proposals have been made about how to justify one's choices, some of them highly implausible and unrealistic. One cf these I shall discuss at some length in a moment: it is the by no means implausible prcposal that a choice is justified, for the limited type of context we are discussing, if and only if it would (or probably would) maximize the net enjoyment or satisfaction of the agent.

Let me now explain the concept of rational preference, and then the alternative proposal. After I have done this, we shall be in a position to consider what meaning may fruitfully be assigned to "increases the welfare of an individual."

Preference

What is it to "prefer"? First, it is convenient to say that what we prefer is always *that one situation be the case* rather than that another be the case. Thus, we may prefer *that* Jones be elected mayor rather than that Smith be elected. We often *say* we prefer *things,* say chocolate to vanilla. But we can always rephrase such remarks in our standard vocabulary; e.g., we can say that we prefer *that* we be savoring chocolate than that we be savoring vanilla.

Now, what I mean by "X would *prefer* that p to that q" (e.g., that he

---

[3] It may be interesting to reflect on whether the accepted standards for inductive inference in science can be given support fundamentally different from that which can be given for choices.

do A rather than that he do B) is "X would *want* that p *more* than that q" or else "would have less of an *aversion* to p than to q," if the alternatives were before him as possibilities. It is perhaps obvious that it does not follow, from the fact that X *chooses* that p rather than that q, that he *wants* that p more than that q. For a person may *select* a cake from a plate of cakes offered him, when he does not prefer (want more) that one to any other cake on the plate, simply because he is busy talking with someone. Moreover, people often act impulsively without attending carefully to what they most want. Further, people can make mistakes about what they want: a person can think he wants a good character, when in reality he simply has an aversion to a bad reputation. Since what a person does is more closely related to what he thinks he wants than to what he does want, there is a further reason why what one does may not be an indicator of what one most wants or prefers.

But what then is it to *want* that p? This is a more elusive concept than might appear at first, as anyone will know who when making a difficult decision has tried to follow the advice "Do what you most *want* to do!" It seems quite clear that wanting something is not a simple introspectible datum like a tickle. The exact logic of the concept of wanting is a difficult matter,[4] but I believe the central portion of the concept of wanting is captured in the following propositions, relating wanting to observable events: (a) If, given that X had not been expecting p but now suddenly judged that p would be the case, X would feel joy, then X wants p. (b) If, given that X had been expecting p but then suddenly judged that p would not be the case, X would feel disappointment, then X wants p. (c) If daydreaming about p is pleasant to X, then X wants p. (d) If X wants p, then, under favorable conditions, if X judges that doing A will probably lead to p and that not doing A will probably lead to not-p, X will feel some impulse to do A. (e) If X wants p, then, under favorable conditions, if X thinks some means M is a way of bringing p about, X will be more likely to notice an M than he would otherwise have been. (f) If X wants p, then, under favorable conditions, if p occurs to the knowledge of X, without the simultaneous occurrence of events X does not want, X will be pleased.[5]

---

[4] See the discussion by R. B. Brandt and Jaegwon Kim, "Wants as Explanations of Actions," *Journal of Philosophy*, 60 (1963), 425-435. For some differences between wants and aversions see Stephen Pepper, *The Sources of Value* (Berkeley: University of California Press, 1958), Chap. 10; and E. C. Tolman, *Purposive Behavior in Animals and Men* (New York: Appleton, 1932). See also Fritz Heider, *Psychology of Interpersonal Relations* (New York: Wiley, 1958), Chaps. 4 and 5.

[5] These propositions are drawn from Brandt and Kim, *Journal of Philosophy*. Some of them require refinement. I do not believe that at present we can give any satisfactory general explanation for "under favorable conditions." We shall wish to include as "unfavorable" conditions such things as extreme fatigue, emotional excitement, and temporal remoteness of the event judged about.

It seems plausible to suppose that evidence for wanting p more than q is provided by occurrence of the events cited in a more intense form, in connection with judgments about p, than with judgments about q.

If the foregoing conception is well taken, then what a person wants is fixed by what he has to *think about* in order for these effects to occur.

I have suggested that there is not a simple relation between what a person wants and the choices he makes. For very similar reasons there is not a simple relation between what a person wants (or wants more or less) and the bets he will lay. It would, of course, be unreasonable to deny that betting behavior is strong evidence about the relative strength of wants.

Rational preference

I have suggested that preference may be called "rational" when it meets certain conditions. Let me explain these more fully.

When we prefer one event p to another q, it is always because we think (at least take for granted or believe) that these events have different properties. (These could be just the properties defining what it is to be a "p" or a "q" occurrence.) For instance, we may prefer the profession of medicine because we think the life of a physician, as compared with that of a philosopher, is one of more contact with other persons or one which produces more definite and tangible results. This fact points to one possible way of criticizing a preference: that of showing that the beliefs on which it is based are incorrect, or even unintelligible. It also points to a second possible way: that of showing that the beliefs on which it is based are incomplete, that there are further facts such that if the agent had thought about them, he would have preferred what he did either more or less. It seems, then, that one condition of a fully justified preference could be this: that it is based on all true beliefs about the object in question which would tend to move the agent one way or the other. I propose calling a preference "rational" only if this condition is met.

There is a second and closely related condition. Sometimes in a sense we *know* all the pros and cons relevant to a preference, but we do not have them *all before our mind*. Sometimes when we think of one feature of an alternative, we feel drawn toward it; when we think of another feature, we feel repelled. This raises the question: What would we prefer if we could get *all* the relevant features before our mind with full vividness—as vividly as if we could actually perceive them all? I propose to call a preference fully "rational" only when it is as it would be if this condition were met.

There is a third defect from which a preference may suffer. It may be formed, and be capable of being formed, only in a peculiar mood or frame of mind. Some features of something may appeal to us more in some frames of mind than others, for instance, under the smart of a wound to our pride. So, again, I propose to call a preference "rational" only when this defect is absent—when the preference is one that would be framed in a state of mind undistorted by temporary mood or emotion or by some temporary craving.

I suggest that we call a preference for p over q a *rational* preference *if, and only if*, these three conditions are met.

We should notice that the question whether a person rationally, in this sense, prefers p to q is one that in principle can be answered by empirical means, by the person and also within limits by other people (assuming they can get information about his wants and aversions)—of course, in some cases by no means easily; for answering requires finding the actual properties of p and q, correct beliefs about which would tend to move a person if he had them.

When thoughtful people have an important decision to make and are in some doubt what to do, I believe that in fact they try to see whether their tentative preference is rational in this sense. If they are convinced it is, they are satisfied with a corresponding decision. The reader is invited to introspect, to determine whether or not this is the case.

But is there any reason, which will be universally persuasive to thoughtful people, why they should guide their conduct by this sort of reflection? (1) For one thing, there is not really a serious alternative, if one is going to be reflective about choices, to paying attention to what we *want* to do. This will be clearer after we have considered the major alternative. (2) *If* we aim to make it a policy to do what we most want to do, presumably the policy will be to do the thing we most want of the *actual* alternatives open to us, as they really are, and not the thing we most want among mere caricatures of the alternatives. And to this end we need knowledge of the relevant facts vividly before us. (3) It is sensible to pay attention to "normal" preferences since we have to live with our decisions. It would be imprudent to favor the fleeting preference of a moment in making a decision we may long dislike and regret. To this it may be replied that no reason has been given why we now should take an interest in whether we shall regret something; but at any rate we can say that it is arbitrary to favor only the preference of the present moment and also that in fact most persons do take an interest in whether they will regret a decision later, when they reflect that they are the very same person who will have to endure the later regrets.

I have already acknowledged that there are other possible systems for appraising choices of the limited kind under consideration. I shall discuss a closely related method in a moment. But there are some quite different ways. A person might think he should choose only what conforms with the "purpose" of the universe, or with God's will. Conceivably reasons might be given for using such a method (although I suspect such reasons would reduce to the method already described). I do not see how we can rule out, in advance, all such possibilities as being absurd. But we also need not worry about them until they are formulated and we know what they are. What we can say now is that up to the present no comparably supported method (aside from the one to be discussed next) has been produced [6] and that a choice which meets the conditions described has met the known possible objections which might seriously be raised against it.

Pleasure, happiness, and satisfaction

There is one possible way of supporting or justifying one's choices (in cases where no questions arise about moral obligation or the rights of others), which is different from the one just outlined, and which has some plausibility. This is the familiar view that an agent's choice is justified if, and only if, it will (or probably will) result in maximizing the agent's pleasure, happiness, or satisfaction. This conception has appealed to many economists and philosophers influenced by the utilitarian tradition.

We can simplify discussion without loss by construing the proposal in terms of maximizing the agent's net long-run *pleasure,* dropping out explicit reference to happiness and satisfaction. At least we can do this if we construe "pleasure" broadly enough so as not to imply merely sensory pleasure but to include such enjoyments as that of reading a book and if we construe "displeasure" broadly enough so as to include such displeasures as those of anxiety and embarrassment in addition to physical discomforts.

It might be objected to this simplification that it distorts and reduces the plausibility of the proposal. But this can hardly be correct, for it appears that we can define "happiness" in all its various senses in terms of "pleasant."

For instance, "I was happy all evening until he said . . ." means the same as "I was enjoying myself this evening until he said . . ." or "I was having a perfectly pleasant evening until he said. . . ." It is often asserted, however, that "happiness" is not a sum of pleasures. In this statement, "happy" is being used in a different and somewhat narrower sense. To be happy in this sense is to be pleased, or at least not discontent, with one's achievements or prospects with respect to one's major goals in life. Indeed, some recent work suggests that people call themselves "happy" if they are pleased, or at least not discontent, with achievement, or prospects, with respect to what they consider their most important

---

[6] I have discussed the merits of the theological proposal in *Ethical Theory,* pp. 63-82 and 252-253.

goals. So we might define "is happy" in this sense as meaning "does not feel any unpleasant emotion at the thought of where he is or is getting with respect to certain major aims in life" and perhaps also "goes about his work with a pleasant cheer and zest." In other words, when one is happy in this sense, one's life is not marred with unpleasant emotions when one reflects on certain matters and by and large one's activities are pleasant. If we conceive "happiness" thus, then it is true that a sequence of sensual pleasures does not amount to happiness; but it is also true that happiness is nothing other than the enjoyment (or absence of displeasure) resulting from being able to take an optimistic view about progress toward important goals. There are doubtless other senses of "happy" which we should recognize; and we must remember that the term is a rather vague one. There is no reason to believe, however, that such other senses cannot be explained in terms of "enjoys" and "pleasant."

Much the same is true of "satisfaction." Suppose a person says he gets much satisfaction out of the progress of his former graduate students in the academic world. What he means is no more than that reflection on the success of certain former students is pleasant. Explanations of other uses of this term will readily come to mind.

With these preliminaries out of the way, the question is this: Might we regard a choice as sensible (in the limited context described above), if it will (or probably will) maximize one's net long-run pleasure, as contrasted with being in conformity with one's rational preference? It will help us adjudicate this question if we consider briefly the nature of pleasure or pleasantness, about which there has recently developed a considerable literature.[7]

---

[7] See G. Ryle, *The Concept of Mind* (London: Hutchinson's University Library, 1949), Chap. 4; also his *Dilemmas* (Cambridge: Cambridge U. P., 1954), Chap. 4; and G. Ryle and W. B. Gallie, "Pleasure," symposium, Aristotelian Society, supplementary Vol. 28 (1954), 135-164. T. Penelhum, "The Logic of Pleasure," *Philosophy and Phenomenological Research*, 17 (1957), 488-503; and T. Penelhum, W. E. Kennick, and A. I. Isenberg, symposium, "Pleasure and Falsity," *American Philosophical Quarterly*, 1 (1964), 81-100. C. W. W. Taylor, "Pleasure," *Analysis*, Supplement, 23 (1963), 1-19. R. M. McNaughton, "A Metrical Concept of Happiness," *Philosophy and Phenomenological Research*, 14 (1953), 172-183. A. R. Manser, "Pleasure," *Proceedings*, Aristotelian Society (1960-1961), 223-238. B. Williams and E. Bedford, "Pleasure and Belief," symposium, Aristotelian Society supplementary Vol. 33 (1959), 57-92. R. B. Brandt, *Ethical Theory*, pp. 304-307. P. Nowell-Smith, *Ethics* (Pelican Book, 1954), Chap. 10.

For interesting psychologists' discussions, see Fritz Heider, *The Psychology of Interpersonal Relations* (New York: Wiley, 1959), Chap. 5; J. G. Beebe-Center, *The Psychology of Pleasantness and Unpleasantness* (New York: Van Nostrand, 1932), 394-413; and his "Feeling and Emotion" in H. Helson, ed., *Theoretical Foundations of Psychology* (New York: Van Nostrand, 1951); P. T. Young, *Emotion in Man and Animal* (New York: Wiley, 1943), Chap. 7; Magda Arnold, *Emotion and Personality* (New York: Columbia, 1960), Vol. I. Perhaps most interesting of all is K. Duncker, "On Pleasure, Emotion, and Striving," *Philosophy and Phenomenological Research*, 1 (1941), 391-430.

The first thing to be noted is that what is pleasant is always some conscious state, or activity, of a person. Things that are pleasant are things like dozing in the sun, listening to a symphony, reading a novel, or hearing good news.

It follows that on this second theory the class of "ultimate reasons" justifying a choice is narrower than on the first theory. The reason for this is that people actually *want* other things besides their own conscious states or activities. Of course, people do want enjoyment and do have an aversion to pain, anxiety, and other unpleasant states. But there are other things they want: such as to get a manuscript in better shape, to have a daughter happy in her marriage and financially secure after her parents' death. Some writers have thought that what a person desires is always some state (or, more particularly, some pleasant state) of himself; but by any reasonable criterion for identifying what a person desires (such as the criteria sketched above), people desire some things which cannot be described as states of themselves. It is true that if one's manuscript gets in better shape, one will feel "happier" about it, and if one's daughter is happily married and provided for, one will feel less unpleasant anxiety about her. But these states of one's self are obviously not the targets of one's desire. For this reason it is quite natural and unconfused for people to ask themselves whether it is sensible to sacrifice personal enjoyments in order to achieve something important; this is a real alternative and some people prefer one course, some another. Of course, it may be that one can *rationally* want something only to the extent that getting it will make one happier; but the rational-preference theory leaves open the possibility that this is not the case. And it is surely not obvious that a "rational" want would be only for some pleasant state of one's self.

A second feature of pleasure is important for our purposes. What precise kind of state or activity is a "pleasant" one? On this the experts are much less fully agreed. Some suppose that "pleasure" consists in relaxation-feelings or bright pressure-feelings, but others find it impossible to introspect such feelings when they are enjoying themselves. Others have held that "pleasure" is always a case of activity in which one is absorbed or to which one attends without effort, but this description hardly fits what is happening when one is dozing in the sun, and one wonders how such writers would describe how one feels when the dentist is drilling. I think myself that the property which most clearly belongs to all pleasant states and activities is simply that *at the time the person wants them to continue for their own sakes* (which is consistent both with not *thinking* that one wants them to continue, and also with *not wanting* to continue them, *everything considered,* in view of consequences or of other things one ought to be doing). And, for one experience to be *more* pleasant than another, is for the person to want to continue it, more intensely, for itself. We should notice that things as diverse as playing a game and having a certain kind of sensation may be pleasant in this sense.[8]

If I am right in this, then pleasure is a *species* of wanting: it is wanting some *present* state or activity to *continue, for its own sake*. Incidentally, one can want a state or activity to continue at the time, but afterward wish it had not. Whether one wants something, and how much, seems to be partly a function of the state of one's glands, so that there may be some inconstancy in what one wants, perhaps even in what one rationally wants. (*If* there is, there may be a limit to the consistent direction we can get for action from appeal to our rational preferences.)

I can now explain why I believe that the traditional hedonist view of how choices (for our limited context) are to be appraised should not be substituted for the "rational-preference" proposal. The major reason is simply that to adopt the hedonist view amounts to an arbitrary decision in favor of conscious states or activities which one wants at the time one has them. It is true that we want these, both at the time and often beforehand, but what is so sacrosanct about them so that all other wants must be dismissed? If a person, after careful reflection, finds that he wants some things (to make an important discovery or the security of his children) more than states of personal enjoyment, it is not clear that there is any persuasive ground for abandoning these desires (as there is for abandoning desires which we would not have except in depressed moments). Of course, the rational-preference proposal leaves open the possibility that a rational want is never directed at anything but a pleasant state of consciousness or a pleasant activity. The rational-preference proposal, therefore, leaves open the possibility that the hedonist is right in his conclusion. But to adopt it at the outset as a method of appraisal is to opt arbitrarily for a special sort of want: for wants directed at the continuance of some state or activity of the self at the time.

There is a second difficulty in the proposal. In order to make rational decisions by the hedonist standard, one must compare enjoyments of certain duration and intensity, for magnitude, with enjoyments of different duration and intensity. But this is impossible: we can compare the intensities of different experiences (strength of wanting to continue at the time), but we cannot compare intensities with durations. We *can*

---

[8] An objection sometimes raised to this proposal is that we can tell directly, by inspection, whether we are enjoying something, whereas we would (it is supposed) have to stop and reflect in order to know that we want to continue some experience or activity for itself (assuming the correctness of the above account of "wanting"). Various points may be made in reply to this. One is that we know, without elaborate reflection, that we would like to have a lot of things: an increase in salary, a trip to Europe, a drink of water, to find misplaced glasses. Another is that it is not impossible to become conditioned to respond with "Yes," when stimulated by the question "Are you enjoying yourself," when and only when we want some present state or activity to continue. Many analogous phenomena have been found in experiments on concept formation.

make the comparisons necessary for decision, however, if we take the notion of preference as basic. We can prefer to endure, say, a certain stretch of pain of a given intensity for the sake of a different stretch of enjoyment of a given intensity. (It does not follow from this that there is *more enjoyment* in the preferred experience.) So it appears that the hedonist can make judgments he needs to make, only if he falls back on the preference standard after all. (He can refuse to do this if he admits that there is no rational answer to questions about conduct which could be answered only by comparisons of the sort described.)

Levels of individual welfare

Thus far I have argued that one might support a choice by showing that it conforms with one's "rational preference" in a sense explained. I have suggested that thoughtful people do appraise actual or possible choices in this manner and that there are reasons which would dispose a thoughtful person to pay attention to his rational preference in deciding what to do. Further, I have suggested that there is no other mode of appraising choices which has a comparable claim on conduct for those cases in which moral obligations and the rights of others are not involved.

We must now revert to the original question what meaning can usefully be assigned to "welfare" or "on a higher level of welfare."

It might be argued that we do not have to "assign" any meaning here, for it is clear that what we *already* mean, in English, by these terms is such that "X is on a higher level of welfare if p rather than if q" just means "X rationally prefers that p to that q" in the above-defined sense of "rationally prefers." (And the same for, "X is better off if p than if q.") At one time I inclined to this view myself, but I believe that "better off" and "welfare" are too vague for this suggestion to be correct. Therefore, if "welfare" is to have a meaning of the kind indicated, it must be an assigned one.

What purpose should guide our assignment of meanings? We need not aim to preserve the vagueness of ordinary language. We need, rather, to have meanings so assigned that things which are important to say can be said clearly and unambiguously. Further, we need terminology related to choice and conduct which enables us to raise and distinguish all the questions it is important to raise, in view of our total understanding of the human scene. And, if I am right in thinking that there is a preferred method for resolving doubts about choices and for appraising choices, we shall need some terms indicative of the status of a choice with respect to the application of this method.

What meaning, then, all these points considered, should we assign to "is on a higher level of welfare"? One possibility is simply to use it as a synonym for "prefers." However, we already have a perfectly good term for this concept. Further, in ordinary speech we often contrast preference with welfare (a person may prefer what is bad for him). I suggest, then, that we are keeping reasonably close to the ordinary associations of "welfare," and are at the same time assigning a useful meaning to the term, if we decide to use "X is on a higher level of welfare if p than if q" to mean "X rationally prefers p to q."

If we adopt this definition, it follows that one person might be put on a higher level of welfare by the very same kind of occurrence that will put another person on a lower level. It also follows that a person's own rational desires are decisive for his own welfare and that the desires of others are not—however much another's wish for him may be more reliable as an indicator of his rational desires than his own actual wishes are. If X conforms to what others want him to do, when their wants are rational, he is adding to *their* welfare, not necessarily to his own. Also, if X wants his son's happiness (rationally), then his son's happiness really does raise X's level of welfare, the extent depending upon how much X wanted it.

Some propositions appear to be true about the rational wants of all persons; but whether they are logically or only empirically true, I shall not discuss. Among them are the following: (1) If a person rationally wants both p and q, and is indifferent between them, he will rationally prefer a given probability of getting p to a smaller probability of getting q. (2) A person will not rationally prefer p to q on account of temporal position *alone*. (3) Knowledge that an event will be pleasant for a person will always arouse, so far, a favorable rational interest in the event; and knowledge that it will be unpleasant will always arouse, so far, a rational aversion toward the event. (4) The rational preferences of a person will be transitive.

Given the above definition, we shall want to specify that a good or service has *utility* for a person if he would rationally prefer to have it rather than not have it. To say that two goods have equal utility for a person will be to say that the person would be rationally indifferent between them.

If the foregoing definition is accepted, "welfare" and "utility" both belong to an empiricist language and at the same time are "value-words" which can function essentially in the expression of a value-judgment.

SOCIAL WELFARE

The foregoing definitions do not commit us to any particular definitions of "social welfare" or "increases social welfare," terms which appear frequently in the literature of welfare economics. Let us now consider what would be a useful way to construe these terms. Our results will enable us to appraise the status of the proposition "The social welfare is increased by the change from S to S' if this increases the welfare of at least one person and the welfare of no one is diminished by the change," a proposition which is viewed by some economists as an ultimate value-judgment. My conclusion will be that this proposition is true by definition.

Space limitations forbid considering various possible meanings that could be assigned to the above expressions. So let us go at once to the heart of the matter: the question what an economist might do, with good reason, to *support* advice he might offer to a public official as to some proposed rule or law. We could follow lines of thought similar to those pursued in the preceding section to justify saying that what one must do, in order to support a recommendation of a rule or law, is show that the rule or law is one *he (or others) would want adopted, if he (they) were rational (in the above-defined sense) and also were a person (persons) whose concern for others were equal to his (their) concern for self or family.*

I shall have to pass by the question what complications are raised by the possibility that two rational and sympathetic persons might disagree in their recommendations. I incline to think that in fact they *would* disagree to some extent, but I also believe there are some principles on which they [9] will necessarily agree—parallel to what was suggested for the case of individual welfare.

Now we could, with some sense, propose to assign to "Rule A will *increase the social welfare* more than Rule B" the meaning "If I [alternatively: anyone] were rational and sympathetic I [he] would prefer to have Rule A adopted rather than Rule B." But in fact this would be inconvenient and misleading, for there are different fundamental reasons on account of which thoughtful people have wanted rules adopted—not only considerations of welfare, but also considerations of justice or equality. (Witness how people have favored equality of income when they have not argued that this would increase the total real income; or they have argued that it should be illegal to purchase ration tickets or to buy a substitute for military service, although they have not denied that such exchanges might increase total welfare.) Indeed, the difference between utilitarians and their critics has been that the utilitarians have said that in the end only increasing welfare is a relevant and forcible reason for adopting an institution, whereas their critics have denied this. In order to preserve at least the possibility of debating these controversial points, it is necessary to assign a meaning to "increases social

---

[9] See my *Ethical Theory*, Chaps. 5, 6, and 11; also *Value and Obligation* (New York: Harcourt, 1961), pp. 433-440; and *Hopi Ethics: A Theoretical Analysis* (Chicago: University of Chicago Press, 1954), Chap. 16 and following.

welfare" so that it is not *self-contradictory* to say "If I [one] were rational and sympathetic I [one] would prefer to have Rule *A* adopted rather than Rule *B*, for reasons of justice, and despite the fact that Rule *B* would enhance social welfare more."

How might we assign meaning to "increases social welfare" so as to meet this condition in a helpful way? I see no alternative to a formulation equating "increases social welfare" with "increases the *sum* of individual welfare" where "individual welfare" is explained as in the preceding section. It remains to be shown, of course, that the welfares of individuals, in that sense of "welfare," *can* be summed. But it is clear, at least, that if "social welfare" is defined in this way, it follows that the social welfare is increased if the welfare of at least one person is increased and that of no one else decreased. It is for this reason that I suggested above that it is an analytic proposition, as we must construe "increased social welfare," that social welfare will be increased under these conditions. Thus, if this definition is adopted, part of welfare economics rests on the sound foundation of an analytic proposition.

It is well-known, however, that if we are to speak of the "sum" of individual welfares and also in principle to be able to determine which of two laws increases the sum of individual welfares the more, certain other propositions must be true. Most important, we must be able to compare for size the prospective utility of one person or persons with the prospective disutility of some other person or persons, if a certain law is adopted. And, if we explain "utility" as above suggested, this means that at least sometimes we must be able to affirm reasonably the following proposition: that *X wants A* more than *Y wants B*. (We are ultimately concerned with a comparison between the *rational* wants of *X* and *Y*, but that problem can be ignored for the present.)

Since the possibility of reasonably affirming propositions of this sort is so central to application of this (traditional) concept of "social welfare" that I am suggesting, and since I happen to think that some economists take an unreasonably purist view about this matter, I shall conclude my remarks with some queries about the epistemology of these economists.

Since according to suggestions made above, the intensity of a person's wanting is measured by various things such as the disappointment he would feel if he did not get it, we may as well simplify our problem by asking simply whether we can know that one person has some conscious state (e.g., disappointment, pain) more intensely than does some other person.

One difficulty a noneconomist has in discussing this problem is that he does not know exactly what is behind the economist's conclusions. If the economist thinks we cannot have sufficient reasons for thinking other persons conscious at all, that is one thing. If, however, he thinks we have sufficient reasons for thinking other persons are conscious, and perhaps for asserting *some* things about their states of consciousness, that is another.

Let us begin with the second possibility. Presumably in this case the purist economist thinks that certain pieces of evidence are good and sufficient for making some assertions about the consciousness of others. Then our question must be: Why draw the line here? Are the reasons you think adequate for these assertions not essentially of the same kind as those available for other affirmations? Suppose the purist economist thinks another person has at least three different colors in his visual field (he may say we cannot know what these colors are like). If this is asserted because it is necessary to explain the other's color discriminations, then one might go on to suggest that the other person's ability to predict that a proctoscopic examination will hurt *me* more than a mosquito bite is good reason for saying that the former hurts *him* more than the latter sort of thing. It is, perhaps, obvious how we might go on. Exactly what we should do is necessarily unclear, of course, until we have information about exactly what the purist is prepared to concede.

The purist economist may be much more radical, however. He may say we have no good reason for making any assertions about the conscious states of other persons, even for asserting that other persons are conscious at all. We should notice, incidentally, that it would not be to the point for him to say merely that we do not have *certain* knowledge about the experiences of others, for this would not disparage our grounds for statements about experiences of others in comparison with grounds for other assertions. If we grant that such knowledge is not certain, it may still be more nearly certain that the man having the proctoscopic examination is in pain than that there will not be a business recession next year. So let us suppose the purist is saying we have *no good and coercive* reasons for beliefs of this sort *at all*.

This position is an extreme one. What are the purist's reasons for adopting it? (One is inclined to say that these reasons are very likely to be more dubious than the reasons for regarding the man having the proctoscopic examination as being in pain.) Presumably the economist thinks that some *type of inference* is required for assertions about the experiences of other persons which is not required in the rest of science and is dubious. (He might go further: he might say we have no good reason for believing, unless it can be shown to *follow logically* from observations, that another person's experience is so and so. But to say this is to condemn all of science, for no law or theory in science anywhere follows logically from a description of the observations.) What kind of inference might this be? Perhaps the purist will reply: "inference *by analogy*." If he does, we must then ask him (a) what he *means* by "analogical inference" (this term is used in many different senses) and

(b) why he thinks that analogical inference in that sense is required for the present context.[10]

It is not unfair to demand that the purist produce *his* epistemology, for he is the one who is departing radically from common sense. The purist obviously does not believe his creed in practice: if his child were about to have an operation, he would not question the advisability of using an anesthetic or of giving morphine after the operation! Nevertheless, it is worthwhile to produce two positive reasons on the other side.

(1) In physics it is thought proper to extrapolate laws confirmed for observable entities, to the unobserved (e.g., Newton's laws are extrapolated to the realm of microscopic entities). It is supposed that if postulates about the unobservables, plus these extrapolated laws, lead to correct predictions, the postulates and the extrapolation are justified. But the logic is the same for inferences about other minds. We know in our own case (a) that we feel pain when having a proctoscopic examination, (b) that we seldom succeed in making witty sallies when in severe pain, (c) that we feel grief when we learn of the death of our mother, (d) that we find it hard to take an interest in things, or to act in a vivacious manner, when we feel severe grief, and (e) that the passage of time reduces the poignancy of grief. On the basis of this, we predict that a man having a proctoscopic examination will seldom come out with witty remarks and that the person whom we have just apprised of his mother's death will not behave vivaciously this evening although he probably will do so in a month's time. These predictions work out magnificently. Why, then, as compared with the physicist, are the extrapolations and assumptions wholly dubious? We use mentalistic assumptions in making a good many predictions about the behavior of others, and it is not clear how we would make them without mentalistic assumptions. The correctness of the predictions would seem to reflect glory on the assumptions, in principle just as in physics (although, of course, the predictions are nonquantitative and much more humble).

(2) Other people succeed in making a good many correct assertions about *our* mental states. One's mother, when dropping iodine on the wound or in stripping back one's injured fingernail, says "That must hurt badly!" How was she able to guess if she has never experienced pain herself? The books on psychology are very successful in predicting all sorts of visual illusions and various facts about the emotional life. How

---

[10] It is possible some economists are influenced by the logical positivism or operationalism which was influential in the 1930's. They may then be saying that statements about the experiences of others are meaningless because in principle we cannot observe them. (We can, of course, observe our *own* mental events, and presumably other persons can observe *their* mental events.) But if he does, is he not condemning most of modern physics? Most of the assertions in the area of quantum mechanics, for instance, are about occurrences which in principle we cannot observe in the required sense.

are the psychologists able to predict how things will look, or feel, if they are unconscious? Indeed, the very availability of a rich language for description of our mental life must be explained by the purist—and also how it was possible to teach us the use of this language. The minimal explanatory assumption appears to be that other persons are built very much along our lines and so there has been a point in the existence of such a language; and they have been able to teach it to us because, on the basis of their own experience, they have been able to know when we have experiences to which these terms properly apply.

Whether the purist in economics will want to deny the force of these lines of reasoning, I do not know. Perhaps he will wish to fall back on the less extreme position, described earlier, that it is only some kinds of information about others which we cannot claim with strong supporting grounds.

We need not deny that it is difficult to know whether an increase in the tariff on bicycles would do more harm than good. But I venture to suggest that some economists are locating the source of the difficulty in the wrong place; they are giving way to a penchant to attribute all our predictive ills to one disease—the philosophical problem about knowledge of other minds—instead of attributing them to the various difficulties of knowing exactly what will happen to various individuals, or classes of individuals, if the tariff were raised. If we knew exactly what difference to the *total conditions of living insofar as these are publicly observable* an increase in tariff would bring about, it seems doubtful to me that the impossibility of observing others' mental states would be much of a further problem. Indeed, if we even knew such a simple fact as that the total effect of a tariff increase would be that one hundred not very sturdy newsboys could not afford bicycles and must, therefore, spend one more hour each day delivering their papers on foot and also (on the credit side) that one man would be able to buy a third air-conditioned Cadillac, it is hard to believe that the purist would doubt that more harm than good was done. Unfortunately the effects of a change of tariff are so hard to predict in detail that we cannot well say just what people are doing, eating (etc.) given the change which they would not have been doing without it. But such effects are essentially knowable, if we wish to spend the time and money.

INDEX

279

Statistical methods in econometrics, 115
problems of verification of econometric
models, 123-28
errors in variables, 126
multicollinearity, 126-27
simultaneity, 123-25
time series nature of observation,
127-28
Statistics, theoretical, relation to economics, 171, 172, 179-80
Steindl, J., 128 n.
Stevens, S. S., 254 n.
Stigler, George J., 45 n., 103 n., 111 n.,
157 n., 193, 231 n.
Stochastic processes:
definition, 122
models, 121-23
programming, 120
theory of, 122-23
Stone, R., 128 n.
Strotz, R. H., 123 n.
Sumner, William Graham, 188
Supply functions, 116

Taylor, C. W. W., 267 n.
Technological change, 7
Teller, Edward, 13
Testing of economic images, see Verification of economic images
Theil, H., 118 n., 125, 203
Theory:
confirmation of, see Empirical con-
firmation of theory
controversy, see Controversy in eco-
nomics
and model, distinction between, 9-10
nature and role of, 25-38
pure theory in economics, 53-64
verification of, 31-33
Thompson, G. L., 128 n.
Thrall, R. M., 231 n.
Time concept, in scope of theory, 48
Tinbergen, Jan, 16
Tintner, Gerhard, 86, 114, 115 n., 117 n.,
118 n., 119, 120 n., 123 n., 125 n.,
126 n., 127 n., 128 n.
Tolman, E. C., 263 n.
Tufts, James H., 82 n.

Unternehmungsforschung, 118 n.
Utilities, intercomparison of, 243-56
Utility function and "economic man,"
227-33

Vajda, S., 116 n.
Value theory:
collective and individual valuations,
254-56
in economic analysis, 221-42
individual and household values, 239-
40
and individualism, 224-25
individual values, structure and substance of, 235-37

Value theory (Cont.)
man's basic value structure:
man as information processor, 244-
45
other minds, information about, 245-
48
measurement of values, 238-39
mechanist-vitalist conflict over values,
243-44
nature of, 222-24
nonmarket values in, 224-25
role of "values" relative to "facts," 249
ultimate and nonultimate consumption,
237-38
values in normative economic theory,
240-42
wants and individual values, 225-27
Vandome, P., 121 n.
Variate Difference Method, 126, 127
Veblen, Thorstein, 81
Verification of economic images:
concept of verifiability, 129-31
definition, 86
economic image defined, 132
economic images classified, 132-37
importance of improved data collection
and processing, 140-41
predictability of dynamic models, 139-
40
testing of equilibrium theory, 137-39
Viner, Jacob, 6
Vining, Rutledge, 179
von Neumann, John, 89, 122 n., 170, 239,
246, 247, 248
von Neumann-Morgenstern utility axioms, 96, 233, 239
von Wieser, Friedrich, 153 n

Wald, A., 118
Walras, Léon, 16, 69, 122
Wants, and individual values, 225-27
Ward, Benjamin W., 146, 184
Waugh, F. V., 127 n.
Weber, Max, 241
Weisbrod, Burton, 171
Welfare economics, 240-42, 255
concept of welfare, 257-76
levels of individual welfare, 270-71
pleasure, happiness, and satisfaction,
265-69
preferences, 262-64
rational, 264-66
welfare of individuals, 258-71
welfare, social, 271-76
Weltwirtschaftliches Archiv., 120 n.
Western Economic Journal, 33 n.
Wicksteed, Philip H., 153 n.
Wiles, Peter, 11
Williams, B., 267 n.
Windelband, W., 82 n.
Wiseman, Jack, 184 n.
Witte, Edwin E., 103 n.
Wold, H., 116 n., 123 n., 128 n.
Wrench, J. W., 28 n.

Young, P. T., 267 n.

Nalen.
Buchanan
Building

25493
14/9/66